STAYING
SAFE

ABROAD

"Ed Lee has written a most timely book which is a must-read for everyone headed overseas, whether for the first or the thousandth time. Ed has culled important stories of things gone wrong and provided smart ways to avoid the problems. His extensive travels and years of work as a security advisor have allowed him deep familiarity with both problems and solutions. Written in a very accessible and compelling way, this book is a wonderful "how-to" guide that I am deeply grateful to have read. Though I am an experienced traveler, I learned a variety of things about personal security that I did not know previously. I am delighted to have learned them the easy way! An important and useful book indeed. Thank you, Ed!"

—Martha G. Miller, PhD,
Consultant on Cross Cultural Communication

"Edward Lee has written a comprehensive and excellent security guide that I would highly recommend for international business travelers, expatriates, students studying abroad, and tourists. *Staying Safe Abroad* should be a "must read" for persons who plan on visiting areas with a high risk for crime and/or terrorism. The book offers numerous critical analyses of real world security incidents, based on Mr. Lee's broad international experience, and provides a wide variety of practical measures for preventing them and/or mitigating their impact."

—G.L. DeSalvo,
Retired Special Agent,
Bureau of Diplomatic Security (DS),
U.S. Department of State and former Director,
DS Office of Training & Performance Support
& the Diplomatic Security Training Center

"Ed Lee has traveled the world for the United States Government for years and uses his knowledge and experience to make international travel easier and safer for the less experienced traveler. His book is as important as your passport for your next trip. As an experienced traveler myself, I have found many useful tips which I intend to put to immediate use."

—Richard A. Marquise,
Retired Special Agent-in-Charge,
Federal Bureau of Investigation

STAYING
SAFE
ABROAD

TRAVELING, WORKING
AND LIVING IN A
POST-9/11 WORLD

Edward L. Lee II

SLEEPING BEAR
RISK SOLUTIONS

Sleeping Bear Risk Solutions LLC
Traverse City, Michigan

Published by Sleeping Bear Risk Solutions LLC
Traverse City, Michigan

Publisher's Cataloging-in-Publication Data
Lee, Edward L.

Staying safe abroad : traveling, working and living in
a post 9/11 world / Edward L. Lee II.—Traverse City, Mich.:
Sleeping Bear Risk Solutions LLC., 2008.

     p. ; cm.

     ISBN13: 978-0-9815605-0-2

     1. Travel—Safety measures. 2. Terrorism. I. Title.

G156.5.S35 L44 2008
910.202-dc22   2008923579

Project coordination by Jenkins Group, Inc
www.BookPublishing.com
Interior design by Brooke Camfield
Cover design by Chris Rhoads

Printed in the United States of America
12 11 10 09 08 • 5 4 3 2 1

Dedication

To Dottie, Vicki, Jen, and Crosby

Contents

Acknowledgments

I would like to express my sincere thanks to my good friend, Sandra Kaye Rose (**http://www.csiofva.com**), whose patience, attention to detail, and hours of assistance in editing this book have resulted in a product that I could not possibly have envisioned. I would also like to thank the Jenkins Group (**http://www.bookpublishing.com**) for its excellent work in designing the book's cover and accomplishing the many production tasks that helped bring this book to the reader. Finally, my deepest thanks go to my lifelong friend Gordon E. Harvey (**http://www.harveypresentations.com**), whom I first met in 1975 when we were Foreign Service Officers together at the U. S. State Department. Gordon's professional insights and the richness of our friendship have contributed to making this book a reality.

Why This Book?

From 1987 to 2002, five editions of my pocket guide, *A Personal Safety Guide for International Travelers*, were published and sold worldwide. This publication primarily offered business travelers specific advice on how to avoid becoming victims of terrorism and crime. The nature of foreign travel has understandably changed since the events September 11, 2001. In light of these changes, **Staying Safe Abroad: Traveling, Working, and Living in a Post-9/11 World** addresses ways to mitigate the new risks we face today.

While **A Personal Safety Guide for International Travelers** was geared toward business travelers and expatriates, this book is for all overseas travelers—novice, occasional, frequent, and seasoned globe-trotters. Of these groups, the travelers most often victimized overseas fall into two categories: (1) the novice with no orientation on safe travel abroad and (2) the seasoned or "old hand" travelers who become overly confident and complacent after a long period of safe, hazard-free travel and life abroad. Both categories become case studies, many of which this book discusses in detail.

xxiv   Staying Safe Abroad

For most Americans, terrorism began with the attacks of September 11, 2001. For me, it began in 1971, when I became a special agent in the U.S. Foreign Service, the overseas side of the U.S. Department of State. Following a period in the United States after working as an investigator and a protective agent in a domestic field office, I was assigned abroad as a regional security officer (RSO) at a number of U.S. embassies, where I was the security advisor to U.S. ambassadors at posts at which I served.

As an RSO, I protected the ambassador and U.S. diplomats, family members, residences, the embassy, and other diplomatic facilities. I worked daily with foreign police agencies to maintain the security of our facilities and staff, responded to criminal and terrorist attacks and threats against U.S. interests, directed the operations of Marine detachments and local security forces, and advised American companies on how to manage criminal and terrorist threats during the turbulent 1970s and 1980s. This may surprise you, but more incidents of terrorism were committed against U.S. interests, diplomatic missions, international airliners, and U.S. companies abroad *during those two decades* than have been committed since 9/11, although the numbers of total fatalities and injuries were fewer. Hence, protecting individuals against terrorism became my life 30 years before most Americans ever gave it much thought.

After retiring from the Foreign Service in the late 1980s, I lectured for 10 years at the U.S. Foreign Service Institute, the U.S. State Department's training center for personnel

assigned overseas. There, I taught more than 8,000 U.S. diplomats and their families how to protect themselves while
living in countries with criminal and terrorist activities.

In 1988, a then-unknown Saudi named Osama bin
Laden formed the al-Qaeda terrorist organization. Thirteen
years later, on September 11, 2001, 19 members of al-Qaeda
hijacked four U.S. airliners and crashed two into the World
Trade Center, one into the Pentagon, and another into a
field in rural Pennsylvania. They claimed the lives of 3,030
people and injured 2,337.

Please reflect on the impact of the events of 9/11, and
then think of three other dates: June 25, 1996; August 7,
1998; and October 12, 2000.

- June 25, 1996: Nineteen Americans died in a truck
  bomb attack on Khobar Towers in Saudi Arabia. That
  attack injured 372 people of various nationalities.
- August 7, 1998: al-Qaeda launched simultaneous car
  bomb attacks on U.S. embassies in Dar es Salaam (Tanzania) and Nairobi (Kenya). These attacks killed more
  than 250 people and injured more than 5,000.
- October 12, 2000: The USS *Cole* was attacked while
  docked at a port in Yemen. Seventeen Americans were
  killed, and 40 were injured.

I mention these three terrorist attacks to demonstrate
that terrorism means very little until it touches us personally. Although a substantial number of people died—many
of them Americans—and the destruction was catastrophic,

the attacks occurred in distant lands. Most of us probably read about them, thought they were awful, felt bad for the victims and their families, and continued with everyday living. We felt protected and believed that this could never happen to us—terrorists attack only in other countries—but then came September 11, 2001.

Other countries have experienced their own versions of September 11. Indonesia suffered two terrorist attacks in 2002. The first was a car bombing of the Jakarta Marriott hotel, and the other was bombings of a nightclub in Bali that killed 202 people. The Bali bombings were the second most deadly terrorist attack since 9/11. The commercial center in Istanbul, Turkey, was bombed on November 20, 2003, destroying the British consulate and killing its consul general. The Philippines was the target of the fourth-largest terrorist attack when al-Qaeda-affiliated Abu Sayeef bombed *SuperFerry 14* on February 27, 2004, killing 116. Spain was the target of the third-largest terrorist attack since 9/11 when terrorists bombed its railway system on March 11, 2004, killing 191. London, England, experienced simultaneous attacks against its transit system on July 7, 2005, killing 57. Months later on November 20, 2005, Amman, Jordan, was the target of simultaneous bombings on the Grand Hyatt, Radisson, and Day's Inn, in which 57 patrons were killed. Egypt, India, Pakistan, Bangladesh, and Morocco, among many other countries, have been victims of terrorist attacks since 9/11.

Despite the events in the preceding paragraph, I believe that terrorism has been excessively sensationalized, politicized, and overcovered by the media, politicians, academia, and U.S. government officials. They continue to warn us of imminent terrorist attacks on American soil. They offer unsubstantiated warnings and, often, nothing more. They do not provide guidelines on how citizens can avoid or mitigate an attack. The result is a public that often feels helpless and insecure, and is confused by government guidance on what to do in the event of an act of terrorism. In the case of chemical attacks, the U.S. Department of Homeland Security continues to discourage that citizens purchase gas masks, even though government employees have them. Duct tape is still being recommended for homes, although citizens may not be home when an attack occurs. What then? . . . Warning people of an imminent terrorist attack has no value, unless they are given specific and reasonable steps to take to mitigate the threat and protect themselves.

Therefore, the purpose of this book is to empower you, the traveler, with experience-tested advice and information based upon facts to help avoid problems. When problems are unavoidable, you will know how to minimize risk. Follow the advice in this book and you will greatly decrease your chances of becoming a victim.

Staying Safe Abroad: Traveling, Living, and Working in a Post-9/11 World does not come with a lifetime warranty promising that you will be free of crime and terrorism while abroad. What it offers is advice that works, advice

I have learned from a lifetime of countering terrorism and crime while living and working overseas and helping others do the same. This book also contains hundreds of invaluable Web sites that enable readers to stay current on critical issues pertaining to international travel; all of the information you can possibly need is at your fingertips. Traveling, living, or working abroad is enjoyable and rewarding. With the confidence that comes with knowledge and capability, you can concentrate on everything that living and working overseas affords you.

Since 9/11, everyone has asked, "Are we safer now [at home] than we were before September 11, 2001?" The short answer is a conditional "Yes." The procedures for tracking visitors to the United States are much more rigorous, and airport screening is technologically advanced. However, in October 2007, *USA Today* reported that Transportation Security Administration (TSA) screeners at Los Angeles International Airport missed about 75 percent of simulated explosives and bomb parts that TSA testers hid under their clothing or in carry-on bags at checkpoints. Similarly, at Chicago O'Hare International Airport, screeners missed about 60 percent of hidden bomb materials packed in carry-ons—including toiletry kits, briefcases, and CD players. San Francisco International Airport screeners, who work for a private company instead of the TSA, missed about 20 percent of the bombs. The TSA ran about 70 tests at Los Angeles International, 75 at Chicago O'Hare International, and 145 at San Francisco International airports.

In contrast to the past, one of the FBI's top priorities today is preventing acts of terrorism before they occur, and police organizations and other agencies are more vigilant and better prepared to counter terrorism. One example is the plot uncovered by British and U.S. intelligence agencies in August 2006 in which extremists planned to use gel-based improvised explosive devices (IEDs) to blow up airliners bound for the United States. The discovery and interruption of this plot was first-rate counterterrorism work by the British and U.S. governments.

Even private citizens are better prepared and more vigilant in countering terrorism. Were it not for a Circuit City employee who became suspicious when asked by a customer in 2007 to copy terrorist training tapes, the terrorist plot against military personnel at Fort Dix, New Jersey, might have gone undiscovered. However, despite the plot's media hype, later investigation revealed this group's questionable capability to execute such an attack.

Another often-asked question is "Which countries are safe?" The short answer is "None." Crime is increasing dramatically in most developed and developing countries, largely because of the preoccupation with acts of terrorism that may never occur. In 2007, the director of the White House travel office spent a few days in Hawaii after a grueling trip to Asia, only to be robbed and beaten outside a Honolulu nightclub at 2 a.m. During the same week, Barbara Bush, daughter of President George W. Bush, was robbed of her purse and cell phone in a Buenos Aires restaurant. On the same trip, an off-duty U.S. Secret Service agent accompanying the Bush twins was mugged. As for terrorism, both domestic and transnational terrorists will continue to select targets in countries that aggressively combat terrorism, which is the reason major attacks have occurred in countries such as the United Kingdom, Spain, the Philippines, Turkey, Indonesia, and Jordan.

This book is a quick read. In fact, you should finish it during a transoceanic flight. It includes narrative on key topics and numerous checkmarks, including tips, advice, and dos and don'ts. The book is formatted for easy stowage in a carry-on bag. It is divided into six major sections.

Section One offers a solid foundation of articles that address the cultural differences and threat environments.

Section Two addresses passports, financial instruments, communications abroad, security for international meetings, airline passenger decorum, cell phone etiquette, and a multitude of issues to consider before arriving at the airport.

Section Three focuses on getting to your destination—from the time you get to the airport to the time you leave the airport—as all of these segments pose their own risks, missteps, and potential problems.

Section Four includes tips and advice on dealing with day-to-day threats and risks you will face abroad.

Section Five includes special topics for those living, working, or studying abroad long-term.

Section Six offers a short analysis and a series of recommendations on how the international community, governments, organizations, and individuals can reduce the perception and actual extent of global terrorism and crime.

Although this book is published in the United States largely for an American traveling audience, I have attempted to provide advice for non-U.S. citizens as well. You may well find other books in the marketplace on how to travel safely abroad, but few have been written by individuals with the real life experience of both protecting travelers abroad and providing solutions to the myriad of international security challenges that can occur. If you have trouble finding a solution to a problem, send me an e-mail, and I will assist you in any way I can.

Finally, remember that one of the most effective weapons you have while traveling abroad is right between your ears: your *brain*. Also, remember that your instincts usually will tell you what to do well before your brain has figured it out. Always keep in mind—chant it, if necessary—the following:

> *I have to anticipate what might happen next and know what action to take if prevention fails. I must consistently and consciously think about the risk-reduction options available to me and choose wisely.*

Because no single book can address every feasible question on crime and terrorism, I urge those of you traveling to a high-risk country to get a security orientation from an experienced firm with international expertise. In addition, I invite you to contact me if you have comments on the book or questions that you feel the book does not adequately address. Please e-mail me at **ed@sbrisksolutions.com** or call me at (231) 938-1176.

Edward L. Lee, II

May 2008, Traverse City, Michigan

SECTION ONE

What You Need to Know about Cultural Differences and International Risks

What Differences Will You Experience Abroad?

Regardless of your destination abroad, you will notice differences—some major, some minor. In all likelihood, differences experienced in developing countries will be more dramatic than those in developed nations. The more you know about the local customs, language, security situation, and environment, the more aware you will become. As I stress throughout the book, the more you know, the safer you will be.

Language

In most cases, you will be surrounded by people speaking an unfamiliar language. Remember that Americans (meaning those from the United States) are among the most monolingual people in the world. Learn as much of the native language as you can before you arrive in the country, or at least show your hosts that you are making an effort by learning to say the basic courtesies (e.g., "Hello," "Good-bye," "It is a pleasure to meet you," "Thank you," and "You are welcome"). You can easily learn these terms from a basic phrase book. If your hosts do not speak English well, speak slowly so that they can understand what you are saying.

Medical Services

We are accustomed to fire and rescue services responding to a scene in fewer than 10 minutes. This is the norm in developed nations but rare in developing nations, where ambulances often take an hour or more to arrive at the scene of an emergency. This extended delay is why the victims of violent crimes and serious automobile accidents often die before they can reach a hospital. Ambulance personnel in many developing nations commonly have little to no training in first-responder skills.

Legal Rights

Once you leave the United States, you have no individual rights, other than those accorded to you by the host country. Some countries often consider foreigners *guilty* until proven innocent. In auto accidents where a foreigner is the driver, police often conclude that you are at fault, regardless of the facts. If arrested, you may not have the right to have an attorney present during police questioning, and you may not have rights against self-incrimination. Moreover, court proceedings in many countries make no allowances for bail pending prosecution or plea bargaining. These are all compelling reasons to be *very* law abiding in countries you visit, including avoiding public drunkenness and illegal drugs. If you are detained or arrested, the police department may or may not employ English speakers and may pressure you to make a statement without the benefit of counsel. My advice: make no statements until you see an embassy offical or a reputable attorney. I will discuss this later in the book.

Police Services

You will find police officers in developed nations as capable as those in the United States. On the other hand, in developing countries, you will soon realize that police officers may be poorly trained and poorly equipped to properly investigate crime. In many cases, institutionalized corruption and police misconduct plague police departments. Moreover, since 9/11, police agencies in both developed and developing countries have been less able to combat crime because their primary role has changed to combating terrorism. Consequently, crime has increased dramatically in many countries, including developed nations.

Cultural Mores

Each country has its laws, ordinances, and mores that prohibit certain behavior. Drinking while driving can result in jail time in many countries; in others, cell phone use is prohibited while driving. Police (e.g., in Mexico and Russia) often solicit bribes during traffic stops as well as during other opportune times. On the other hand, in some countries (e.g., Chile), offering a bribe is a criminal offense. In parts of the Middle East, possessing a copy of *Cosmopolitan*, *Vogue*, or *Playboy* can result in confiscation, a fine, or temporary detention. Loud and vulgar language, profanity, and spitting on the sidewalk can also subject you to fines. Police in Singapore can even impose a fine if you fail to flush a toilet, jaywalk or bring chewing gum into the country. In a business context, foreign business representatives can often be harassed and/or arrested simply because of a dispute with a local business. In many Islamic countries, the use of alcohol in public may be either prohibited or discouraged. In December 2007, a British teacher in Khartoum was arrested and jailed (and faced 40 lashes, six months in jail and a fine) for naming a Teddy Bear in her class, "Mohammed," an action that upset the parents of some of her students. Fortunately, British parliamentarians pleaded with the Sudanese president for clemency, who ordered her release and permitted her return to the U.K.

Treatment of Women

In much of the developing world, particularly the Middle East, women do not have the same rights, wages, working conditions, and professional acceptance as they do in developed countries. Men in some countries view Western women as promiscuous. Consequently, women may face harassment, especially when alone or dressed in a manner the locals may deem provocative—sleeveless blouses, short skirts, shorts, jeans, etc. The local women are as "offended" as the local men are and often show their displeasure by pinching the offender. Even jogging or other forms of exercise do not provide an excuse to wear fewer or more formfitting clothes. Some cultures interpret making eye contact with local men as an expression of romantic interest. Public displays of affection—even to a significant other—are frowned upon in many, although not all, countries. I remember that years ago in Lima, young lovers would "make out" in large numbers in the park across the street from the U.S. Embassy because their homes had many occupants and they did not have cars.

Ethnic and Physical Differences

Blond-, red-, and fair-haired foreigners are ogled in cultures where most of the locals have dark or black hair. I first encountered this in Greece as well as in Asia, Africa, and the Middle East. Conversely, foreigners whose ethnicity is Asian, African, or Latin American are ogled in rural areas of countries where most people are fair-skinned and homogeneous. People of all ethnic backgrounds should also be aware of the potential for hate crimes because of skin color, religion, and country of origin.

Currency, Electricity, and Measurements

Currency will be different, as will electrical plugs and measurements. Study the currency carefully—if you do not know the equivalent in your own currency, you can easily get ripped off. Most cell phones, iPods, PDAs, and laptops can accommodate both 120 and 220-plus volts, but verify this before using. As for the metric system, learn about meters, kilos, and kilometers. Use these Web sites for further inquiry:

- **http://www.oanda.com** (an excellent source for converting global currency)
- **http://www.walkabouttravelgear.com** (information on electric plugs required for countries abroad; the company also sells them)
- **http://www.onlineconversion.com** (a Web site that converts every possible measurement)

Infrastructure

As with many items discussed in this section, infrastructure (electrical, communications, and transportation) in developed nations will be similar to that with which you are familiar. In some developing nations, however, power interruptions may occur frequently or may last up to several hours a day, phone service may be sporadic, and transportation may be poorly administered and often unsafe. In many developing countries, you will find that the majority of government and business entities operate principally on cell phones.

Photography

Photographing areas such as airports, government buildings, military installations, and police headquarters is prohibited in most countries. Many locals (especially women and military or police officers) do not want their pictures taken. Men and women can also become angry or aggressive if you photograph their children without asking and may demand money if you take photographs of them without permission. Failure to get permission can often result in seizure of your film, digital media, or camera; questioning by police; a severe fine or even incarceration.

The Iraq War and Anti-Americanism

You will be viewed in many countries as aggressive, arrogant, and other unflattering adjectives that have surfaced since the invasion of Iraq. Foreigners see you as an American, and the United States, by their way of thinking, is responsible for the war in Iraq, and the considerable loss of life that has occurred. Others may chide you over the U.S. government's luke-warm stand in dealing aggressively with global warming. Consequently, one consistent message in this book is to maintain a *low profile* regarding your identification as an American. I suggest the following:

☐ Avoid wearing apparel that identifies you as an American (including company logos and university T-shirts, ball caps, and sweatshirts). Also avoid apparel with the U.S. flag or military affiliations.

☐ If traveling on business, have an inexpensive card printed with just your name. This provides you the option of writing down your contact information without having to show the company or country with which you are associated.

Unquestionably, many Americans wear their citizenship on their sleeves. If you are in an international airport or a foreign country, you can usually pick out the Americans. All you have to do is close your eyes and *listen*: the Americans are often the loudest among those talking. If you cannot identify them by sound, look around at how people are dressed. Look for the logos and insignia. Another easy way to determine who in a group is American is to look for young men and women wearing baseball caps. Usually, the young men will be wearing the caps backward.

Citizens of other developed nations also display arrogant, loud, disorderly, and intoxicated behavior abroad. For example, Liam Donaldson, the British government's chief medical officer, recently was quoted as saying: "In our culture, getting drunk is seen as an exciting and status thing to do. We need to try to get away from that." However, if the problem is bad at home, it is magnified when Britons travel abroad. Surveys have confirmed, time after time, that Britons are some of the world's "worst tourists" because of their drunkenness, loud behavior, and cultural arrogance. In fact, a recent study issued in 2007 by the government, **Britons Abroad: Great Race or Disgrace**, showed that more than 90 percent of respondents believe that Britons behave badly when abroad.

For the first time, the United Kingdom's Foreign Office exposed the extent of British bad behavior in a report released in August 2006. It showed that between April 2004 and March 2005, 1,663 Britons were arrested in Spain, 1,460 in the United States, and 170 in Greece. Britons lost 4,774 passports in Spain, 1,370 in the United States, 1,273 in Germany, 983 in Italy, and hundreds more in other countries. The Foreign Office report said binge drinking was behind much of the trouble, and it hoped that by releasing the figures, travelers would become more aware of the environment around them while abroad. Interestingly, the United Kingdom is becoming so bogged down with Britons getting into trouble abroad that embassies may soon be asking travelers to pay an hourly charge of $160 for consular services. This trend could also be considered by the United States and other foreign ministries.

As we go to press, a 26-year-old Finnish tourist, Marko Kulju, broke the ear off of a Moai on Easter Island, one of 400 statues carved from volcanic rock representing ancestors of island residents. Unfortunately, a thirteen-day house arrest and payment of a fine hardly seems commensurate with vandalizing one of Chile's precious national treasures.

How to Help Prevent Anti-Americanism

Although most of us can do little about U.S. foreign policy, we can individually help change the "ugly American" image that some Americans promote knowingly or unknowingly when they are:

- Outwardly arrogant and boastful
- Intolerant of culture, languages, and social mores of other countries

- Loudly voicing the opinion that other nationalities should speak English
- Unwilling to speak the language, even nominal greetings and expressions

Below are some pointers on how not to be an ugly American:

☐ **Adapt to the local customs.** Unfortunately, Americans are often impatient and always in a hurry—even when dining. In contrast, most foreigners move more slowly and are frustrated with American impatience. In Greece or France, for example, lunch or dinner can easily take two or three hours.

☐ **Study the country.** The best way to learn quickly about a country is to pick up a good guidebook that includes in-depth sections on its culture, language, history, customs, and popular industries. Pay particular attention to the local culture so that you know what is considered offensive behavior—and *don't do it*. Publishers of good guidebooks include:

- **http://www.lonelyplanet.com**
- **http://www.footprintbooks.com**
- **http://www.fodors.com**
- **http://www.frommers.com**
- **http://www.roughguides.com**
- **http://www.worldtravelguide.net**

☐ *Time and schedules.* At home, you may be tethered to your Day-Timer, appointment book, Blackberry, Treo, or other multitasking support devices. Abroad, save yourself frustration and time by not expecting to get as much done as you do at home. In some cities, such as Bangkok, traveling three miles may take an hour—or more. In Latin America, you often have to adapt to the afternoon siesta. In most countries, businesspeople do not start working before 9 or 10 a.m. People in most countries dine much later than we do in the United States. Do not be surprised at receiving a 10 p.m. dinner invitation. In some places, stores are rarely open late in the evening and may not be open at all on certain days of the week. If you are conducting official business in some countries, you will be lucky to hold three key meetings a day. In many cultures, your meetings will routinely be interrupted by subordinates.

☐ *Personal space.* In the United States and Western Europe, personal space is generally about two or three feet. However, in Latin America, Asia, the Mediterranean, and Africa, it can be as close as a foot. This may offend you, but try to get used it—locals are not knowingly being rude. Backing away, on the other hand, can be considered rude or may be interpreted as not being approachable.

☐ *Make a good impression.* Find out the customs of greeting both men and women and how to present business cards. In most parts of the world, first meetings are normally spent getting to know each other and sharing refreshments, usually coffee or tea. Always accept refreshments that are offered. Declining is considered rude and an affront to the generosity of the host. If you rush quickly into business discussions, you may **not** make the proper impression. Let your host be the first to begin business discussions. Follow his or her lead.

☐ *Avoid asking judgmental questions.* If visiting Indonesia, for instance, asking an Indonesian how he or she copes with the pollution and congestion will not be well received. In Kenya, asking why there are so many armed carjackings is not a good starting point in making a good impression with Kenyans.

☐ *Understand local etiquette.* Educate yourself on dining etiquette. If you are going to Asia, learn to use chopsticks and do not decline food. Take small servings to leave your plate empty and convey how much you enjoyed the meal. In a Muslim country, realize that alcoholic beverages normally are not served.

☐ *Speak the language.* As mentioned earlier, make an effort to use as much of the local language as possible. Not attempting to use the language will be looked upon unfavorably by the locals.

☐ *Be careful with written communications.* If a foreign counterpart sends you an e-mail, letter, or fax written in his or her language, respond in kind unless you are sure that your counterpart speaks English fluently and will not mind a response in English. Below are some Web sites that can assist you with translation services and verbal interpretation assistance:

- **http://www.certifiedlanguages.com**
- **http://www.atanet.org/onlinedirectories**
- **http://www.mlsolutions.com**
- **http://www.alsintl.com/interpreting**
- **http://www.translation-services.com**

☐ *Do not overtip.* Overtipping can be interpreted as flaunting your wealth, so seek a local's advice on the proper tipping percentage. It may seem low to you, but overtipping could increase your risk to crime.

☐ *Be careful of gestures.* Hand gestures that are acceptable at home are not always interpreted the same way overseas. For example, the "okay" sign and the "come here" gestures are offensive in some countries. Others can be perceived as being in poor taste.

- *Blunders in International Trade* (David A. Ricks)
- *Do's & Taboos Around the World* (Roger E. Axtell)
- *Do's & Taboos of International Trade* (Roger E. Axtell)
- *Do's & Taboos Around the World for Women in Business* (Roger E. Axtell)

☐ *Dress respectfully.* A T-shirt and khaki shorts for a man or a midriff shirt and a short skirt for a woman may be great outfits for going to lunch at home, but they may be offensive in many countries. Find out the appropriate dress, and pack accordingly. Keep in mind that lunch, dinner, and business meetings often require business dress.

☐ *Display humility and avoid being boastful.* Locals you meet may have lower salaries, modest homes, and a lower socioeconomic level. Avoid discussions of wealth, possessions, or lifestyle. Being soft-spoken and asking questions about the country and its language are always well received.

Americans as Desirable Targets

Why the emphasis on the ease of picking an American out of a crowd? Criminals usually know (or believe, which is just as dangerous) that Americans invariably carry more money, credit cards, and electronics than do travelers of most other nationalities. For terrorists and extremists, Americans are the most desirable targets, followed by Israelis and citizens of nations with aggressive counterterrorism policies. The following case study highlights this point:

On December 27, 1985, terrorists belonging to the Abu Nidal Organization (ANO), a Palestinian group connected to the Fatah Revolutionary Council, simultaneously walked into the international airports in Rome and Vienna and took positions near passengers gathered at the El Al and TWA ticket counters. They pulled AK-47s from their gym bags and fired at anyone appearing to be Jewish or American. They killed 18 and injured 140.

The following are more examples of targeting individuals based upon citizenship:

- June 2004: A gunman in downtown Dar es Salaam accosted two British tourists by pointing his gun at them and demanding to know whether they were Americans. The gunman left the scene only after the tourists convinced him that they were from the United Kingdom.

- January 2004: A U.S. citizen was hiking alone on the outskirts of La Paz, Bolivia, when two Bolivian men approached her and asked her nationality. They then demanded money, threatened her with a knife and gun, and sexually assaulted her. Both assailants told the victim they attacked her because of what the United States had done to Bolivia.

A potential risk for Americans today is still at airports, even after the multibillion-dollar buildup of current passenger screening by the U.S. Transportation Security Administration (TSA). In most airports—in the United States and abroad—ticket counters, luggage check-in, stores, concessions, restaurants, and newsstands are in the public-access part of the terminal. Passengers do not encounter the TSA screening process (x-ray units, magnetometers, screeners, etc.) until they are well into the terminal. Ironically, despite the billions spent on airport security, the attacks in Rome and Vienna could happen just as easily at any airport today. Terrorists using small arms, wearing explosive belts, or carrying explosive backpacks could easily kill hundreds of outbound passengers with little opposition from the occasional patrolling police officer. Although the risk of such an attack is remote, it still exists. To counter this threat, I offer the following:

- ☐ Get to the airport two and a half hours before departure so that you can check in *quickly*.
- ☐ Proceed to the security screening area and the passengers-only area of the terminal as soon as possible.
- ☐ If you observe anything unusual or suspicious, report it to airport personnel.

Hate Crimes and Ethnic/Religious Bias

Travelers of certain ethnicities (e.g., African-Americans, Arabs/Persians, and Asians) have been harassed, threatened, or assaulted by extremists in a number of countries. In general (but especially if you are of one of these ethnicities), research the countries to which you are traveling to determine whether an increased potential for harassment exists. Both Jews and Muslims should be aware of the potential risk they face in certain countries that are intolerant—or distrustful—of those faiths and ethnicities.

Traveling Abroad: A Risk-Rich Environment

At the beginning of this book, I mentioned that one of my objectives is to give you insights, knowledge, and solutions that will empower you to act prudently and avoid situations that might sabotage your entire trip, cause financial loss, or result in injury or death. Again, my intention is not to scare you but rather to educate you by looking at situations that can potentially happen abroad and giving you the knowledge and skills to successfully handle a situation and/or prevent injury or loss.

Fatalism

Travelers have often asked me whether I believe that we really have *no* control over the outcome of events in our future. My response has always been an emphatic "No." What they are saying is that they believe they have no control over what may or may not happen to them during a trip abroad. For many of us, our religious beliefs often mold our perceptions that we have no control over what will happen to us tomorrow. At the same time, I firmly believe that the choices we make now (based upon available data) can and do change the outcome of events today and tomorrow. From personal experience, I can tell you that this approach has saved my life more than once. For instance, I do know that travelers who drink excessively become crime victims or get involved in adverse situations more often than do those who drink moderately or not at all. I also know that travelers who go out late at night while abroad expose themselves to increased risk, simply because the criminals are out late at night in greater numbers, darkness conceals their behavior, and police presence is often diminished.

Possibility and Probability

Will you *possibly* become a victim of crime or terrorism, be involved in a serious automobile accident, or get caught up in a natural disaster or political unrest while abroad? Yes, of course. Now, are these calamities *probable*? The answer depends largely on the number of behavioral, physical, procedural, and situational vulnerabilities that are simultaneously occurring. The risks you face abroad could easily go from being possible to being probable, depending on your choices and how much risk you are comfortable with.

Let's assume that you are in Mexico City, where street crime is among the highest in Latin America. Examine two threat situations:

Target 1 (*possibility* of being a crime victim)

Time of day: 1100 hours
Type of watch worn: Inexpensive digital watch ($25)
Rings and necklaces: None
Dress: Casual
Attitude: Confident, observant
Wallet location: Front pocket
Wallet style: No credit cards visible when opened
Activity: Orders taxis by cell phone

Target 2 (*probability* of being a crime victim)

Time of day: 2330 hours
The type of watch worn: Gold Rolex ($7,500)
Rings and necklaces: Wedding ring w/diamond ($4,500)
Dress: Pin-striped suit
Attitude: Looking lost and confused, walking with map
            in hand

Wallet location: In back pocket or in open purse
Wallet style: When opened, five credit cards on each side
Activity: Hails taxis from street or walks several blocks

I exaggerated the variables to demonstrate the dramatic differences between the two targets and to better make my point. As you see from the characteristics of Target 1, he/she is cognizant of the security threat and dresses and acts accordingly. Conversely, Target 2 is unaware of the threat and behaves in a manner that increases the probability of becoming a crime victim. Street criminals simply will not pass up a target as tempting as Target 2, where the jewelry alone will encourage them to abandon other less desirable—or more security-conscious targets.

Defining Risk

Risk encompasses many definitions, but in the context of this book (staying safe), I define *personal risk* as the "potential of harm to you or others as a result of a multitude of events" (e.g., earthquake, disease, auto or bus accident, lost passport, injury, victim of crime or terrorism, political unrest, or detention by police). Any event can pose risks. For example, in July 2006, a U.S. tourist was paralyzed from the waist down after being injured in the Running of the Bulls at Pamplona.

As a foreign traveler, you have four approaches to managing your risk overseas:

- *Risk avoidance.* This might involve choosing not to travel at all or deferring travel. However, business travelers, diplomats, aid workers, academicians, and students do not always have that option.

- *Risk ignorance*. This is my *least* favorite because ignoring the threat can produce irreversible negative results. Risk ignorance often stems from fatalism, the belief that regardless of what you do or do not do, most events are preordained and behavioral modification plays **no** role in reducing risk.

- *Risk transfer*. This is a good step. In this approach, you would, for example, obtain international medical and evacuation insurance for your trip and transfer some of your risk to an insurance company.

- *Risk reduction*. As you probably suspect, this is my personal favorite. An example of reducing your risk could be purchasing a local phone card for calls made during your trip rather than carrying your long-distance card abroad. This way, if your wallet is stolen, you will not return home to find extraordinary expenses on your phone bill. By reducing risks and vulnerabilities, you will reduce the *probability* of an event actually occurring. Even if your wallet is stolen, the financial impact (known as criticality) will be minimized. Sections 3, 4, and 5 will focus heavily on how to reduce risks and vulnerabilities.

Knowing the Threat

If you have traveled internationally often and arranged your own flight reservations through travel agents, how many times have the agents cautioned you about the security risks in a particular country? How many times have they directed you to the Department of State (DOS) Web site (**http://www.travel.state.gov**) or to those of other governments' foreign offices and foreign ministries? In all likelihood, this does not happen often because most travel agents are more concerned with selling tickets than in the the safety of travelers abroad. Of course, most travelers no longer use travel agents, but rather plan their trips on line. If traveling on business, your employer's security managers may require that you be provided briefing materials or attend pre-depareture security training, but most do not, which is why you should go to: **http://www.travel.state.gov**, where travel information provided by the State Department's Bureau of Consular Affairs (effective January 7, 2008), has changed. In contrast to the past, State now offers *Travel Alerts* (short-term conditions affecting travel and risk), *Travel Warnings* (advise to defer or reconsider travel due to a dangerous situation), *Worldwide Cautions* (general warnings to be vigilant) and *Country-Specific Information* (which gives a complete treatment on travel information for all countries). Of course, unless you check the DOS Web site, you will not know the risks.

By way of example, the DOS currently has travel warnings on the following countries because of dangerous or unstable situations:

East Timor	Nepal
Eritrea	Yemen
The Philippines	Uzbekistan

Congo	Sri Lanka
Afghanistan	Algeria
Central African Republic	Liberia
Kenya	Burundi
Nigeria	Israel, the West Bank/
Serbia	Gaza
Haiti	Indonesia
Lebanon	Saudi Arabia
Côte d'Ivoire	Pakistan
Chad	Syria
Iran	Sudan
Iraq	Somalia
Bosnia-Herzegovina	Colombia
Cameroon	Nepal

Additionally, DOS has active travel alerts on Guyana, Zimbabwe, Mali, Tajikistan, and Mexico due to imminent risks to U.S. citizens.

Essentially, these warnings are for the U.S. citizen who catches a plane and a day later is in Nairobi and is soaking up the local sites and acting as though he or she is still in Minneapolis. DOS issued the Kenya warning on February 6, 2007, in response to a series of armed carjackings that involved fatalities. In January 2007, two American women—family members of a U.S. diplomat—were shot and killed during an armed carjacking in Nairobi simply because they did not move quickly enough to exit the carjacked vehicle. In another case, a U.S. Embassy employee and his son were shot and killed in another carjacking outside the capital. In September 2006, a U.S. diplomat was shot in the chest by a carjacker, and the Russian ambassador was stabbed while helping his grandchild on the side of the road. In yet another carjacking, the regional director for CARE was shot and killed in January 2007 in an attempted carjacking.

Unfortunately, the majority of untrained foreign travelers without good threat information have difficulty going from a relatively low-threat situation at home to one of the most dangerous countries in the world. For example, in Kenya, where foreigners are the primary target of carjackings, few travelers have really focused on how they would respond if carjacked. This and other factors result in a high-risk environment.

Do not become complacent just because the country to which you are traveling does not have an official travel warning. The lack of a posted travel warning does not mean you can leave this book at home and read it when you get back from your trip.

In addition to checking the DOS Web site, I strongly suggest that you go to the international travel Web sites of the British, Canadian, and Australian governments to get slightly different perspectives. Review them and draw your own conclusions:

- **http://www.fco.gov.uk** (United Kingdom)
- **http://www.dfait-maeci.gc.ca** (Canada)
- **http://www.smarttraveller.gov.au** (Australia)

You might logically ask whether statistics are available on crime and terrorism incidents against foreign travelers. The answer is "No." Few diplomatic missions maintain or release reliable statistics on incidents in which their nationals have been involved, although the Canadian and British governments have begun doing so. One study, conducted by the Canadian government, reports that more Canadians were assaulted in Mexico than in any other destination. Of 1,133 Canadians who reported assaults or violent crime on foreign soil between 2000 and 2006, 173 said these incidents took place in Mexico. China was second on the list, with 105 reported crimes. Rounding out the top five were Cuba, with 62 reported assaults; Thailand, with 45; and the United States, with 40. Canadians also reported high numbers of incidents in both the Dominican Republic and South Korea, with 38 assaults each. The report lists France with 35 assaults, Guatemala with 34, and Japan with 33. A February 2007 Ipsos Reid survey revealed that 60 percent of Canadians said if they had a choice of going or not going to Mexico for a vacation this winter, they would not go because of the recent crimes committed against their fellow citizens.

Speaking of Mexico, during the summer of 2007, there was a rash of violent attacks on American tourists along the beaches of Baja California. In one case, an American who arranged surfing tours to Baja was robbed at gunpoint, his girlfriend raped and his laptop, camera equipment and credit cards stolen. Another young American couple, with their two children, were pulled over by a gang of armed, masked men as they were returning to California, thinking that the flashing red lights that came pulled up behind them was the police, wanting to shake them down. Subsequently, the family was terrorized, roughed up, guns were pointed at them and they were robbed of everything they had, including their truck and trailer, before the gunmen left. At least seven attacks on foreigners took place during late 2007 on a 190-mile stretch of road between Tijuana and San Quintin. Of course, these attacks don't include the some 20 to 30 Americans and Mexicans who have been kidnapped by criminal gangs on both sides of the United States border.

Even if foreign governments do track assaults against their citizens abroad, the numbers are rarely valid because of the many unreported incidents. Insofar as those governments reporting and/or releasing crime data, the information invariably ranges from incomplete to unsupported statistics. Consequently, a far better strategy is to learn from anecdotal cases and concentrate on reducing personal risk rather than calculating chances of being assaulted according to statistics. In actuality, rape and murder statistics are of little value if you are raped or murdered. The avoidance of crime should be based on vulnerabilities, not on numbers.

Why are foreign travelers victimized abroad more often than at home? Many factors contribute to this increased risk, including:

- They are jet-lagged and fatigued
- They are more visible in a foreign environment

- They are creatures of habit whose movements are predictable
- They are naive
- They often are ignorant of the threat
- They are viewed as wealthy
- Americans, in particular, are victimized because of their nationality

Below, in descending order of frequency, are the threats that foreign travelers face abroad. Although no government maintains credible statistics in terms of their nationals being victims in these categories, in the course of my thirty-year career in protecting diplomats, expatriates and travelers abroad, tracking of news accounts over a twenty-year period and focus groups have resulted in my conclusions that travelers have been victims of these types of events in priority order:

1. Illness
2. Non-Vehicular accidents
3. Crime (nonviolent)
4. Vehicular accidents
5. Crime (violent)
6. Natural disasters
7. Terrorism

It may be interesting to note here that according to the **Seventh United Nations Survey of Crime Trends**, of 62 nations whose statistics of homicide were assessed,

23 nations had **higher** levels of murder per 1,000 citizens than the United States, including South Africa, Jamaica, Venezuela, Russia, Mexico, Thailand, Costa Rica, and Poland.

In Many Countries, You Really Are on Your Own

One of the reasons I stress the importance of knowing the threats you will be facing in *developing* countries, knowing how to avoid them, and knowing how to respond to them is because fire, rescue, and police services are ill-equipped, poorly trained, and slow to respond. Although such countries may have emergency systems equal to our 911, they may be unable to respond promptly, may not have the necessary professional skills, or may not understand you. Self-sufficiency is important, especially when traveling abroad.

As you will see, this book contains myriad case studies that I offer for two reasons. First, lessons learned are the best way to look at an event, analyze what happened, see others' mistakes, learn from them, and plan ways that you can avoid making the same—sometimes fatal—mistakes. Second, these case studies relate the experiences of people like you and me. They chose to live in, work in, or visit distant, exotic places and thought that the same rules at home apply abroad as well. They made quick decisions that, in many cases, cost them injury and/or death.

Consider the following case studies. After describing these incidents, I will provide recommendations on how different courses of action might have produced safer results:

- April 2000: A German expatriate employed by Daimler-Benz AG and his wife and two children, 14 and 12, were stabbed to death in their Nanjing (China) villa after two young Chinese burglars gained access to the second floor of the villa. The expatriate heard footsteps upstairs and went to investigate. He subsequently confronted one of the burglars, who stabbed him to death. The burglars then went downstairs and killed his children and his wife.

- October 2002: A British couple in their late 50s, staying at a resort 250 miles northeast of Pretoria, South Africa, was confronted by a gunman who demanded money as they walked to their hotel room. When the couple refused, the gunmen opened fire, killing the wife and injuring her husband.

- January 2006: A 21-year-old British woman was walking alone on a beach in Thailand on New Year's Day while talking on a cell phone to her mother in Scotland when two men came up behind her and hit her several times with a wooden club. The assailants raped her and dragged her into the sea. The victim's mother told police that while she was speaking to her daughter, she heard her scream and then the line went dead.

- March 2006: Twelve U.S. retirees from a Celebrity cruise ship were killed in northern Chile when their tour bus swerved to avoid a truck and plunged off a cliff. The bus was not registered, nor was it authorized to carry passengers. The tourists—not the cruise line—had arranged for the bus.

- June 2006: An American couple traveling in Quetzaltenango, Guatemala, was abducted off the street by gunmen, forced into a car, and taken to a house. There, the couple was robbed, and the woman was raped.

- September 2006: A group of European tourists was visiting the Roman ruins outside Amman when, without warning, Nabeel Ahmed Issa Jaourah, 38, approached from behind and began shooting at the tourists as they walked up the steps of the 2,000-year-old amphitheater. One Briton, Christopher Stokes, 30, was shot in the head and died instantly. The 14 rounds that Jaourah fired before witnesses restrained him, hit two British women, an Australian, a New Zealander, a Dutch national, and the Jordanian tourist guide. Several survivors of the shooting spree later said that they thought they were hearing firecrackers—not the sound of an assailant's pistol.

- November 2006: A Dutch couple honeymooning in the Bay of Islands in New Zealand was sleeping in a camper in a parking area when awakened by two men armed with a shotgun. The men tied up the couple and drove around for hours in the camper while they repeatedly raped and sodomized the wife in front of her husband. Finally, the gunmen forced the couple to withdraw money from the ATM and left with the couple's passports, credit cards, and possessions.

- February 2007: A 70-year-old American retiree killed one of three assailants who attempted to rob him and 12 other seniors in Limon, Costa Rica, during a tour arranged by the tourists. Local authorities chose not to press charges against the passenger, who also broke the clavicle of one of the armed assailants.

- April 2007: A 40-year-old U.S. Peace Corps volunteer was beaten to death while hiking alone in an isolated region in the northern Philippines. Her assailant apparently mistook her for someone else, against whom he had a grudge. The victim had only two weeks remaining on her tour of duty.

- April 2007: Two gunmen confronted a customer leaving a bank in Rio de Janeiro, only 20 yards from the U.S. Consulate. The robbers demanded the man's money and shot him in the chest when he resisted.

- April 2007: Two employees of a U.S. multinational company were staying in a five-star hotel in Caracas. As the executives talked in the lobby, one placed his briefcase (which contained a laptop) on the floor. The two men noticed a woman standing nearby. Suddenly, the man looked down to check on his briefcase, only to realize that it was missing.

- May 2007: A U.S. Mormon group was traveling by bus from Quetzaltenango, Guatemala, to Mexico when five gunmen opened fire on the bus to halt it. The gunfire wounded the driver and killed a 52-year-old Ogden, Utah, architect. The assailants ordered the rest of the passengers to lie down, and they stole their passports, money, and other belongings.

- August 2007: A drunken British tourist, 21, was sentenced to 14 months in prison on the island of Rhodes after biting a police officer who was attempting to break up a bar fight.

Learning from Travelers Like You:

- ***Burglary/murder in Nanjing.*** At the time of the burglary, the family of four was downstairs. When they heard the footsteps on the second floor (and recognized them as evidence of an intruder), the family should have left the house and gone to a neighbor's home to call the police. Even if the family members had lost some of their belongings, they would at least have been alive to replace them.

- ***British couple visiting South Africa.*** Knowing that gunmen in developing countries have no compunction about killing their victims, the victims made a bad decision in refusing to give the assailant their money. No property or money is worth your life. In December 1997, a U.S. executive employed by Cushman-Wakefield hailed a taxi in Mexico City, even though the U.S. embassy strongly warned Americans not to do so (largely because criminals have stolen so many taxis). When the executive got into the taxi, he soon realized he was being abducted. Rather than give up his money, the American—a former U.S. Navy Seal—resisted and was shot and killed. After two unsuccessful attempts at prosecution, the man's assailants were acquitted.

■ *Rape in Thailand.* The victim had left the company of her friends on New Year's Day to call her mother. She put herself in a vulnerable position by being preoccupied with the cell phone conversation and by walking alone in a remote area. Because she was preoccupied, she was unaware of the two men approaching her from behind with a weapon, hence she was unaware of the impending attack.

■ *Chilean bus accident.* Rather than setting up their own bus trip, the cruise passengers should have either participated in a cruise line tour or used a reputable tour operation to set up transportation for them. Using a vehicle not authorized for passengers cost 12 Americans their lives. Bus accidents on mountain roads are very common throughout Latin America and other parts of the world.

■ *Quetzaltenango abduction and rape.* Quetzaltenango, Guatemala's second-largest city (pop. 300,000), is near the Mexican border and has always been a magnet for criminals. Foreigners should not be on the streets of Quetzaltenango late at night. That is when local criminals look for vulnerable victims. At 0100 hours, the couple should have arranged for a reputable taxi. Many travelers make decisions and take chances away from home that they would never consider taking in their own neighborhood in the United States. Just because a place is beautiful, peaceful looking, or exotic does not mean that you can throw caution to the wind.

- *Random shooting at Roman ruins in Amman.* If you hear any sudden noise or repetitive popping or see people falling nearby you (suggesting the use of a pistol silencer), **get down, make yourself small, and seek cover**. It is better to be embarrassed than it is to be shot. The assailant, a Palestinian, had been brooding for years over the death of his two brothers at the hands of Israeli soldiers in 1982. It is very possible that the violence in Lebanon during the summer of 2006 precipitated Jaourah's attack on the group of tourists. Interestingly, Jaourah was not a member of a terrorist organization. He was the hardworking father of five children and had no history of mental disease. He was, however, a Jordanian from the town of Zarqa, the birthplace of Abu Musab al-Zarqawi, the late al-Qaeda leader in Iraq who also planned the 2002 assassination in Jordan of U.S. diplomat Lawrence Foley. Lone assailants such as Jaourah rarely appear on the radar screens of police or intelligence agencies, yet they can strike at any time with no warning. No level of security could have prevented the attack on the European tourists. This same type of attack could just as easily have occurred in any city in the world.

- *Dutch couple in New Zealand.* The honeymooners' first lapse in security was not checking on the security threats in New Zealand. The second lapse was not parking in a designated campground area, where they would have had security protection. Setting up the camper in a parking area created a major vulnerability.

- **Cruise line robbery in Costa Rica.** My advice to international travelers is **not** to resist an armed robbery. Although such crimes are traumatic and may leave the victim outraged, they are usually over in minutes. On the other hand, I have seen too many cases of travelers being wounded (and sometimes killed) when they resisted an assailant who had a firearm, a knife, or even a machete. The natural and instinctive reaction is to resist a robbery: DON'T DO IT. Even hesitation, as was the case in Kenya, can be deadly. Tell yourself repeatedly that nothing is worth your life

- **Murdered Peace Corps volunteer in the Philippines.** This case really centers on a naive American traveling alone in a rural area with little law and order. Hiking alone in an isolated area anywhere in the world is inadvisable—an unfortunate reality of modern life. The victim's failure to hike with friends in a remote area was imprudent. Overconfidence in traveling in an unfamiliar area made her vulnerable when an unanticipated threat presented itself. Recall the "old hand" travelers mentioned at the beginning of this book—past safe experiences does not necessarily translate into safety in the future.

- **Bank customer shot near U.S. consulate.** Rio is one of the most dangerous cities in South America. Criminals in this city will often shoot victims who resist their demands for money or valuables. Remember that no amount of property is worth your life.

- **Stolen laptop from lobby of five-star hotel in Venezuela.** More laptops are stolen abroad than at home, largely as a result of high duties for computers in some countries but also because of the proprietary information contained on laptops carried by many foreign travelers. The executive could have prevented this theft by simply placing his briefcase on the floor between his legs, where he could keep a tight grip on the case and its contents.

- **Death of U.S. missionary in Guatemala.** Buses are the frequent targets of criminals, smugglers, and drug traffickers in rural areas throughout many Latin-American countries. Missionaries often do not have the funds to travel by air; however, given the current vulnerabilities of bus travel, these types of tragedies will continue to occur frequently.

- **Drunken British tourist.** Travelers who drink excessively and are prone to rowdy behavior usually get a chance to meet the local police. Excessive drinking also puts travelers at risk in threat situations because they usually do not make the right choices.

- **Non-Vehicular Accidents.** Not being familiar with your surroundings in a foreign country, particularly in developing countries with considerable risks, can indeed lead to serious injury and death. Examples that come to mind include the countless foreigners who have been permanently disabled and/or injured while "running with the bulls" in Pamplona. Some have even been killed. In 2006, for example, a Bank of America bond trader was partially paralyzed after being injured by a bull. Seven others were also hospitalized after being gored.

Other interesting examples include a German tourist killed in a crocodile attack in Australia in 2002, when she ignored signs not to swim in reservoirs at Kakadu National Park. Accidental falls are also on the list of accidents befalling tourists, as was the case of an American tourist who died after falling from a bridge at Jordan's famous ruins at Petra. Unfortunately, tourists were advised by officials to stay away from Petra at the time because of slippery conditions caused by snow. In another Petra incident, an Australian tourist fell to his death when he ventured into a fenced-off area that was marked as out of bounds to visitors. And in 2005, an Australian woman was killed by a hippopotamus in Kenya when she ignored warnings to avoid hippos at night by her tour guide.

I myself was nearly fatally bitten by a King Cobra in Thailand, while photographing a mongoose and cobra fight that caused me to lose sight of another cobra nearby. As a result, I backed within striking distance of the hooded snake, but for some strange reason, he failed to bite me.

Roadway Accidents: A Major Concern

In the summer of 2006, I received an e-mail from my former office at the State Department in Washington that informed me that my coworkers had been involved in a serious automobile accident on a highway between Nairobi and the Mt. Kenya Safari Club in Kenya. One contract employee was killed, the bus driver and an embassy employee were injured, and a former subordinate of mine was severely injured and required extensive facial surgery. The minivan, driven by an embassy driver, was approaching the crest of a hill on a two-way highway when an oncoming bus, passing on the wrong side of the road at the top of the hill, hit the minivan head-on. Unfortunately, accidents such as this happen regularly in developing countries. Passersby came to the accident, but instead of rendering first aid, they stole the victims' luggage, laptops, expensive camera and media equipment, and other personal belongings.

Seventy percent of the world's auto fatalities occur in developing nations. According to the World Health Organization (WHO) and the World Bank, road accidents claim an estimated 1.2 million lives per year worldwide and disable another 20–50 million people. Roughly 70 percent of the accidents occur in developing countries. Sixty-five percent of these deaths involve pedestrians. Thirty-five percent of pedestrian deaths are children. Since 1975, an estimated *6,200 Americans have died in road accidents abroad* (twice the number lost on 9/11), for an average of approximately 200 per year. These road accidents involve automobiles, taxis, buses, trucks, and other motorized road vehicles. The WHO predicts that road fatalities will reach 2.3 million by 2020, nearly double the number of today's fatalities. The U.S. State Department also reports that in the past three years, more than 700 U.S. citizens were killed in auto accidents abroad. That is roughly 233 American deaths annually and 4,666 American deaths during the past 20 years. For more information, see **http://www.makeroadssafe.org**.

In many rural areas in developing countries, foreigners often face great danger when involved in automobile accidents, especially if the vehicle they are driving or riding in hits a person or an animal. In such cases, victims will demand payments from foreigners. The foreigner also can be fined and jailed, particularly if he or she is intoxicated.

Know what to do in the event of a road accident. Make sure that you check with the embassy or consulate to learn what to do if you are involved in an automobile accident. In some countries, you will be advised to go to the nearest police station and report what happened; in other countries, you will be advised to go to the embassy. It is important to know *before* you are involved in an accident.

Americans preparing to travel or live abroad should be aware of certain realities that typify ground transportation in foreign countries. Note that the trends listed below largely describe driving in developing countries. Travel and traffic law enforcement in *developed* countries are generally similar to—or better than—conditions in the United States and Canada.

When driving in developing countries, remember that:

- Driving habits and patterns are more aggressive and dangerous than those found in developed countries.

- Foreigners often are involved in automobile accidents in developing countries because they do not adapt quickly to local driving conditions and because they do not understand the local rules of the road, if they exist.

- Foreigners coming from right-hand-drive (RHD) countries experience a much higher number of accidents when driving in any of the 42 left-hand-drive (LHD) countries.

- Few developing countries have mandatory inspection of motor vehicles. The result is a greater number of accidents and broken-down vehicles, which are especially hazardous at night. In many developing countries, you may suddenly encounter a vehicle—often a large truck—broken down in the middle of the road and abandoned with no lights or warning cones. This situation has caused numerous serious accidents.

- Driving is especially hazardous at night, in general, and should be avoided if possible. Many drivers in developing countries often drive at night with their headlamps *off*.

- People, buses, trucks, cars, motorcycles, bicycles, donkey carts, rickshaws, caribou, water buffalo, cows, sheep, goats, and even the occasional camel or elephant may all share the road—each going in a different direction.

Although most countries use international road signs, some do not. This could be unfortunate unless you can speak (and read) the local language.

In addition to the high risk of traffic accidents in developing countries, the risks of auto theft, armed carjacking, kidnapping, and armed robbery are also very high. For example, in Rio de Janeiro, motorists are permitted to proceed through red lights between 2200 and 0500 hours if they feel threatened by carjackers.

Don't be eager to rent a car abroad. As a rule, travelers should ***not*** rent cars in developing countries unless they are comfortable with the driving environment and speak the language. Foreigners who rent cars and are not familiar with the environment and language face enormous risks for the following reasons:

- Foreign travelers have no special legal protection (unless, of course, they are diplomats). If foreign travelers are involved in a serious traffic accident and they are at fault (which is invariably the case), they will likely be arrested and incarcerated, pending adjudication and/or prosecution.
- If involved in traffic accidents, they face an increased risk of civil suits brought by injured parties or their families.
- In countries where armed carjacking is a major risk for foreigners (e.g., Kenya, Nigeria, Ivory Coast, South Africa, Mexico, Venezuela, Brazil, etc.), renting cars may put foreigners at an increased risk of being victims of violent crime (for those readers who will be living abroad long-term, I'll address this issue later).

On the basis of deaths per distance driven, the most dangerous nations for motorist fatalities are Egypt, Kenya, Greece, South Korea, Turkey, Morocco, Yemen, Austria, South Africa, Bulgaria, Portugal, Hungary, and Macedonia. In these countries, deaths per million miles driven range from 15 to 29; the U.S. rate is 1.8.

Before driving in any foreign country, consider the following:

☐ Ensure that you know the regulations before you drive a vehicle in a foreign country. In many countries, you cannot turn on a red light, pass on the right, enter a tunnel without lights on, or drive without engaging a seat belt. In Mexico City, you cannot drive unless your license plate number is odd or even, depending upon which day one of the two can enter the city center.

☐ Make sure that you have insurance coverage.

☐ If you drive in a LHD country (e.g., Thailand, Cyprus, the United Kingdom, or Kenya) and you have never driven on the left, first drive during a period of light traffic (e.g., early on a Sunday morning). This will help with the transition before you venture out into the morning rush hour.

☐ If possible, avoid driving a RHD vehicle (which has the steering wheel on the left) in a LHD nation. If you do and you are driving on a two-way roadway, you must expose your entire vehicle to the oncoming lane just to determine whether you have enough room to pass safely.

☐ Ensure that you have the maximum collision and liability coverage. You cannot use your domestic car insurance to cover rental cars abroad.

☐ Ensure that you have an authorized driving permit.

☐ Invest in a hands-free device for your cell phone. Forty-four nations require them. Only four of the 50 states in the United States ban cell phones while driving without a hands-free device. In Italy, the fine is $124, Ireland $380, Norway $600, and Poland $1,000.
See **http://www.cellular-news.com/car_bans**.

☐ Know your legal responsibility if you are involved in an accident.

☐ Know what to do if a police officer stops you and solicits a bribe.

☐ Understand and obey all traffic signs.

ASIRT has the best reports on road travel abroad. The Association for Safe International Road Travel (ASIRT), founded by Rochelle Sobel, is one of the best resources for international road travel. Ms. Sobel's son and 21 others were killed in a bus accident in Turkey in 1995. ASIRT sells road travel reports, which are invaluable to anyone driving on roadways abroad (**http://www.asirt.org**).

Even if business travelers do not rent vehicles and drive abroad, they should still obtain an international driving permit (IDP). This document is useful for the following reasons:

- The IDP is accepted as an authorized driving permit in 150 countries, many of which do not recognize driving permits issued by the United States.

- It serves as a legitimate second form of photo identification (after a U.S. passport).

The U.S. Department of State, in keeping with Article 24 of the United Nations Convention on Road Traffic (1949), authorizes only two organizations in the United States to issue IDPs: the American Automobile Association (AAA) and the National Automobile Club (NAC). IDPs also function as the official translation of a U.S. driver's license into 10 foreign languages. IDPs are not valid in the country of issue.

To apply for an IDP, you must be 18 years of age. You must present two passport-size photographs and a valid U.S. driving permit. The cost of an IDP from either AAA or NAC is $15.

- **http://www.aaa.com/vacation/idpc.html**
- **http://www.thenac.com/international_driving**

Weapons of Mass Destruction

The highly-charged global political environment sometimes makes remaining apolitical difficult, especially when discussing world events, terrorism, and weapons of mass destruction (WMDs). Prior to 9/11, Weapons of Mass Destruction (WMD) were invariably defined only in nuclear, radiological, biological or chemical context, where large-scale mass casualties were likely. Yet, today, according to some, a letter bomb is defined as a WMD. To demonstrate the ambiguity of the U.S. Government's definition of the term, Lake Superior State University (Michigan's smallest public institution of higher learning) has included WMD in its banned list of "misused, overused and generally useless words."

For the sake of our discussion in this chapter, let's simply define a WMD as a "nuclear, radiological, biological, chemical or explosive/incendiary event that produces casualties in excess of 200, which could easily challenge any hospital management system, regardless of motivation. This definition would also include the use of conveyances as suicide instruments of destruction (i.e, the events of 9/11), causing mass casualties." As a comparison, the 1995 sarin gas attack on the Tokyo subway system, killed only twelve, but forced the treatment of over 5,000 injured at medical facilities.

Each terrorist attack—no matter where it occurs in the world—has indicators. For an excellent resource on pre-incident indicators, I would suggest that you consult with the online version of the **9/11 Commission Report (http://www.gpoaccess.gov/911.**)

Admittedly, governments cannot possibly prevent every attack, every time. If a potential target is "hardened," the terrorist will strike another "softer" target. For example, government buildings and military installations have hardened security and decreased their vulnerabilities. So, terrorists respond by choosing softer targets. In this case, emulate the government—become a harder target and decrease your vulnerabilities.

Let's say you are traveling, working, or living abroad in a country that experiences a WMD attack. Such an incident will probably involve the use of high explosives, given the tactics used by terrorists during the past six years. If the attack happens in a developed nation, the police and emergency response should be professional and timely, as they were after the transit attacks in Spain and the United Kingdom. This level of response should minimize casualties.

On the other hand, if the WMD attack occurs in a developing nation—where most ambulances are not staffed with certified EMTs and paramedics trained in advanced life support—a mobile victim is probably better off using a taxi for immediate transport to the hospital. In either situation, the prudent traveler will need to make several of the following assumptions:

In an attack, cellular phone service probably will not work, depending on the severity of the attack. If you recall, most cell phone service was inoperable on 9/11. Service will eventually return, but traffic will be snarled, and chaos will prevail, so try to be patient.

Naturally, you cannot predict a major terrorist incident in which a WMD is used. Therefore, while abroad, prepare yourself. In any event, here are some suggested tips:

☐ Always carry the phone numbers and addresses of the best full-service hospitals in your location, your embassy or consulate, and people on whom you can depend in the country and in the United States.

☐ Always register your overseas trip with the embassies or consulates in those countries to which you will be traveling. We'll cover this later.

☐ Women should not wear high-heeled shoes while abroad. As 9/11 and the European attacks demonstrated, high-heeled shoes are ill suited for walking over broken glass and debris or running from the scene of a WMD attack. Always wear comfortable shoes abroad for both normal conditions and emergencies.

☐ Preselected gas masks or respirators will be of little use: conditions are often too unpredictable to preselect the correct protective equipment at the right time, especially in the case of biochemical attack.

☐ Always carry a briefcase, purse, or tote bag while abroad. This piece of luggage should hold several key items listed below. While the list may seem like a lot to carry, the individual items are quite small. Be prepared. Stock your bag with:

- Cell phone and an extra battery
- Power supply to recharge your phone
- Documentation on your international medical care and evacuation coverage
- List of medications, allergies, and your blood type
- Your passport or a photocopy of both it and your entry visa
- Small AM/SW radio with extra batteries
- Small flashlight with extra batteries

- Whistle
- Surgical mask (to reduce smoke and dust)
- Map of the city

☐ If you can, get as far away as possible from the scene of the incident.

☐ Render first aid to those around you who may need help. Take a Red Cross course on first aid and CPR before you leave the United States.

☐ Assuming the area is safe, you should go to your hotel or residence if you can.

☐ Send text messages to your family, friends, or colleagues to let them know that you are all right, and give them your location.

Improvised Explosive Devices, Improvised Incendiary Devices & Suicide Belts

As seen throughout the world in the types of terrorist attacks which have occurred since 9/11, currently used bomb tactics fall into four categories:

- Improvised Explosive Devices (IEDs)
- Improvised Incendiary Devices (IIDs)
- Suicide, or Explosive Belts
- Vehicular Bombs

IEDs (outside of Iraq and Afghanistan) are generally defined as a bomb that is non-military in design and constructed of high explosives (commercially made or improvised) using differing types of energy sources and detonation initiators. Unfortunately, all improvised bombs are often described as IEDs, which they are not, as many types of bombs are incendiary in nature, and do not include high explosives.

IIDs are designed in a similar fashion to IEDs, in that they often need an energy source and an initiator, but in contrast to IEDs, IIDs are defined as "thrown or detonated incendiary bombs, which are designed to cause casualties." IIDs are constructed of differing types of igniting fuels and gases, including propane. Included in IIDs are Molotov Cocktails (see page 270).

Suicide, or explosive belts, are often used by suicide bombers who carry the belt on their person under a coat, robe or other apparel, and who can use a variety of devices to detonate the bomb, as well as themselves, causing casualties to those within hundreds of feet of the bomber. Belts are usually packed with nails, screws, bolts, and other objects that serve as shrapnel to maximize the number of casualties following the explosion. An explosive belt is essentially a body-worn claymore mine. Once the vest is detonated, the explosion resembles an omni-directional shotgun blast.

Vehicular Bombs (cars and trucks) can be constructed of IEDs or IIDs and generally pose high risk to buildings and people a like. An excellent example of a car bomb is the one used at the Marriot hotel in Karachi in March 2006, that killed 4 people, including a U.S. diplomat. The Marriot was just yards from the U.S. Consulate. The blast destroyed windows on ten floors and destroyed ten vehicles. Since 9/11, five Marriot hotels have been attacked by al-Qaeda.

Placed IEDs/IIDs

An IED/IID can look like any imaginable object. Terrorists disguise devices in boxes, radios, cans, propane cylinders, vehicles—*anything*. Some years ago, in Chile, a Canadian expatriate was killed by a bomb built into a baseball bat. A leftist guerilla built the bomb and left it on the ground amid other bats at a game played by foreign and Chilean executives. Unless a targeted facility has extremely good physical security, alert security personnel, and meticulous inspection of goods and vehicles transiting the facility, most placed devices escape detection: bombers choose opportunities in which they are not subject to scrutiny. However, in the June 2007 case in London in which an IED was discovered in a Mercedes-Benz, an ambulance driver who was en route to another scene noticed smoke emitting from the vehicle. That observation and the resulting timely action prevented the device's activation.

Suicide Bombers

Suicide bombers can be male or female. Eighty-three percent of suicide bombers are single. Approximately 30 percent are women.

Suicide bombers typically are used in two ways: (1) they drive an explosive-laden vehicle or (2) they wear "explosive belts," a vest packed with explosives and armed with a detonator. Explosive belts are often packed with nails, screws, and bolts, which serve as shrapnel to maximize casualties. Explosive belts were first introduced by Sri Lanka's Tamil Tigers in 1991, when a Tamil bomber detonated herself, killing Rajiv Gandhi. Today, explosive belts are the weapon of choice of many terrorist groups.

Suicide bombers equipped with explosive belts, which can weigh up to 40 pounds, often display a number of characteristics:

- Long, heavy coats or apparel, regardless of the season
- Torsos often seem larger than expected, as if they have a coat beneath the outer garment
- An unusual gait that could suggest that someone is forcing or willing himself or herself to go through with the attack
- Facial expressions that seem unusually preoccupied or intense
- Tunnel vision—many suicide bombers will be fixated on their target and often will look straight ahead
- Signs of irritability, sweating, and nervous behavior
- An appearance of being drugged (which often helps a bomber carry out his or her mission); enlarged pupils, a fixed stare, and erratic behavior may also be common
- On men, a freshly shaven beard (obvious lighter skin on lower face area)
- A hand in the pocket, which might suggest clutching a detonator or a trigger for an explosive belt

- Evasiveness—avoiding eye contact or security cameras and guards
- Repeatedly fidgeting with an overstuffed backpack, as was the case with one of the London bombers

What protective steps can travelers take to protect themselves from IEDs and incendiary devices while abroad? First, some realities:

Countries that are most likely to be targeted by Islamic extremists include the United States, Canada, the United Kingdom, Turkey, Indonesia, the Philippines, Germany, Jordan, Egypt, Pakistan, and other nations that have joined the U.S. in the "war" on terrorism.

Travelers must observe everything around them and report anything unusual or suspicious to authorities.

Unfortunately, while travelers can take many steps to avoid and counter street crime, con games, air travel hazards, credit card fraud, and other calamities, IEDs and suicide bombers represent threats we can personally do little about. The best counter to these threats lies in being observant.

On the other hand, multinational companies, nonprofits, NGOs, governments, and international organizations that hire staff to travel, work, and live abroad can do a great deal about countering the threat posed by IEDs and incendiary devices. These entities can offer seminars on safe foreign travel, develop crisis management plans, provide international insurance and medical evacuation coverage, institute rigorous security controls at workplaces, and have a contingency plan for virtually every type of emergency that might occur overseas.

The following are specific steps available to the traveler to reduce the risk:

☐ Take a Red Cross class on emergency first aid and CPR. This knowledge will be invaluable if an IED/IID detonates nearby or if injuries are sustained during an accident or act of terrorism.

☐ If you are traveling in a high-risk country where car bombs have been used in the past, ensure that any vehicle you use is quickly searched for IEDs.

☐ Ensure that vehicles for which you are responsible are locked, guarded by an attendant, or safely garaged to prevent access. Would-be bombers or car thieves will steal these vehicles to use in a car bombing.

☐ When riding in vehicles, keep the windows rolled up. A closed vehicle window provides good protection against Molotov cocktails: tests show that these incendiary devices will inflame the window and the outer part of the vehicle but the flames will eventually burn out. If they do not, drive to a safe area and exit the vehicle.

☐ Never loiter in hotel lobbies, particularly in countries where hotels and other public places have been targets of terrorist bombings.

☐ Avoid waiting outside with a large group for regularly scheduled vehicular or bus transportation, where you could be targeted by IED detonations, hand grenades, or small arms attacks. Extremists have also been known to use nearby refuse containers to conceal IEDs and detonate them remotely.

☐ Never open delivered packages (even by reputable couriers) unless you expect the delivery and are certain the package is legitimate. If you suspect that a package or object may contain a suspicious object, do not touch it! Call the police.

☐ Take the appropriate action following a bomb threat. Carefully analyze telephone calls in which the caller announces the presence of a bomb; follow established search procedures in response to such a threat. Evacuating the building is not always the appropriate response.

☐ In countries where hand grenade attacks against crowds are possible, those close to such an attack should always keep their mouths open and fall away from the device. These actions will reduce the likelihood of injury to the head and/or torso. When falling to the ground, cover your head with your arms and seek available cover.

☐ Some suicide bombers will raise their hand(s) into the air before detonating the device to ensure that their bodies do not deflect any of the blast and to ensure that most of the injuries to victims will be above the waist. Injuries to the head and chest are obviously the most severe.

☐ Realize that bomb detonations shatter window glass into thousands of pieces and cause injuries from the force of the blast bouncing off brick or concrete walls.

In 2007, authorities in London discovered functional incendiary devices inside two suspicious vehicles. In addition, the terrorists launched a failed attack in which they attempted to drive a flaming vehicle into the inner perimeter of Scotland's Glasgow Airport. In light of these events, below are some tips for identifying vehicle bombs equipped with explosive or incendiary devices. Travelers should be suspicious of:

☐ Vehicles parked in no-parking areas or other areas they normally should not be

☐ Vehicles with an uneven weight distribution, suggesting an excessive load of improvised explosives or incendiary materials

☐ Vehicles that have wires stemming from the gas tank or engine hood

☐ Vehicles that emit strong odors of fuel, oil, or other suspicious materials

☐ Vehicles with expired tags

Letter and package bombs. Although letter and package bombs generally have become unpopular with extremists since the events of 9/11, employers abroad should have a formal mail screening program. Keep in mind that letter and package bombs typically have excessive postage, often have oily stains, have incorrect spelling of the addressee's name, are lopsided, or bear markings such as "confidential" and "addressee only." Note that most packages delivered by courier services are not screened. Incidentally, in December

2007, a letter bomb killed a French secretary and injured a lawyer working in a Paris law firm where French President Nicolas Sarkozy once worked.

Surveillance: Conducted by Governments, Terrorists and Criminals

Governments, criminals, and terrorists watch foreigners for many reasons. We call this *surveillance*. One of the best examples of surveillance by terrorists included the pre-attack surveillance of the U.S. commercial airline system by the 9/11 hijackers. Another example is the surveillance of the late U.S. diplomat Larry Foley, who was surveilled by al-Qaeda operatives before they assassinated him in front of his house in Amman in 2002. Criminals use surveillance techniques often to guarantee the success of a robbery, burglary, rape, home invasion, and other crimes. Below are some examples of government surveillance:

- April 1997: Donald Ratcliffe, Asian area sales manager for a Litton subsidiary, was arrested by South Korean intelligence agents for allegedly obtaining military secrets from Korean arms dealers. Ratcliffe was tried along with three other defendants and received a two-year suspended sentence.
- December 2000: Retired U.S. Navy Captain Edmond Pope was surveilled by Russian FSB (formerly KGB) agents, arrested, and charged with purchasing military

plans that were publicly available. Pope eventually became the first American to be convicted of espionage in Russia and received a 20-year sentence. After eight months in prison, Pope received a pardon from Russian President Vladamir Putin.

- December 2006: Haleh Esfandiari, an Iranian American and head of the Middle East program at the Woodrow Wilson Center in Washington, D.C., was pulled from her taxi en route to the Tehran airport. Iranian authorities prevented her return to the United States, seized her U.S. and Iranian passports, and placed her under house arrest. Iran does not recognize dual citizenship and considers Esfandiari an Iranian. In May 2007, Esfandiari was taken to the notorious Evin Prison. In 2003, journalist Zahra Kazemi (who held both Canadian and Iranian passports and lived in Montreal) was accused of taking photographs of the prison. She was taken into custody, sent to the same prison, and died from beatings received there.

- April 2007: Retired FBI Agent Robert S. Levinson disappeared in Iran while working as a security consultant. Considering that he has been missing over a year, with no leads to support that he is still alive, it is expected that he will soon be declared dead.

The above incidents share one commonality: the victims became caught up in political games. The cases of both Esfandiari and Levinson, whose travels to Iran coincided with a period of particular hostility and contention between Tehran and Washington, stem from imprudence, bravado, and poor judgment.

Foreigners may find themselves under surveillance for a variety of reasons:

- The local government wants to know what they are doing.
- The local government suspects they are engaging in illegal behavior (e.g., illegal currency exchange, immigration violations, or drug possession).
- The local government does not want anything bad to happen to them. They may be guests of the government, on a diplomatic mission, or senior business executives.
- Local criminals use preincident surveillance to ensure they can successfully commit a crime against them.
- Terrorists conduct preincident surveillance to ensure a successful attack against a vital installation, national landmark, soft targets, or a transportation system (e.g., the London transit attacks).

Laurence Foley was assassinated because of his predictable behavior, even after embassy diplomats were warned that the embassy or its staff might be attacked. Foley was the executive officer for the U.S. Agency for International Development (USAID). While he was in his driveway and was getting into his car to go to work, he was shot several times with a pistol equipped with a silencer. The late Abu Musab al-Zarqawi ordered Foley's assassination.

Unfortunately, Foley did not heed the embassy's advice to vary routes and times. Consequently, he came under preincident surveillance by a Libyan and a Jordanian working for al-Zarqawi. Jordanian authorities subsequently arrested and convicted Foley's two assassins; on March 11, 2006, both men were executed.

Surveillance is conducted from stationary or mobile positions by a single person or teams of several *surveillers*. They may follow on foot, in vehicles, or even on public transportation. Targets should not assume that surveillers will be male; women are often used, and children may be manipulated or rewarded to watch foreigners.

How to Determine Whether You Are under Surveillance

- You notice something that is *not* normal (e.g., a person dressed in business dress but idle for hours; a man working on a broken-down car that is never fixed or removed; a utility van with no obvious work being conducted; a person with a camera or a camcorder who is taking photos in your direction).
- You see someone sitting in the same car near your hotel or residence and he or she appears to do nothing for lengthy periods.
- You suddenly see a street vendor you have never seen before.
- Local acquaintances tell you that strangers have been asking questions about you.

- You notice people who always check their watches when you walk by them.
- You observe people in areas you frequent who wash the same car repeatedly.

How to Confirm You Are Being Surveilled

This task is tricky. You do not want to alert a surveiller that you are suspicious. If handled improperly, the actions you take to confirm surveillance could cause the person or team you suspect to shut down operations. Conversely, the surveillance could continue but with different surveillers. If the surveillance is a precursor to a kidnapping or crime attempt, your obvious suspicions could cause the surveillers to move up their timetable. Here are some steps to take discreetly.

☐ If on foot, stop occasionally to look into a store window. Use this pause to determine whether the person you suspect of surveilling you stops or simply walks on. Do this several times to confirm whether the same person always stops or whether other surveillers key in on your movements.

☐ If in a vehicle, drive around the block several times to see whether the driver of a suspect vehicle continues to follow you. If so, try to memorize the trailing vehicle's license plate without being obvious.

☐ Vary your routes and times of departure and arrival to determine whether suspected surveillers remain with you.

☐ Do *not* attempt to outrun or "slip up" a surveiller, as this could make the situation worse.

☐ If you believe you are the target of surveillance, do *not* drive to your home; the surveiller may not yet know where you live.

If you believe you are under surveillance:

☐ Contact the security representative at your embassy or consulate. If you are an American citizen, ask to speak to the RSO. If you are calling after hours, ask to speak to the embassy duty officer.

☐ If you are working abroad, report the matter verbally and in writing to your employer's security representative or general manager.

Never think you are being silly to report a suspected surveillance. Remember that our instincts tell us what to do well before our brain figures it out. Trust those instincts. The target that remains ignorant of his or her surroundings or succumbs to denial often moves from a bad situation to a worse situation.

Practice proactive *countersurveillance* by doing the following:

☐ Be predictably *unpredictable* in high-threat environments.

☐ Avoid "chokepoints," a place you can always be expected to be at a particular time.

☐ Vary the routes you take and your departure and arrival times in environments in which you feel the risk of surveillance.

☐ Be observant of people around you; pay attention to abnormal or suspicious behavior.

☐ When driving, use rear-view and side mirrors periodically to examine what is going on behind you. (In many cases, foreigners leaving restaurants have been followed by criminals who then commit a home invasion robbery.)

Ransom Kidnapping, Abduction, and Hostage Taking: What Is the Risk?

In early 2001, I flew from Chicago to Bogotá to conduct a vulnerability assessment of new office space for a multinational company. I sat next to an American executive who was flying to San Juan (via Miami). He asked me where I was going. When I replied, "Bogotá," he asked me whether I was aware of the dangers in Bogotá. I responded, "Less dangerous than San Juan if you stay in the capital and don't do anything stupid." I told him that I had been traveling to Bogotá, Medellin, and Cali for more than 20 years and had never had a problem. He asked me how that was possible if Colombia was "the kidnap capital of the world." My response was the same one that I recommend in this book: "Be careful, know the threat, know areas to avoid, anticipate what might happen next, and know what to do if it *actually* happens."

Nevertheless, Colombia has the edge on the number of kidnappings (roughly 1,500–2,500 a year), but most kidnappings are not in the capital city. Most occur in small towns and rural areas. Remember that statistics are unreliable because of the high number of unreported abductions. Nevertheless, the actual number of kidnappings has declined in the past two years because of changes in the criminal code, computerization of kidnap cases, and development of prosecutorial/police task forces to increase arrests and convictions. Since 1980, roughly 100 Americans and about the same number of Europeans have been kidnapped in Colombia.

Mexico has the second-highest number of kidnappings (1,000–2,000), followed by Brazil, the Philippines, Venezuela, India, Guatemala, Nigeria, Argentina, Ecuador, Russia, Trinidad and Tobago, Haiti, and South Africa. Approximately 70 percent of abductions (across all categories) occur in Latin America.

Long-Term Kidnapping

Despite common misconceptions, few kidnap victims in Colombia are foreigners; however, when Colombian kidnappers seize foreigners, the results often are tragic. The period of captivity frequently is a year or longer. Below are just a few examples:

- January 1993: Three U.S. missionaries with the New Tribes Mission were kidnapped in Panama by the Revolutionary Armed Forces of Colombia (FARC) and taken to Colombia. In October 2001, the three men were eventually declared dead.

- September 1994: U.S. agronomist Tom Hargrove was kidnapped by the FARC outside Cali on his way to work. He was held for 11 months in the jungle. Two ransom payments were made before he was released. See Hargrove's book entitled, *Long March to Freedom*.

- April 1998: One day before they were scheduled to return home from Bogotá, four birdwatchers from the United States rented a car and drove an hour from the capital to go birding. The four ran into a FARC roadblock; the rebels held them along with other kidnap victims for a month before releasing them. *Comment: This case demonstrates how ignorance and naiveté can really get people into serious trouble.*

- March 1999: Three U.S. citizens on a mission to help organize schools for the indigenous U'wa were kidnapped by the FARC in Arauca. The victims (one woman and two men) were beaten, tortured, and shot to death. Their bodies were found near the Colombian-Venezuelan border approximately a week after the kidnapping.

- February 2003: Three American Northrop-Grumman contractors flying on an antidrug mission crashed in a rebel-active area in southern Colombia and were subsequently kidnapped by the FARC. A Colombian police officer, who had been held by the FARC for eight years before his escape in April 2007, confirmed that the contractors were alive.

Currently, the FARC is holding perhaps as many as 100 kidnap victims. Few are foreigners. However, most diplomats, multinational executives, and expatriates almost never travel by road in Colombia, unless no other option exists.

Fortunately, long-term kidnappings of foreigners are not a frequent occurrence in Colombia or Mexico. When foreigners are abducted, they are usually in rural areas and vulnerable to either rebels or criminals, who kidnap individuals for a living. Some individuals foolishly enter areas where kidnappings are known to occur. Although foreign travelers have been kidnapped for ransom in some of the countries listed earlier, the targets are usually locals of means—expatriates, ranchers, geologists, petroleum engineers, and multinational business executives. Global figures report between 8,000 and 10,000 long-term ransom kidnappings, most of them in Latin America.

Mass-Hostage Incidents

The section above discusses "traditional" forms of detention. This section includes examples of mass-hostage situations, which can be stationary or mobile:

- April 1997: In December 1996, Peru's Tupac Amaru Revolutionary Movement seized more than 600 hostages (some foreigners) at the Japanese Embassy in Lima. The takeover lasted 126 days and ended with an armed assault by the government. All of the hostage-takers were killed.

- October 2002: Chechen militants took over the Dubrovka Theater in Moscow and held 850 hostages. The militants demanded Russia's withdrawal from Chechnya. The incident lasted nearly three days and ended when the Russian government pumped fentanyl into the air conditioning system, thus killing 33 terrorists and 129 hostages.

- August 2003: In February 2003, 14 European tourists on a desert safari in Algeria were kidnapped by the Salafist Group for Call and Combat (linked to al-Qaeda). Originally, a portion of the group of 32 (13 were released and one died of heat stroke) was held for six months and moved from Algeria to Mali, where the Malian government helped secure the victims' release.

- February 2007: A Moroccan man with two handguns hijacked an Air Mauritania B-737 after it left the capital for the Canary Islands. He demanded transport to France. After the passengers and crew overpowered the hijacker, the pilot landed the aircraft at a military airport in the Canaries. Police stormed the plane and arrested the hijacker. Twenty-one passengers sustained minor injuries.

- May 2007: Four British and three American oil workers in Nigeria were kidnapped by militants representing the Movement for the Emancipation of the Niger Delta. This group had been demanding a greater share of oil revenues for the Delta region, where more than 200 foreign oil workers have been kidnapped in the past 18 months.

Kidnap victims are usually released after the payment of ransom, although many companies refuse to pay.

You are unlikely to become a victim of any of the foregoing forms of detention—unless, of course, you are unaware and wander into a rebel-infested area, as did the U.S. bird-watchers in Colombia.

Express Kidnappings

Although long-term and mass-hostage kidnappings are rare, *express kidnapping* (aka *secuestro express*) can happen to anyone, particularly those traveling throughout much of Latin America. The number of express kidnappings is increasing in Africa and elsewhere.

An express kidnapping is a short-term abduction, usually lasting less than than 36 hours. Armed kidnappers abduct a target, either a pedestrian or an individual in a vehicle (often in conjunction with a carjacking). Kidnappers take the victim to an isolated ATM and force him or her to make the maximum withdrawal. In some cases, the kidnappers hold the victim until the next day so he or she can make another withdrawal. A variation of this tactic is to hold the person until family or friends provide a specified amount of cash, jewelry, or valuables.

In many cases, victims of express kidnappings who resist are injured or killed. Unfortunately, less than 10 percent of these crimes are reported to the police. If you are ever a victim of an express kidnapping, report the crime, especially if you have been injured or harmed or your vehicle has been stolen as a result of the crime. Also, report the crime for insurance purposes. The following are some examples of express kidnappings:

- March 2000: In 2000, while playing golf outside the capital of Georgetown, Guyana, U.S. Embassy regional security officer Steve Lesniak was kidnapped. The kidnappers threatened to kill him if a ransom of $300,000 was not paid. When the U.S. government refused the kidnappers' demand, Steve's girlfriend and family facilitated a ransom payment of a lesser amount, and Lesniak was released.

- July 2005: A Mexican businessman arriving at the international airport in Caracas, Venezuela, from Mexico City, Mexico, was confronted by a man as he used an ATM in an isolated area of the airport. The man, who had approached the victim earlier in the arrival area to offer services, lifted his shirt to display a handgun tucked in his waistband. The man escorted the businessman to a taxi, where another assailant was waiting. The businessman was taken into Caracas and driven to several ATMs to withdraw money from his accounts. He was later released unharmed.

- April 2007: After picking up two friends in his vehicle, a 38-year-old Sao Paulo, Brazil, topographer was forced to stop by a car driven by three men brandishing firearms. The three victims were taken to an isolated area, where they were pushed into a dark, deep hole in the ground. The victims were forced at gunpoint to hand over their credit cards and PINs. Two of the kidnappers left with the credit cards to withdraw money from an ATM, while the third remained with the victims. The topographer had a preexisting medical condition that resulted in chronic cramping in his elbows. The kidnapper mistook a sudden movement the topographer made to ease the elbow pain as an aggressive act and shot the topographer in the head. When the other two kidnappers returned and saw that the topographer was dead, they decided to kill the other two victims. The gunmen opened fire on the two remaining victims, who feigned death. The kidnappers fled in the victims' vehicle; the surviving victims notified the police.

Ransom Insurance

Although a substantial percentage of Fortune 500 companies purchase kidnap and ransom (K&R) insurance for employees who live or travel in high-risk countries, insurance companies that sell such coverage stipulate that K&R policy details are to be kept secret from those the policy protects. Companies with major exposure in developing countries derive definite advantages from this coverage, considering that roughly 65 percent of kidnap cases involve ransom payments, whereas less than 20 percent involve release without ransom payments. In addition, most underwriters have formal relationships with experienced consultants who deploy to a country in the event of a kidnapping and provide strategies to negotiators, intermediaries, family members, and underwriters' management.

The downside of K&R coverage is that payment of the ransom is often on a reimbursable basis. That is, a company must have assets that can be liquidated for the ransom payment; the underwriter reimburses the company or individual only after the ransom is paid. Travelers and expatriates should ask employers about the extent of the corporate commitment to gain their freedom if kidnapped. The Web sites listed below link to underwriters that provide K&R coverage. The last URL links to the Control Risks Group, which has probably handled more kidnap responses than any other global company:

- **http://www.piu.org**
- **http://www.willis.com**
- **http://www.chubb.com**
- **http://www.crg.com**

This chapter places the threat of various forms of detention in context. As you can see, the likelihood of your risk for most forms of detention is actually quite low (although express kidnappings should be considered when traveling in certain high-risk countries). To learn how to avoid, prevent, or survive a detention, please go to pages 279–283.

U.S. Policy

The policy of the U.S. government prohibits negotiating with criminals and terrorists who kidnap U.S. citizens.

The U.S. government will not pay ransom, release prisoners, provide weapons, or facilitate the escape of hostage takers. This applies particularly to employees of the U.S. government and their family members. In cases where U.S. citizens are seized or abducted, the United States always leaves the resolution of the kidnapping or hostage taking to the government of the nation in which the crime occurred.

Although the U.S. government will not pay ransom or make concessions, most U.S. multinational companies that operate in developing countries invariably pay ransom when their executives are kidnapped. Ironically, this inconsistency works: looking back on the three decades in which Colombia has led the world in kidnappings, only one U.S. government official has been abducted, compared to 99 kidnappings of Americans without government ties. Most of these victims were released after a ransom payment; in other cases, the victims were killed. Very few escaped.

It should be noted that the U.S. policy on hostage-taking evolved during President Richard M. Nixon's administration when Uruguay's Tupamaros kidnapped USAID officer Dan Mitrione in July 1970, while he was working as a police advisor in Montevideo. At the time, the USAID Office of Public Safety program had drawn criticism for not promoting democratic police tactics in Latin America, which, at the time, was facing an upsurge in leftist terrorism. The Tupamaros demanded that the Uruguayan and U.S. governments release 150 Tupamaros prisoners. When the United States urged the Uruguayan government not to give in to the demand, the Tupamaros executed Mitrione and dumped his body in the back of an abandoned car. The Mitrione case subsequently led to the formulation of the "no negotiations, no concessions" policy regarding international hostage taking that the U.S. government follows to this day.

Fraud and Scams Played on Travelers
Nigerian 419 Scams

One of the most prevalent forms of fraud directed at foreigners is the *Nigerian 419* scam; the number comes from the section of the Nigerian criminal code that addresses such fraud. These scams have victimized thousands of foreigners, including successful senior business executives. One such scam is advance fee fraud (AFF). Potential victims are convinced that they have been selected to share in multimillion-dollar windfall profits for doing virtually nothing. AFF scams often begin with a letter, a fax, an e-mail, or a telephone call from a person purporting to be an official in Nigeria or another African country. The main content of the call appears (at first glance) to be a legitimate proposal for transfer of a huge sum of money from one account to another. In the notification, the sender informs the recipient that he is seeking a reputable foreign company or individual into whose account he can deposit funds ranging from $10 to $60 million that the Nigerian government overpaid on some procurement contract. Initially, the target victim is instructed to provide company letterheads and pro forma invoicing that will be used to show completion of the contract. One reason for the request is to use the victim's letterhead to forge letters of recommendation to other victim companies. The victim is told that the completed contracts will be submitted for him or her.

Indications are that AFF grosses hundreds of millions of dollars annually. In all likelihood, some victims do not report their losses to authorities because of fear or embarrassment. For additional information, refer to the DOS publication *Nigerian Advance Fee Fraud* (**http://www.state. gov/regions/africa/naffpub.pdf**).

In many cases, victims of these scams are invited to Nigeria or other African countries to meet real or bogus government officials. Some victims who do travel are instead held for ransom. In some cases, victims have even been smuggled into the country without a visa and threatened into giving up more money. The penalties for being in a foreign country without a visa can be severe. Some specific cases involving Nigerian fraud highlight the severity and desperation that result. For instance:

- Danut Tetrescu, a Romanian who flew from Bucharest to Johannesburg to meet with con men in the Soweto area of Johannesburg, was kidnapped in 1999 and held for $500,000.
- Mary Winkler, who was sentenced to 210 days in prison for voluntary manslaughter in the shooting death of her pastor husband in Tennessee, was defrauded of $17,500 in a 419 scam in 2006.

■ A bookkeeper for a Michigan law firm in 2002 emptied the company bank account of $2.1 million in expectation of a $4.5-million payout from a 419 scam.

The Financial Crimes Division of the U.S. Secret Service receives daily approximately 100 telephone calls from victims/potential victims and 300–500 pieces of 419-related correspondence. If you have already lost funds or feel you may be a potential victim of the above scheme, please contact your local Secret Service field office in the United States or overseas (**http://www.secretservice.gov**) or the RSO (**http://www.osac.gov/posts**). If you have received communication asking you to participate in one of these scams but have not lost any money, forward the letter or e-mail to **419.fcd@usss.treas.gov** or fax it to (202) 406-6930.

Even the most experienced traveler can be duped by confidence artists abroad. Fatigue, jet lag, unfamiliar surroundings and customs, and, occasionally, verbal misunderstandings result in travelers being victimized. Some examples of scams to be on the alert for are:

☐ *Bogus porter.* An individual outside the airport terminal approaches you and claims to be a porter. He may even have a cap and a uniform. Be cautious to whom you give your bags. Never place your carry-on bag on a porter's cart, as an assistant for the "porter" may suddenly appear, grab your carry-on luggage, and disappear into the crowd, with the porter feigning dismay.

☐ *Accidental spill.* This is a commonly used scam world-wide. Someone passed by close to you and suddenly spilled a drink or food on your clothing, only to apologize profusely while a confederate lifts your wallet or passport from your pocket or purse.

☐ *"Watch for Pickpocket" signs.* This is a very innovative scam. Pickpockets place signs on walls near tourist sites that urge tourists to be alert for pickpockets. The pickpockets watch tourists to see how they react to the sign. Tourists' reactions help determine what the pickpockets target—for example, if a tourist tightens her grip on her purse, that is where she is carrying the "goods." If a man pats his back pocket, he unwittingly signals to the pickpocket where his wallet is located.

☐ *Faulty taxi meter.* Inoperative meters and exorbitant fares are commonplace, particularly in countries where taxis are not regulated. Insist upon using the meter, or, better yet, always agree on the fare before you get into the car.

☐ *Use of drugs to weaken defenses.* Criminals can lace your drink with one of several drugs (including date rape substances; see pages 239–241) to make you susceptible to both nonviolent and violent crime. These drugs can be used in liquids, sprays, and powders. To prevent this from happening, never leave drinks unattended, and be suspicious of particularly attentive new friends.

☐ *Counterfeit gems and antiques.* Be extremely cautious in purchasing gems and antiques. Insist on a certificate of authenticity so that if it later proves to be unauthentic, you have documented evidence of fraud. Furthermore, before you purchase antiques, find out what type of genuine antiquities cannot be exported. Often an unscrupulous merchant will sell an item to a visitor and then alert an accomplice in the customs service who seizes the item upon your departure and levies a heavy fine. The item is returned to the merchant and resold to another unwitting foreigner.

Protecting Laptops, Cell Phones, MP3 Players, and Proprietary Information

A laptop computer is stolen every 53 seconds. This figure does not include those laptops left in rental cars, at airports, and in hotels. According to FBI reports, 97 percent of those laptops are never returned. We have heard the stories of 200 laptops missing from the FBI and throughout the government. Companies, too, suffer losses. Multinational companies lose computers loaded with trade secrets and proprietary information. The situation is even worse in other countries. In many cases, the thefts are more serious because thieves are paid to steal laptops from foreign business executives. Many foreign travelers are simply too complacent about laptop security.

In an upcoming book, ***Economic Espionage: Protecting Laptops, Trade Secrets, and Proprietary Information***, scheduled for release in February, 2009 (see page 327), I address in detail protecting sensitive information abroad. In this chapter, I give a brief overview of laptop and information security; however, if you work abroad, you will get the message from the tips below:

☐ If you travel with a laptop, cell phone/PDA, MP3 player, digital camera, flash drives, external hard drives, or a camcorder, insure this equipment for accidental damages or losses. Not long ago, a British couple rented a car upon arrival in South Africa, parked in front of a luxury resort, and entered the office area to confirm their reservations. When they returned to their car 20 minutes later, they discovered that the car was gone, along with their laptops, cells phones, outbound tickets, and traveler's checks. Before you leave home, ensure that electronic components are covered by your homeowner's policy, renter's insurance, or international travel insurance. Review seriously the underwriters' list at **http://www.safeware.com**. This company provides international breakage, accidental damage, and confiscation coverage. This coverage is also beneficial to students on a foreign study program.

☐ Consider permanently affixing your name, address phone and cell numbers and email address on your laptop, along with a statement that a reward is offered for its return, if lost. This could help you recover the laptop if it is lost, and it will discourage fencing. Or, tape your business card to your laptop with a note promising a reward if returned.

☐ Always carry a laptop in a padded protective sleeve in a zippered bag. I have seen travelers carry laptops without a sleeve in open tote bags or under their arms while walking through airports. I have seen many laptops dropped in airports; this issue needs to be stressed.

☐ While traveling on airplanes, waiting for flights, or in cafes while working on your laptop, be cautious of people glancing at your screen if you are working on proprietary files. I prefer using 3M privacy filters, which will prevent others from reading your work (**http://www.3Mprivacyfilter.com**).

☐ Do not believe that a password secures your laptop. It does not. The only way to increase the security of your laptop is to purchase software designed to safeguard access to your folders and files (see pages 78–79).

☐ Do not go abroad without a firewall, comprehensive antivirus software, and high-level security on your wireless configuration.

☐ Free Wi-Fi hotspots are convenient, but imagine the number of hackers at airports, hotels and coffee shops. If your laptop's wireless configuration is secure, the following two Web sites will help you find free Wi-Fi zones: **http://www.jiwire.com/hotspots** and **http://www.wififreespot.com**.

☐ Do not leave your laptop unattended in fee-based airline hospitality lounges. Criminals often rent a mailbox, join an airline club, and buy a cheap ticket for admittance to the passengers-only area to gain access to unattended luggage and laptops.

☐ Do not place your laptop, MP3 player, or other electronics in the aircraft's seat pocket in front of you. You could forget them.

☐ Purchase a backup battery for your laptop to ensure available power. Purchase a cable that allows you to connect to the seat power systems on many airplanes.

☐ Use a cable lock on your laptop. Almost 80 percent of laptops come with a security port that, when used with a cable lock, will secure them to a heavy piece of furniture. One of the best sources for cable locks is **http://www.secure-it.com**, which also carries a wide range of computer security products.

☐ Ensure that your laptop power supplies are dual voltage. If not, bring the proper plugs (see page 6) so that you can recharge your computer.

☐ Do not take a conventional black laptop bag overseas. These bags scream, "Take me!" Purchase a padded backpack instead. Your laptop will be inconspicuous inside that backpack. The following two companies offer many options: **http://www.targus.com** and **http://www.mobileoffice.about.com**.

☐ If you use a laptop that stores trade secrets, client lists, business strategies, and/or proposals, use Pretty

Good Privacy (PGP) software. For approximately $150 (**http://www.pgp.com**), you can encrypt the entire hard drive or specific folders. PGP safeguards the information on your computer, even if a foreign intelligence service mirror images your hard drive, if your laptop is left in your hotel room.

☐ If PGP is not an option, carry a travel laptop with only MS Office and applications you need. Do not place your working files on the laptop. Rather, keep files on a 4-GB flash drive, and always carry it with you. Of course, this approach does not solve the security of your e-mail system, so the only safe way to deal with this problem is to use an e-mail-capable cell phone. Turn off the phone when it is not in use, and rely upon voice mail to respond to callers' messages.

☐ Assume that calls made from your hotel room are monitored. A more secure option is a quad-band unlocked cell phone that you can use in a coffee shop.

☐ Do not place sensitive business documents in the wastebasket in your hotel room, and do not leave documents unsecured in your room.

☐ Do not ask the business center to duplicate sensitive business documents; you do not know whether an extra copy is made.

☐ Travel with a few inexpensive flash drives. If you copy a file to a flash drive, use a business center computer, and make changes to the file, destroy that flash drive.

DO NOT use it in your laptop. You may risk the contamination or destruction of your hard drive.

How the U.S. State Department or Your Foreign Ministry Can Assist You

The foreign affairs components of most governments offer information, support, and assistance on:

- Passport issuance, renewal, and replacement (for theft or loss)
- Referral lists of medical providers and English-speaking attorneys
- Registration of travelers
- Location of missing citizens
- Intermediary services in the event of arrest or incarceration
- Emergency services to citizens, including authorized evacuation from a foreign country

They also offer assistance to travelers who have been victimized by crime.

Registration of your trip. I suggest you take advantage of a very important service that the U.S. Department of State and several governments provide their citizens: registration of your travel itinerary abroad. Before automation, citizens had to stand in line and register at an embassy or consulate. Today, this is done electronically on the Department's

Web site (**http://www.travel.state.gov**) before you leave home. During the 2006 hostilities between Hezbollah and Israeli forces in Lebanon, some 60,000 foreigners were trapped in Beirut, many of them because their embassies were unaware of their presence in Lebanon. Other reasons to register your travel involve your government being able to reach you in case of an emergency or death in your family or in the event of natural disasters in the country you are visiting. To register, go to the Web site listed above and complete the requested information. If you are not a U.S. citizen, contact your country's foreign affairs department to learn how to register with the embassy or consulate at your destination.

Lists of medical providers and attorneys. Go the Web sites of your embassies and consulates, which have such lists, or contact the underwriter of your international medical care and evacuation coverage (*see Web sites at the end of this chapter*).

If you are victimized by an act of crime or terrorism while abroad, contact the consular section or duty officer of your embassy. If you cannot reach your embassy/consulate and are an American citizen, contact the State Department's Office of Overseas Citizens Services 24-7 at (202) 647-5225. If you have been a crime victim, embassies and consulates can assist you with the following:

- Replacing stolen/lost passports
- Contacting family and friends

- Obtaining medical care
- Getting advice on the pros and cons of prosecution and obtaining information on the handling of your case

Traveling Americans should also realize that consular officers can advise U.S. citizens on how to request compensation or reimbursement for costs following victimization by criminals or terrorists while abroad, primarily through the U.S. Department of Justice's Victims of Crime Act (1984). Such programs are described in Section 7 of the State's *Foreign Affairs Manual*, section 1960. Currently, 30 foreign governments have victim compensation programs, and many are available to foreigners victimized abroad. For further information, refer to the following:

- **http://www.ojp.usdoj.gov/ovc**

If you are injured, robbed, or assaulted or require medical attention, obtain a copy of the police report, and get a certified translated copy of it. This could help with submitting insurance and reimbursement claims. Finally, obtain copies of reports that describe medical treatment.

If you have been a victim of crime abroad, have been arrested, or have encountered some other type of major problem, it is possible that occasionally you may receive less than a sympathetic response from the staff of some U.S. embassies or consulates. If you feel like you're not receiving adequate support from State Department representatives:

☐ Do not be unreasonable, and never ask for help while intoxicated.

☐ Always get the name of the embassy officer you encounter. Get his or her title and phone number.

☐ Firmly but diplomatically request to speak to the consul general or the ambassador to get your problem solved. If you are denied this request, ensure that you get the name of the person who denied you access.

☐ After you get name(s), title(s), and number(s), simply say something to the effect, "I know that your inclination is to be helpful to me, but actually you're not being helpful at all. I guess my only option is to write the ambassador a letter or contact the Secretary of State and/or my congressperson. Thank you." Embassy officers do not want external pressure that will eventually require them to explain how they treated you.

☐ If you are told that the *Foreign Affairs Manual* (FAM) precludes the embassy from helping you on a particular issue, ask to see that section of the FAM that precludes it.

☐ Before every trip abroad, make a copy of the list of key officers of the embassy or consulate at your destination (from **http://www.state.gov**) so you know the right person to contact. This information will also give you the embassy or consulate fax number.

☐ Carry with you the names, e-mail addresses, and contact information of your congressional representatives. You may have to contact them to exert pressure on the State

Department. Cabinet department heads must respond promptly to letters from congresspersons or senators.

Death of an American citizen. Roughly 6,000 Americans die while abroad each year. In such cases, the U.S. State Department can be helpful in registration of a death; however, most details and arrangements, including financial ones, are the responsibilities of families of decedents. I suggest you not leave the responsibility for these arrangements to people you do not know.

Determining the whereabouts of American citizens. The U.S. State Department can attempt to contact U.S. citizens who are abroad. In many cases, there may be a family emergency in the United States or cases where a U.S. family or employer cannot contact an American abroad, which is why the registration of your trip abroad is so important. Most missing Americans usually are located, but hundreds and perhaps more are not. Two examples include Brigham Young University student David Sneddon, who disappeared while hiking alone near the Tibetan border in China in 2004. He remains missing (**http://www.helpfinddavid. com**). Another missing American is Christine Feld-Boskoff, a famous mountain climber who disappeared during a climb in Litang, China. The body of Feld-Boskoff's climbing partner, Charles Fowler, was found in December 2006. Feld-Boskoff remains missing, although she is presumed dead. One excellent service that enables friends and families to attempt to locate travelers abroad via cell phone and e-mail is **http://www.sendwordnow.com**, which will be described later in the section on emergency evacuation.

Child exploitation. U.S. citizens should also be aware of the Child Protect Act of 2003, which reaches beyond U.S. borders to help protect children under the age of 18 and combat child sex tourism. Since the law was enacted, eight U.S. residents have been arrested on charges of child sex tourism. The U.S. Immigration and Customs Enforcement (ICE), a component of the Department of Homeland Security, continues to investigate cases of U.S. citizens who have sexually exploited children. ICE has also assigned 32 agents in countries where child sex tourism is particularly active. Under the Act, conviction could result in a mandatory 30-year imprisonment for each offense related to the sexual exploitation of children. ICE maintains a toll-free telephone number to report suspected child exploitation perpetrated by U.S. residents. The hotline number is 1-866-347-2423. Information can also be e-mailed to ICE investigators at **3@ dhs.gov**. Other organizations involved in combating child sex tourism include:

- **http://www.ncmec.org** (the National Center for Missing and Exploited Children)
- **http://www.ecpat.net** (End Child Prostitution, etc.)
- **http://www.worldvision.org** (World Vision)
- **http://www.state.gov/m/ds/** (U.S. Diplomatic Security Service)

Embassy Web sites. Below are several Web sites that provide additional information:

- **http://www.embassyworld.com** (embassies worldwide)
- **http://www.osac.gov/Posts** (information on RSOs worldwide)
- **http://www.usembassy.state.gov** (Web sites and resource information on all U.S. embassies)

Conducting Your Own Country Assessment Prior to Departure

If you work for a company or an organization that employs a security manager, ask for a country-specific briefing before traveling abroad.

If you are a tourist, an entrepreneur, an independent consultant, a freelance journalist, or a student, you may have to conduct your own threat assessment.

Note that many travelers who get into trouble abroad know little about the country they are visiting and are unaware of potential misfortunes. As such, research the security threats, learn about the culture and language, and know what you should *not* do and where you should *not* go. If you have no choice but to go to a high-risk country, read *carefully*. Here are some other good sources:

☐ Go to the following Web sites and search for information and advisories concerning the countries to which you will be traveling. I suggest you visit *all* the sites because each source approaches security issues differently.

- **http://www.travel.state.gov** (United States)
- **http://www.fco.gov.uk** (United Kingdom)
- **http://www.dfait-maeci.gc.ca** (Canada)
- **http://www.smarttraveller.gov.au** (Australia)

☐ Refer to the *CIA World Factbook* (**http://www.cia. gov/library** and the State Department's *Background Notes* (**http://www.state.gov/r/pa/ei/bgn**).

☐ Refer to **http://www.osac.gov** for global security alerts and information. Note that you must be an approved constitute of the Overseas Security Advisory Council (OSAC) to access some password-protected reports.

☐ Refer to **http://www.ediplomat.com**, which is a highly useful Australian resource that enables you to choose extensive and informative country reports on each country.

☐ If you want to know where your destination country fits in comparison to other nations on quality of life (including personal security and health), read Mercer Human Resource Consulting's (**http://www.mercer. com**) annual quality of life annual report of 350 global cities.

☐ Go to the Internet and type in "crime in [the name of your destination]." You will find, depending on the threat, reliable and unreliable reports and news accounts pertaining to security and crime issues. For example, if you search "crime in Kenya," you will see the significance information on the criminal threat and OSAC's crime report on the country. Moreover, if you visit **http://www.travel.state.gov** and click on "Travel," you will see a path to travel advisories that provide more in-depth information on the criminal threat in Kenya.

☐ Purchase a reputable travel guide on the country to which you will be traveling. The travel guide should cover crime, terrorism, unrest, and cultural "dos" and "don'ts."

☐ Purchase a map of the country you will visit so that you can become familiar with the area before departing:

- **http://www.onemapplace.com**
- **http://www.store.randmcnalley.com**
- **http://www.borders.com**
- **http://www.barnesandnoble.com**

☐ Purchase city maps of the cities and towns you will be traveling in upon arrival in the country.

SECTION TWO

What You Need to Know before Departure

What You Need to Know about Passports and Visas

☐ Do not leave passport issues until the *last minute* because the U.S. State Department is severely backlogged with passport applications. Routine applications can take months before passports are issued. Most travelers focus early on flight and hotel reservations, ground transportation, meetings, and tours but delay dealing with their passport and visa requirements until the last minute.

☐ If you have never had a passport, you must apply for it in person (for details, go to **http://www.travel.state.gov**).

☐ If your current passport expires within six months, you could be denied entry at your destination. Make sure it is valid for at least six to eight months after your expected return from abroad.

☐ Many nations are *not* flexible on requirements that you have a visa. If they require a visa and you do not have one, you could be denied entry or be deported.

☐ Some nations are extremely slow in issuing visas, so do not assume you can get a visa at the airport or in a day or so. In most cases, you cannot.

☐ If you will be conducting *business* in another country, get a business visa; otherwise, you could be fined or arrested for a violation of the country's immigration laws. Having a business visa may also authorize you to bring in a laptop or business products/materials; otherwise, you may be forced to pay a surety bond on your electronic equipment or pay customs fees on business samples.

☐ Most countries are extremely strict on foreigners working within their borders (either as nonresidents or as residents) without a work permit or visa authorizing them to earn income within the country. In some cases, foreigners have been prosecuted criminally for not having a work visa and/or a work permit and for tax evasion.

☐ Pay careful attention to visa applications. In some cases, they require sponsorship letters, an explanation of your purpose of travel, and/or a statement of financial responsibility. In addition, the photos you had taken for your passport will not suffice for visa applications in many countries (e.g., the Philippines requires photos **without** eyeglasses and your signature on each of the two required photos).

For further information, please refer to:

- **http://www.travel.state.gov/passport**
- **http://www.travel.state.gov/passport/get/renew**
- **http://www.unitedstatesvisas.gov**

In compliance with the Intelligence Reform and Terrorism Prevention Act of 2004, citizens of any country (including the United States) traveling by *air* between the United States and Canada, Mexico, Central and South America, the Caribbean, and Bermuda must have a passport, effective January 23, 2007. Effective January 31, 2008, all travelers entering the United States from Mexico, Canada, the Caribbean or Bermuda will require a government-issued photo identification card *and* proof of citizen, such as a birth certificate. Further, on a date to a be determined later, anyone traveling to the United States from any of the aforementioned sovereignties will be required to travel on a passport or other authorized identification. Note: These requirements do not apply to persons traveling to or from a U.S. territory.

These new requirements are one of the reasons that resources are so limited and routine issuance of new and renewed passports can take weeks or, in some cases, months if you go through the normal process. Foreign ministries, embassies, and consulates worldwide are feeling the strain of this additional workload and resultant backlog.

The U.S. State Department does have an expedited process for getting new or renewed U.S. passports to you in two or three weeks. In this case, additional fees are required for expedited service and for overnight delivery. See **http://www.travel.state.gov/passport**. A word of caution, though: the expedited process takes closer to six weeks, despite State Department promises.

For those planning to travel in fewer than two months, Travisa may be an option. The company is based in Washington, D.C., and has offices in New York City, San Francisco, Chicago, Los Angeles, Miami, London, and Beijing. It has excellent connections at the State Department and on Embassy Row to help you get new or renewed passports, additional passport pages, visas, and second valid passports. Travisa also handles Indian and British passports. The company's website is **http://www.travisa.com**, and its phone number is (202) 463-6166 or (800) 222-2589.

There are three types of U.S. passports: (1) regular (issued to all citizens), (2) official (issued to citizens on official assignments abroad for the U.S. government), and (3) diplomatic (originally reserved for accredited diplomats only to foreign governments, but in recent years issued to expedite government officials who are not accredited diplomats).

Important travel tips:

☐ Do not purchase or use a passport holder/wallet to protect your passport *if it is affixed with the great seal of the United States*. Most are, and they advertise that you are an American. However, Travisa, mentioned above, does have a travel store on its Web site that sells blank passport holders at a reasonable cost.

☐ Before leaving on your trip, ensure that you have a photocopy of the photo and information page from your passport (particularly the section that contains the passport number) and extra passport photos tucked away in your carry-on luggage. This will expedite replacing a lost or stolen passport if you are one of many travelers who lose their passports.

☐ Remember that the U.S. is not the only country that has rigorous entry regulations for non-citizens. Even though six years has passed since the events of 9/11, governments aligned with the United States in the GWOT continue to institute rigorous rules for foreigners traveling abroad. Examples include the Government of Japan now requiring all foreigners over 16 to be subject to fingerprinting and having their photograph taken by immigration officials. Further, the European Union proposed in February 2008 a plan to store significant personal information (including credit card information) on foreign travelers without a clear strategy of how it will be used.

Using Financial Instruments Abroad

The disadvantage of using currency abroad is that carrying too much cash increases your risk of becoming a victim of crime. Hence, the advantages to using other financial instruments are considerable.

In most countries, credit cards, ATM cards, and check and debit cards are accepted although with varying levels of compatibility. The downside is the risk of fraud. Be aware of the following:

☐ *Foreign exchange transaction.* Before arriving at your destination, print a copy of the currencies used, and learn what they look like by denomination. Not knowing the currency and the general exchange rate can result in legitimate and black market money changers cheating you.

☐ *Credit card switch.* The credit card returned to you after you make a purchase is not yours. Instead, it is an expired or stolen card. Always examine your card when merchants return it to you and verify that it is yours.

☐ *Credit card fraud.* If possible, observe that merchants process only one transaction. Dishonest merchants, assuming you will never check your statement, can process two or more transactions. I returned home from a trip to Colombia to find more than $3,000 in charges on my card for tires and auto parts. Always check your statement. Before you sign for a transaction, ensure that the name of the merchant is printed on the transaction slip.

☐ *Police impersonating money changers.* In many countries where currency is tightly controlled, dishonest police will often impersonate a money changer. When a foreigner uses the unauthorized money changer, the police officer identifies himself and demands several hundred dollars in exchange for not arresting him or her. Convert currency at authorized vendors only.

One new concern in credit card use abroad is credit card issuers adding surcharges from 2 to 4 percent on purchases. This trend emerged in 2004 when Providian Financial Corporation began adding a 4-percent surcharge to overseas card transactions. Citibank followed with a 2-percent fee and First USA with a 3-percent fee. When the media reported the surcharges, First USA rescinded its fee. The credit card issuers attributed the surcharges to the increased costs of transactions and the rise of credit card fraud. Interestingly, both Visa and MasterCard have levied a 1-percent surcharge on overseas card transactions for years. American Express currently levies a 2-percent surcharge.

Before using your credit card overseas, call your credit card issuer and ask it to explain its policy regarding a special surcharge on overseas transactions. If it does add a surcharge, find out the percentage that is added. The answer helps you determine the financial transaction strategy you will use overseas: currency, credit card, debit card, traveler's checks, or traveler's check cards.

As you plan for your business trip abroad, here are some suggestions for getting the most benefit financially from the options available:

☐ Get enough foreign currency before leaving the United States to cover initial expenses (e.g., porters at the airport, taxi fares, hotel bellhops, and perhaps a meal or other incidentals on the day of travel). You can purchase foreign currency through the following sources, but remember that the least beneficial rates of exchange will be at airports. Exchanging a large sum of money at an arriving airport also has associated risks. Criminals often observe travelers exchanging a lot of cash and later rob them. If you must exchange money at an airport, exchange $100 or less.

- http://www.americanexpress.com
- http://www.ezforex.com
- http://www.foreignexchangeservice.com

☐ Traveler's checks are available, but their use has declined since the traveler's check card became available from Visa, MasterCard, and AMEX. Traveler's check cards have the protection of traveler's checks if lost or stolen. DO NOT tape your PIN to the card. You can get these cards from participating institutions before you leave the country. Some can be ordered online. The cards are compatible worldwide at any ATM where the issuer's logo is posted, and they can be reloaded anywhere. The AMEX traveler's check card can be purchased in dollars, pounds, or euros.

- http://www.americanexpress.com
- http://www.mastercard.com/us/personal/en/aboutourcards/prepaid
- http://www.usa.visa.com/personal/cards/prepaid

☐ If you use your ATM card abroad, ensure that it is compatible in the countries you are visiting. Take at least one major credit card in the event you cannot find a compatible ATM and are forced to get a cash advance on a credit card. Both Visa and MasterCard have ATM locator information available on their Web sites:

- **http://www.visa.via.infonow.net/locator/global**
- **http://www.mastercard.com/us/personal/en//atmlocations**

☐ Use credit cards if you are carrying a surcharge-free card or one that does not exceed a 1-percent surcharge (e.g., Visa and MasterCard).

☐ Remember that ATM fees are usually less than the fees for obtaining a cash advance on a credit card.

☐ Using a designated ATM card at an ATM is less expensive than using a credit card at an ATM. For example, if you use an ATM card or a debit card to get cash in London, you pay a fee of $1 or $1.50 per withdrawal. Conversely, if you use a credit card to get cash from an ATM, you may pay a minimum fee of $5 or 3 percent of the transaction amount, whichever is greater. The cost is four times greater to withdraw $200 with a credit card than with an ATM card.

☐ Note that four-digit personal identification numbers (PINs) are common in most countries. If the PIN you use is not numeric, you may have to change it before leaving the United States.

☐ Before you leave for your overseas trip, secure some cash ($200–$300) in case you have difficulty getting local currency upon arrival.

☐ Although a debit card is generally easier to use abroad than a credit card, the disadvantages of using a debit card are:

- It often does not have the same protection as a credit card, particularly if you do not report loss or theft in a timely manner.

- You are in a weaker position when disputing a debit card purchase than when disputing a credit card purchase. If the financial institution that has issued your debit card is notified of loss or fraud within two business days, the cardholder's liability is generally capped at $50. If the notification of loss or fraud is made after two days but before 60 days, the loss is often capped at $500, and if notification is made after 60 days, the cardholder potentially risks the complete loss of all assets in his or her account.

- Using a debit card to place a deposit on a car rental or hotel reservation is not always possible.

- Using a debit card does not benefit your credit score. Debit card transactions are not reported to credit agencies.

Voice Communications Abroad

For years, I have told my "Safe Foreign Travel" workshop attendees that the ability to communicate 24-7 in an emergency is the *one* capability that will ensure their safety while abroad—*not* a firearm, pepper spray, or other security hardware or device.

During the 1990s, a friend of mine was working with an NGO in Honduras. On the long drive from Tegucigalpa to San Pedro Sula, his car broke down. He had no means of communications, so he simply waited by the side of the road and hoped that a helpful motorist or the police would pass by. Some time later, a car stopped, but instead of helping, the occupants shot and killed him and stole everything of value from his vehicle.

Communications Infrastructure

Before departing the United States, find out the reliability of the local communications system. Western Europe, Asia, some of the Middle East, and a large portion of Latin America have reliable landline or cellular service. In fact, the cellular phone service in Asia and Europe is superior to that in the United States.

Sub-Saharan Africa, Central Asia, and some parts of the Caribbean, particularly some of the poorer nations, depend almost exclusively on cellular service. Their landline communications are inadequate. If you need cellular service while traveling, ensure that you have the necessary plugs and voltage converters to keep your cell phone powered. Also, make sure the power supply for your cell phone is dual voltage—most are. See **http://www.walkabouttravelgear.com** or **http://www.radioshack.com**.

Keep in mind that during national emergencies (terrorist attacks, earthquakes, violent regime changes, etc.), cellular service is the *first* means of communication to stop functioning. That is why I have included information on VHF/UHF systems and satellite phones in this section. This information is especially useful for travelers who will be working abroad in high-risk areas or living long-term as expatriates and need an alternate means of communication.

Using a Cell Phone Abroad

This section can save you hundreds, if not thousands, of dollars. If you have a cell phone and subscribe to one of the many U.S. wireless carriers (AT&T, Sprint, Verizon, and T-Mobile), you possibly can use your cell phone in many countries. However, cell phone usage abroad may have an exorbitant cost and can be considerably inconvenient.

A majority of the world's cell phone users (82 percent) use Global System Mobile (GSM) technology. AT&T and T-Mobile use GSM, and Sprint and Verizon use Code-Division Multiple Access (CDMA) technology. More than 185 nations use GSM, whereas CDMA phones work only in 26 countries (North America, a few Asian nations, the Caribbean, and parts of Latin America). CDMA phones are practically inoperative in most of Europe. Although subscribers to GSM and

CDMA phones in the United States can technically have their carrier service roam in compatible countries, roaming charges range from $.50 to $1.00 per minute for CDMA phones and $1.00 to $5.00 per minute for GSM phones. For instance, one T-Mobile (GSM) subscriber on a 10-day trip to Tanzania was charged $5 a minute, or $800. Had he called T-Mobile and unlocked his phone from overseas restrictions, he could have replaced his GSM SIM (subscriber identity module) card with one for another country, which would have cost him $1.15 in Tanzania, not $5 per minute. Also, CDMA phones do not store the SIM in a removable card but in the hardware. For these reasons, you may want to consider avoiding using CDMA phones abroad.

Another point is that U.S. GSM phones use two frequencies outside the United States. Consequently, the preference is a *quad-band unlocked* phone that is not tied to a wireless company and that works worldwide. Unlocked phones are a bit more expensive than locked phones, but having one overseas will prove invaluable. (I paid $160 for my quad-band unlocked phone, which comes with international plugs.) Good online sources from which to purchase this type of phone include:

- **http://www.cellular-blowout.com**
- **http://www.cellularabroad.com**
- **http://www.telestial.com** (This source also sells SIM cards for most countries, but you can buy them much more inexpensively at kiosks when you arrive at your destination.)

For a U.S. phone to work easily abroad, the unit must be either tri-band or quad-band. These technologies enable the phones to bridge varying frequency levels. Confirm whether your phone can function at the prevailing frequencies in each country of interest. The following Web sites will help:

- **http://www.wireless.att.com**
- **http://www.sprint.com**
- **http://www.verizon.com**
- **http://www.t-mobile.com**
- **http://www.gsmworld.com** (GSM compatibility and frequency levels)
- **http://www.cdg.org** (CDMA compatibility and frequency levels)

I recommend that you have two cell phones: one that works in the United States and one that works overseas. The only disadvantage is that when you buy an unlocked phone and purchase a SIM card for a specific country, you will have to reload your address book. One solution is to carry your U.S. or home-based phone abroad for access to the address book.

On the other hand, if you want to use your U.S. phone abroad, call your wireless company to see whether it will unlock your phone so you can avoid high roaming charges. Note that many carriers have riders attached. For example, they will unlock you phone if (a) your contract has expired, (b) you paid full price for the phone and it was not subsidized by your employer, or (c) you have had service with the company for at least 90 days. Finally, many wireless carriers will give you an unlock code *once* every 90 days only. If you need this service more often, the two companies below will unlock your phone for a small fee:

- **http://www.thetravelinsider.com**
- **http://www.unlocktelecom.co.uk**

Purchase (preferable) or rent a quad-band **unlocked** GSM phone if you travel abroad more than once a year. The rental cost for an unlocked phone may run $70 a week. Keep in mind that T-Mobile charges $.99 a minute to use its service in the United Kingdom. Insert a British SIM card, and local calls drop to $.26. Calls to the United States are $.09 to $.14 per minute.

If you buy a quad-band unlocked phone, take the following steps:

1. Buy the phone and charge it before you leave on your trip.
2. After you arrive in the country of your destination, go to a newsstand, convenience store, or a cell phone kiosk and purchase a SIM card and prepaid load card. This adds anywhere from an hour to several hours of talk time to your phone beyond the nominal talk time included on the SIM card. If you have difficulty inserting the SIM card into the phone, ask clerks to help you. They usually accommodate foreigners.
3. Turn on your phone. Your phone number (in that country) will appear on the display.

4. Make sure you write down the number so you can give it to others. Incoming calls are free.

5. Take your load card and scratch off the back of the card, much like you would for a prepaid phone card. This will give you a code that you need to type into the phone to make local or international calls.

6. When your minutes run down, buy another load card, and simply repeat the process.

The most effective, useful, flexible and clearest cellular systems in the world are not in the United States. They are in Europe, Latin America, Asia and even in Africa, given the control and restrictions wielded by the American cellular carriers. Hopefully, one day, we will cease to be the laughing stock of the mobile world.

Other Communications Options

Cell phones invariably become inoperative in the midst of a crisis. *Communications redundancy*—having more than one means of communicating—in an emergency abroad is crucial. This book briefly covers the options; however, if you have further questions, please contact me directly.

- **HF/VHF Radio Systems.** These radio systems are generally best suited for a *long-term-resident* situation because of the high cost of procurement, configuration, installation, and long-term maintenance. For example, two base stations, mobile vehicular units, and 12 handhelds can run into six figures, depending upon the terrain and whether the system is operating in duplex (with repeaters) or simplex (without repeaters), which is very risky. If you use HF/VHF radio systems, you must obtain approval from the country's Ministry of Telecommunications to use a series of frequencies. If your employer is an NGO directly affiliated with the United Nations, you may be able to use UN frequencies. Another option is to purchase a system from a local radio distributor and use its frequencies. Note that the distributor is likely to monitor your traffic unless you use a disciplined call sign system to conceal users, places, and situations or shift to much more expensive equipment that will encrypt your radio transmissions. Reputable companies that can help you design and set up a system include:

- http://www.motorola.com
- http://www.qmac.com
- http://www.barrettcommunications.com
- http://www.codan.com
- http://www.yaesu.com

- **Satellite Phone Systems.** These self-contained systems are ideal for both long-term and short-term operations and are particularly suited for large-scale emergencies. I cannot tell you the number of times I have seen *satphones* save lives. They are preferred for operations in developing countries. They eliminate the need for government approvals, are cheaper, and cannot be shut down by the host governments. On the other hand, they are expensive

($1,500–$2,000 per unit) when supporting a large number of people. Satellite phone charges can be $3 to $15 per minute. Cell phone and/or HF/VHF radio systems should be used for routine communications. Satphones provide high-quality direct-dial, voice, fax, and e-mail capabilities and require virtually no installation. They are similar to radios in that they communicate by line of sight (the antenna must "see" the satellite). Most briefcase-configured satphones weigh about 20 pounds and can operate on direct and alternating power supplies. The following companies are the major providers of satphones. However, buyers beware. Promises of coverage are often just promises. Ask for testimonials, and test the equipment over real distances if you can.

- http://www.iridium.com
- http://www.globalstar.com
- http://www.inmarsat.com

Coordinating Security for International Meetings and Conferences

Given that the best conference cities throughout the world are susceptible to acts of terrorism and violent crime, meeting and conference planners of events abroad have a responsibility to ensure the safety of attendees and participants. Consequently, the following steps are suggested:

☐ Engage professional security advisors to discuss the proposed meeting/conference site, political climate, and history of incidents against attendees, or confer with embassy security representatives and business organizations.

☐ Prepare a written threat assessment on which security arrangements should be based.

☐ Engage appropriate hotel and conference site managers, hotel security managers, diplomatic missions, tourist bureaus, chambers of commerce, and local police to inform them of the meeting. Document how they view the threat, and ask for suggestions on how to reduce attendee risk. Where necessary, request traffic controls or other police assistance near the meeting site.

☐ Confer with airport security officials, and make arrangements that will ease customs clearance of luggage. Arrange for a vehicle dedicated to the transportation of luggage. Arrange for an airport expediter to assist attendees in clearing airport formalities and transporting them quickly to the meeting site. If the conference site is in a high-threat location, hire a reputable security firm to transport attendees, and provide a security escort. On January 26, 2006, 33 elderly European tourists were traveling by tour bus from the Rio de Janeiro airport to their hotel. A gunman stopped the bus and robbed the tourists of their passports, jewelry, money, cameras, and credit cards. Such robberies are common in Rio. Meeting planners should ensure that transportation arrangements emphasize security, which may include the need for an armed guard on tour buses and vans.

☐ Obtain the names of reputable transportation companies from the embassy, visitor's bureau, chambers of commerce, and hotel officials to support the transportation of attendees. Do not permit attendees to hire their own transportation.

☐ As appropriate, employ local guards or off-duty police officers to provide security for meeting and reception areas.

☐ Ensure that hotel staff and security personnel are designated security representatives for the meeting and reachable by cell phone.

☐ As necessary, hire a reliable, vetted interpreter to assist in making security arrangements with local police. This eliminates misunderstandings.

☐ In the case of large numbers of attendees (eight or more) from the same organization, recommend that they fly on different flights, and ensure that selected airlines have good safety records.

☐ Depending upon the threat to participants and the subject, sensitivity, and size of the meeting, use identification cards. Use off-duty police to check participant ID cards and operate walk-through magnetometers.

☐ Do not use the organization's name when making airline reservations. This draws attention to the passengers' affiliation. Omit the titles of executives on hotel preregistration.

☐ Maintain a control room in the hotel from which emergencies can be managed for the meeting's participants.

☐ Locate the best medical facilities and pharmacies available for emergencies. Determine whether the hotel has an on-call physician and whether participants have serious medical conditions.

☐ Instruct hotels, restaurants, and transportation companies to avoid using the organization's name in public announcements or on reader boards. Use an inconspicuous acronym to identify the organization at certain events and to mark vans/buses for use by attendees.

☐ Prepare a brief written handout on security, such as safe and unsafe areas for walking and jogging, protection of valuables, areas frequented by criminals, and emergency phone numbers.

☐ Consult with hotel officials to determine the quality of fire safety features. Ideally, a site should have a sprinkler system, an automatic fire detection system, external emergency stairwells, and a fire station within five minutes of the site, although these may not always be available.

☐ Determine the scope of press converge you want for the meeting, if any. If you do not set the ground rules in advance, the press may arrive unannounced. If you do not want publicity, ensure that the hotel does not list the meeting on the daily meeting marquee.

☐ Depending on the threat, consider providing participants or key participants with a cell phone. Their regular cell may not work in the country.

How to Use Interpreters and Translators

Not everyone who travels, works, or lives abroad will need
interpreters or translators. Those that do may include businesspersons, government officials, academicians, journalists,
NGOs assisting foreign governments or diplomatic missions,
or international organizations.

Be aware that a bilingual person is **not** necessarily an
interpreter or a translator. Professional interpreters and
translators have years of training and experience in their
fields. Using a bilingual person for important meetings or
projects can produce inaccurate or incomplete results.

An interpreter is a professional who simultaneously
interprets verbally in two languages. A translator is a professional who translates written documentation from one language to another. Both are normally certified by a recognized
association in the field of interpreting and translations.

Below are some useful tips from lessons learned:

☐ If possible, interview at least two or three interpreters or
translators before hiring one. Interpersonal chemistry is
important. During the interview, review a list of projects the individual has worked on and corroborate his
or her work.

☐ After you select a person, review acronyms, slang, or technical terms with him or her. Many words in one language do not have an equivalent word in another language. The interpreter or translator will balk at a glossary of unfamiliar terms that may not be in his or her native language.

☐ If possible, determine the interpreter's or translator's political biases. If you work with the opposition, this could cloud his or her objectivity.

☐ If sensitive or proprietary issues are going to be discussed, consider asking the interpreter or translator to sign a nondisclosure statement.

☐ In the case of simultaneous interpretation, speak slowly. This will produce a more accurate result.

☐ If possible, give your interpreter periodic breaks during a day of meetings or consider hiring a backup interpreter. Simultaneous interpretation is physically and mentally challenging.

☐ A good gesture is to give the interpreter(s) a gift to express gratitude for making your meetings, speeches, or discussions successful. An appropriate gift would be something from where you live, music CDs, or an appropriate gift affixed with your organization's logo. The interpreter will appreciate your thoughtfulness, which will solidify a continuing professional relationship and leave a good impression.

Contact the American Translators Association (**http:// www.atanet.org**), which allows you to search for reputable translators or interpreters from the online directory. Another useful source is the American Chamber of Commerce (**http://www.uschamber.com/international/directory**). The Web site on commercial attachés at U.S. diplomatic and consular posts is **http://www.usembassy.state.gov**.

To impress a foreign counterpart or associate who does not speak your language well, do not call him or her and say, "Do you speak English?" Rather, show your sensitivity and call LLE Language Services (**http://www.lle-inc.com**, 877-405-8764). The service helps you set up an account (prices are very reasonable) and interprets for you during your conversation while you are speaking your language and your party is speaking his or hers. It is that easy. LLE has 1,000 certified interpreters, representing more than 100 languages, who can interpret a phone conversation for you on a 24-7 basis.

Learning the Language

Although Americans are not known for trying new languages, I strongly recommend that you attempt to learn as much as you can. As I have said, the more you know about the country in which you will be visiting or living, the more aware and comfortable you will become, making your stay more satisfying. Nothing is more exciting than being able to order a meal, ask for directions, or carry on a conversation in a language other than your own.

I have studied Vietnamese, French, Greek, and Spanish in immersion-type learning situations and believe that total immersion is by far the *best* and *quickest* way to learn a language. On the other hand, I have tried self-study and found it less *productive*, although I am pleased with the learning methodology of RosettaStone (**http://www.rosettastone.com**). If you cannot attend an immersion program, purchase both the basic and the advanced programs in RosettaStone and *complete* them. You will find that this method works very well, particularly if you go abroad immediately afterward. Another method is to go through the entire RosettaStone program and work one on one with an *experienced* language instructor for a week or two before you travel abroad.

Being a Considerate Airline Passenger

When traveling overseas, the enjoyment of flying commercially is rapidly deteriorating because of rigorous security screening, overbookings, delayed and canceled flights, pilot shortages, crowded cabins, and stressed-out gate agents and flight attendants. So, by the time the traveler boards the plane, he or she is often agitated, tired, and stressed. Whether you are an experienced or inexperienced traveler, below are a few tips to help reduce stress on transoceanic flights:

☐ If you cannot lift a bag into the overhead bin, please check it. Not doing so takes up extra stowage space, and carrying it around exhausts you on a long flight.

Not lugging a heavy bag onboard affords you more over-head room for your smaller carry-on luggage. Hence, you have more legroom in front of you for 8–14 hour trips.

☐ Do not rearrange other passengers' luggage in the over-head; people are protective of their personal belongings, particularly computer bags. If something needs to be moved, ask the owner or flight attendant to move it.

☐ Even though the middle seat and the space under the seat in front of it might be empty, this does not mean they belong to you.

☐ If you have a window seat, go to the bathroom before you board the flight. It may be more than an hour before you will have access to the restroom.

☐ Experienced passengers choose an aisle seat. It gives them more room and easy access to the restroom.

☐ Before you recline your seat completely, check to see that the passenger behind you does not have his or her legs crossed. Alert the passenger behind you that you are going to recline your seat. Be considerate; do not push the seat back all the way, particularly if you are in coach class.

☐ Two armrests in a row of three seats mean that three passengers have to share.

☐ Limit your use of alcoholic beverages. Drinking exces-sively will worsen jet lag.

☐ If flying with children, plan your arrangements in advance so that your family can sit together and you can conduct your parental responsibilities. Flying 12 hours with a five-year-old sitting next to you and one of the parents sitting several rows away is not enjoyable; parents have to realize that not all passengers love their children as much as they do.

☐ Comply fully with your aircrew. Belligerent behavior, noncompliance with a flight attendant's instruction, arguing, or becoming disorderly can result in you being charged with a crime.

Cell Phone Etiquette

Be considerate. If you are, you will make a favorable impression regardless of where you are going or what you are doing. Having worked with more than 80 cultures, I found that all nationalities multilaterally dislike *a jerk*. Distaste for rudeness is universal, and poor cell phone etiquette probably tops the list for rudeness. So, below are a few tips for using cell phones abroad:

☐ *The 10-foot rule.* If someone is closer to you than 10 feet, you are forcing noise pollution on him or her. Be considerate.

☐ *Before the aircraft door closes.* Remember that microphones on cell phones are very sensitive. The other party hears you, so there is no need to shout. Speak softly, and do not invade the hearing space of those sitting next to you.

☐ *Make your calls short.* There are times when you must make or receive a call. Be considerate of those around you.

☐ *Keep the volume of the ringer turned down.* Cell phones have a vibration mode for a reason. If you cannot use this mode, at least turn down the volume of the ringer.

☐ *Public places.* Turn your phone to silent or vibrate when you are in public places. Seek privacy to take or make calls. Also note that, increasingly, restaurants abroad are posting signs discouraging the use of cell phones and often ask customers who use their cell phones to leave.

☐ *The one-phone rule.* Please, one phone only. I was flying to Manila some months ago and saw a man boarding the flight with three cell phones on his belt. Are you being considerate if more than one phone rings?

☐ *Get a hands-free device.* Regardless of the local law, dialing or talking on the phone while driving is dangerous, inconsiderate, and arrogant.

☐ *Remove earpieces after use.* Cell users who leave the earpiece or Bluetooth in all the time is annoying.

Critical Issues If You Do Business Abroad

The Overseas Security Advisory Council (OSAC). OSAC is a Federal Advisory Committee with a U.S. government charter to promote security cooperation between American business and private-sector interests worldwide and the U.S.

Department of State. The OSAC currently has a 34-member core council, an executive office, more than 100 country councils, more than 3,500 constituent member organizations, and 372 associates. Companies from the United States doing business abroad will derive considerable benefits by becoming associate members of OSAC (**http://www.osac.gov**). Membership grants access to OSAC's country security reports and other invaluable information.

Liability for crimes against international travelers. Courts are increasingly holding hotels, cruise ship lines, travel agents, employers, and others accountable for taking reasonable steps to warn, and in some cases protect, clients and staff who are victimized, injured, or killed in conjunction with foreseeable criminal and terrorist acts abroad. Consequently, concerned readers may want to confer with their legal counsel and review *Tourist Industry Liability for Crimes against International Travelers*, authored by Dennis B. Kennedy and Jason R. Sakis. See *22 Trial Lawyer* pp. 301–310, 1999.

Failure to provide adequate security support. This shortfall prevails when global companies lack vision; concern for safety of staff and assets; and will to implement effective security policies, procedures, training, services, and infrastructure to safeguard travelers and expatriates (and families) abroad. Threats such as nonviolent and violent crime against travelers and expatriates, trade secret compromises, truck hijackings, labor problems, theft, and acts of terrorism must be addressed, as should business continuity following natural disasters and political unrest.

Case studies cited earlier show that criminal and terrorists acts abroad are foreseeable events. Consequently, global organizations should confer with legal counsel on the liability that employers face when they send employees abroad. This conference is important where there are known risks of violent crime and terrorist acts against foreign interests and where an established international security program designed to manage risk does not exist. For a multinational company to adequately safeguard its executives, staff, facilities, products, and proprietary information in a developing country, its security budget should be roughly 5 percent of its annual operating budget. Anything less may result in unexpected injuries, deaths, costs, or losses that could adversely impact annual profits.

Ideally, the essential components of an international security program for an organization that sends staff abroad on temporary or long-term assignments should include:

- Policies and procedures on international travel and expatriate security support
- A formal communication plan educating staff on threats they could face abroad, how to respond, and the organization's support role
- Comprehensive health care and medical evacuation coverage for travelers, expatriates, and family members

- A method for periodically reviewing security issues abroad to ensure that staff and organizational assets are protected
- A global crisis management plan that lists the organization's strategy for responding to emergencies, to include evacuation of staff
- Predetermined resources that can respond to on-site emergencies in countries in which expatriates, local staff, and travelers reside

An example of poor risk management by a multinational company occurred in Mexico some years ago when the company hastily contracted for security guards to protect a 20,000-square-foot warehouse containing pharmaceutical merchandise worth $4 million. The company failed to check references or to investigate the security firm. Worse, the company had no contract with the hired security company that specified liabilities and negligence. Within weeks, a major break-in occurred at the company warehouse. A contract guard who was working with a criminal gang shot the second guard, who was unaware of the plot. The thieves stole nearly $2.5 million in merchandise that was later sold on the black market. The victimized company soon realized that paying two guards a total of $10 a shift and having no redundant security, such as alarms or covert CCTV coverage, caused it to suffer a significant loss. In addition to the loss of the second guard's life and the loss of the inventory, the company's insurance premiums rose dramatically.

A second case of poor risk management involved the theft of Peru's priceless *tumi mochica*, a pure gold ceremonial knife used by the Moche, a pre-Inca civilization, for the human sacrifice of its enemies. The ritual, performed some 1,500 years ago, was conducted with surgical precision whereby the face of the victim was peeled away and the heart removed while the victim was still alive. The one original *tumi* was considered a masterpiece of Mochica metalwork. Unfortunately, it was stolen in 1983 from a museum in Cuzco (near Macchu Pichua) that was protected by a guard paid $1 a day. Thieves later melted the knife down for its gold before they were eventually arrested. Tragically, the *tumi* was as priceless to the Peruvians as the *Mona Lisa* is to the Italians. Nevertheless, the *tumi mochica* was lost forever because inadequate security of a museum whose holdings were priceless.

Foreign corruption and bribery practices.

Any company conducting business abroad needs to learn the extent of foreign corruption practices in the countries in which it will operate for several reasons:

- Corrupt practices in some industries may pose extreme obstacles, making doing business unprofitable in the country.
- Unethical competitors may pay bribes to government officials and make competing equitably difficult for foreign companies.

- Government regulations may make operating in the country impossible because of the payment of required "licenses and fees" imposed selectively or discriminately.
- Unethical governments often exert extreme pressure on your intermediaries to pay bribes and call them something else. This can get you into trouble.

By far, one of the best and most authoritative resources is Transparency International (**http://www.transparency. org**), which was founded by a former World Bank official. Among other products, each year TI issues its *Corruption Perception Index*, which lists 163 countries and their level of ethical transparency. Some of the countries at the bottom of the list (most corrupt) include Indonesia, Bangladesh, Chad, Sudan, Iraq, Ecuador, Venezuela, Kenya, Nigeria, Haiti, Iraq, Cambodia, Pakistan, and Belarus. Conversely, the top-10 nations that TI considers the least corrupt include Finland, Iceland, New Zealand, Denmark, Singapore, Sweden, Switzerland, Norway, Australia, and the Netherlands (the United Kingdom is no. 11, Canada is no. 14, and the United States is no. 20).

The Foreign Corrupt Practices Act of 1977 is a U.S. Federal law that was enacted predominantly to include companies that have publicly traded stock to maintain records that accurately and fairly represent the company's transactions and that have an adequate system of internal accounting controls. Additionally, the law applies to all companies in the United States and those associated with them. As a result of U.S. Securities and Exchange Commission investigations in the mid-1970s, more than 400 U.S. companies admitted making questionable or illegal payments in excess of $300 million to foreign government officials, politicians, and political parties. The abuses included bribing high foreign officials to secure favors to ensure that government functionaries perform certain ministerial or clerical duties.

The act was amended in 1998 by the International Anti-Bribery Act of 1998, which was designed to implement the antibribery conventions of the Organization for Economic Cooperation and Development (OECD). Regarding payments to foreign officials, the act draws a distinction between bribery and facilitation or "grease payments," which may be permissible if they are not against local laws. However, a company's legal counsel has to approve such payments. The primary distinction is that grease payments are paid to an official to expedite the performance of duties he or she is already bound to perform (e.g., customs clearance and issuance of licenses or permits). References on how to comply with FCPA can be found at **http://www.usdoj.gov/criminal/fraud/fcpa**.

As an example of how the FCPA can penalize companies, the largest foreign bribery case against a U.S. company occurred in 2005. The Titan Corporation pleaded guilty and paid a $28-million fine to settle allegations that it covered up unauthorized payments in six countries, including millions of dollars funneled to an associate of an African president to influence an election. Ironically, Titan's bribery was uncovered by Lockheed Martin during acquisition negotiations. In a much larger case, in October 2007, Germany's Siemens AG in a Munich court, accepted responsibility for paying bribes in the amount of 12 million Euros for business in Nigeria, Russia and Libera, and as a result, agreed to pay fines in the amount of 201 million Euros. For a complete summary of 2007 FCPA cases and inquiries, refer to an excellent report prepared by the U.S. law firm Vinson & Elkins (**http://www.vinson-elkins.com/resources**).

A growing threat: economic espionage (EEA). The U.S. Economic Espionage Act of 1996 makes the theft or misappropriation of a trade secret a federal crime. This law contains provisions for criminalizing two types of activity. The first provision criminalizes the theft of trade secrets to benefit foreign powers, and the second criminalizes the theft for commercial or economic purposes. The EEA also has extraterritorial jurisdiction when the offender _or_ the victim is a U.S. citizen. The EEA is a broad law that provides criminal prosecution of individuals who steal, appropriate, buy, receive, or possess a trade secret without authorization. It also provides prosecution of individuals who conspire to steal a trade secret. Maximum penalties for an individual include a fine of $500,000, 15 years in prison, or both. In some cases, organizations convicted under this law can face much higher penalties.

Although the law tries to protect the trade secrets of U.S. entities, individuals or organizations that are victimized by economic espionage must produce documentation showing that reasonable steps were taken to protect trade secrets from theft and compromise. If effective security controls cannot be established, the success of prosecution under the EEA can be severely jeopardized. The following would represent documented efforts to effectively protect trade secrets:

- ☐ Clear written policies and procedures regarding trade secrets and information security.
- ☐ A formally established security unit tasked in writing to protect trade secrets.
- ☐ Nondisclosure statements for employees and contractors.
- ☐ Physical, technical, and electronic security protection of trade secrets.
- ☐ Access to trade secrets on a need-to-know basis.
- ☐ Periodic and random technical countermeasure surveys to reduce the risk of electronic eavesdropping.
- ☐ A formal background investigation of all employees and contractors having access to trade secrets.
- ☐ A formal mechanism for investigating breeches in the security of trade secret protection.

A landmark case prosecuted under the EEA shortly after the enactment of the law involved a case of economic espionage in which more than $60 million worth of Avery Denison documents, adhesive formulas, tapes, and primers was stolen by an AD employee (Ten-Hong Lee) who was a "mole" for Taiwan-based Four Pillars. Lee was paid $160,000 to steal Avery's trade secrets. Ironically, a Four Pillars employee alerted Avery to Lee's activities. Lee was persuaded to cooperate with authorities after the FBI arrested him in a sting operation. When the top executives of Four Pillars came to the United States to meet with Lee, he was wired with audio and video equipment as he provided Avery documents to them. The executives were arrested as they attempted to leave the United States, convicted under the EEA, and ordered to pay $5 million in fines.

A recent case that was not prosecuted under the EEA involved funneling controlled U.S. defense documents to the Chinese government. Chi Mak, 66, a naturalized U.S. citizen, was employed by Power Paragon, an Anaheim, California–based defense contractor, when he, his brother, and his sister-in-law were arrested in 2005 as they boarded a flight for Hong Kong. FBI agents subsequently found three encrypted CDs containing documents on submarine propulsion. In May 2007, Mak was convicted of being an unregistered foreign agent, attempting to violate export-control laws, conspiracy, and making false statements to the FBI. He could face 35 years in prison when he appears for sentencing. Mak passed sensitive documents to his brother for years. Documents were eventually passed to the handler representing the Chinese government. As a matter of inter-est, the majority of defendants tried under the EEA have had direct or indirect links to China and Taiwan.

In another recent case, American citizens Gregg Berg-ersen and Greg Chung were both charged in February 2008, of handing over military secrets to the Chinese government. Bergersen was employed by the Department of Defense and

Chung was retired from the Boeing Co. If found guilty, both men face lengthy prison terms.

Below are useful Web sites on the EEA and economic espionage:

- **http://www.cybercrime.gov/eea** (information on the substance of EEA, as well as resulting convictions)
- **http://www.fbi.gov/publications**
- **http://www.ncix.gov/publications** (access the *2005 Annual Report to Congress: Foreign Economic Collection and Industrial Espionage*)

Electronic eavesdropping. Business executives must be aware that the magnitude of economic espionage in the global marketplace mandates that sensitive discussions concerning business strategies, new products, mergers and acquisitions, and new investment need to be safeguarded. Consequently, it is vital that conference rooms, boardrooms, executive offices, aircraft, and executives' vehicles undergo periodic technical security countermeasures (TSCM) inspections, which ensure that transmitters, "bugs," and phone taps are not compromising sensitive discussions. Of course, this presumes that those responsible for the control of such spaces and vehicles are trusted. Additionally, a TSCM specialist may also recommend the installation of in-place monitoring systems (IPMS) in high-risk spaces, which permits monitoring of eavesdropping activity in the space while sensitive meetings are being conducted.

Business executives working abroad should be aware that eavesdropping devices can be purchased inexpensively and monitored and recorded from almost anywhere. If sensitive areas have to be cleaned or maintained, a trusted staff member should observe the visitors. Eavesdropping risks occur for the following reasons:

- Aggressive competition, particularly among top companies
- Distrust of subordinates, cleaning crews, and repair technicians
- Lack of legal prohibitions against the use of electronic eavesdropping equipment
- Unchecked use of electronic eavesdropping by law enforcement

If you are a business executive operating abroad and need a firm that can assist with the full range of TSCM services, contact Murray Associates (Spybusters LLC), operated by Kevin D. Murray, CPP, one of the best in the business with a solid track record of ethical and discreet operations (**http://www.spybusters.com**). Kevin can also be reached at (908) 832-7900 or by e-mail at **murray@ spybusters.com**. Kevin's advice to global companies is:

- Conduct proactive eavesdropping inspections on a regular basis. Discovery of eavesdropping—during the information collection process—gives you time to neutralize an attack *before* harm can be done.

■ Think of your eavesdropping detection program as being a very cheap insurance policy. If you have vital trade secrets, failure to have periodic technical inspections is tantamount to driving a new car without insurance.

Executive security abroad. The personal security of presidents and CEOs is one issue about which companies operating abroad should be concerned. Small companies should not conclude that their principals and executives are not subject to being targeted as well. Issues that should be reviewed are (a) safety of airlines selected; (b) assessment of the threat to executives while traveling; (c) press issues, including the executives' photos appearing in local media; (d) security of ground transportation and circumstances that warrant the use of ballistic-resistant vehicles and security drivers/escorts; (e) medical preparedness if the travelers have health issues; (f) protection of sensitive documents and meetings; (g) special hotel security arrangements; (h) rural travel and the use of domestic flights or charters; and (i) potential for criminal, terrorist, or governmental surveillance. This subject cannot be discussed at length in this book; therefore, companies are urged to contact me for a copy of our complimentary ***Executive Travel Checklist***. The adverse impact of life insurance payouts and the ramifications of refused assignments, lawsuits, business continuity, and negative press should be factored into why comprehensive executive security of visible CEOs should be considered.

When ballistic-resistant vehicles are warranted. Executives of profitable global companies are often targeted for
kidnapping, carjacking, assassination, extortion, robbery,
and acts of terrorism. This is true for companies and organizations operating in developing countries, particularly
high-threat countries such as Mexico, Colombia, Guatemala,
Venezuela, the Ivory Coast, Nigeria, Kenya, South Africa,
Pakistan, Indonesia, and the Philippines. Consequently, any
threat assessment of an organization's senior management in
a particular country should consider whether a fully armored
vehicle (FAV) or a light-armored (LAV) vehicle is necessary
or appropriate for the threat.

A FAV is a vehicle that has been disassembled and essentially rebuilt to include an enhanced suspension and engine
and the installation of transparent and opaque armoring materials (360 degrees). It also includes the installation of windows
and door panels capable of deflecting bullets from various types
of handguns and rifles. This process also includes equipping
the vehicle with run-flat tires and an external speaker system
so that the driver can communicate with those outside the
vehicle without opening a door or window. *If you would like to
know the appropriate specifications for a protected vehicle needed
for a particular level of threat, please contact me.* Some FAVs
can defeat AK-47s, 30-06s, and NATO rounds; others are
modified to defeat mainly handguns and light machine guns
(9 mm). FAVs can easily cost $130,000–$175,000, depending on the type of vehicle modified. In Mexico, for example,

some companies armor the Volkswagen Passat, which is more adaptable to the country and roads.

LAVs can be either factory installed or, less desirably, field installed. They generally do not have the higher defeating capability, but they are a less expensive option for users primarily concerned with kidnappings, carjackings, robberies, and rapes, as compared to FAV users, who may be senior governmental or corporate executives with a protective detail that includes LAV-protected lead-and-follow ("chase") cars.

Unquestionably, protected vehicles can save your life from most of the threats encountered in countries where local and foreign executives are targeted by criminals, rebels, and terrorist groups. These vehicles can protect you against kidnappings, assassinations, carjackings, and some bomb attacks. Some companies do not believe that a protected vehicle is worth the money. However, individuals who have been in a position where they have needed protected vehicles are very likely to disagree. So, who really needs a protected vehicle?

- Targets who have received *documented* threats of violence
- Targets whose compatriots have been threatened or attacked by political extremists or criminals
- Senior multinational executives living in developing countries where corporate executives are threatened often
- Heads of state and senior foreign dignitaries

- Political candidates on whom an assassination attempt is highly likely
- Well-known CEOs traveling in high-threat countries

One consideration before purchasing an FAV or an LAV is the obvious risk of theft by criminals, narcotics traffickers, smugglers, rebels, and terrorists. Consequently, these vehicles need to be guarded, and their drivers should be trained. Protected vehicles handle differently than unarmored vehicles.

Organizations or executives contemplating the purchase of an FAV or an LAV should cautiously examine the type of vehicle to be armored, particularly if they are a highly visible American operating a vehicle abroad. They should remember to lower their profiles and select an automobile that fits into the local environment, particularly in countries where BMW and Mercedes-Benz vehicles are common. Also, know that maintenance on an FAV or an LAV can be problematic. Below are some reputable companies that can produce FAVs and LAVs:

- http://www.centigon.com
- http://www.worldwidearmor.com
- http://www.armoured-vehicles.com
- http://www.firstdefense.com
- http://www.lascointl.com

The benefits of the ATA Carnet. An ATA Carnet, which can be issued within 24 hours, is an international customs document issued by 70 countries (**https://www.atacarnet. com**) and administered in the United States by the U.S. Corporation for International Business on behalf of the U.S. Council for International Business (**http://www. uscib.org**). A carnet is needed if your business operations require you to have specialized equipment or products (laptops, LCD projectors, samples, prototypes, commercial samples, aircraft, yachts, and items for conferences and exhibits). Generally, having a carnet prevents unexpected tax and duty payments on equipment, helps avoid lengthy customs inspections, and reduces aggravation.

The carnet is obtained upon entering a carnet country with merchandise or equipment that will be exported within 12 months. The carnet serves as the U.S. registration of goods and permits the equipment or merchandise to clear customs without the owner having to pay duties and taxes. Typically, the U.S. Council annually issues more than 10,000 carnets for goods valued at more than $1 billion. For information on the carnet, go to **https://www.atacarnet. com** or call (800) ATA-2900. Readers who reside outside the United States should contact their ministry of trade for information on how to obtain a carnet.

Predeparture Considerations
The Importance of a Predeparture Physical Examination.

Nearly 6,000 U.S. citizens die abroad every year. *If you learn nothing else from this book, do not leave home with any doubt about the status of your health*. Early in 2003 while working for the State Department, I made a number of trips to Greece to help the government prepare for potential acts of terrorism during the 2004 Summer Olympics. On one trip there, I met my friend Mike, a retired Federal agent, who would be working along with me and the Greek police until the Olympics began.

The night before we were scheduled to leave Athens, Mike and I had dinner at the home of embassy friends. We had an early flight back to Dulles the next morning, so we said good night in the lobby and agreed to meet there the following morning.

From details that we later pieced together, Mike had gotten out of bed the next morning and collapsed next to the bathroom from a massive heart attack . . . A week later I escorted his body back to his family in the U.S. An autopsy revealed that Mike's heart had been barely functioning and he should never have gone on the trip.

Unlike Mike, who had less than a healthy lifestyle, I have been health conscious most of my adult life. Ironically, though, I would soon be facing the same disease that killed Mike. I had no idea when I traveled to some of the unhealthiest, highest-altitude, and highest-threat countries in the world that I, too, was a walking time bomb, in need of a quadruple bypass and aortic valve replacement that was successfully performed two years later. Because of Mike and 6,000 others, I offer the following:

☐ Schedule an annual physical examination with comprehensive blood and urine tests before you travel abroad.

☐ Visit the Web site of the U.S. Centers for Disease Control and Prevention (**http://www.cdc.gov/travel**) to obtain country-specific health condition reports and *required* and *suggested* vaccinations.

☐ Visit an international travel clinic that can administer the vaccinations you need for your destination, and document them in a vaccination record. If you have a record of previous vaccinations, take it to the clinic and have it updated. Contact the nearest clinic by visiting **http://www.istm.org**, the Web site of the International Society of Travel Medicine. Remember to get vaccinated against both hepatitis A and B (**http://www.hepfi.org/living**). If headed for a developing country, consideration should be given to getting the three-dose series of pre-exposure vaccinations for rabies and malaria medication, if you'll be traveling in regions where malaria is prevalent.

☐ Visit your dentist before departing for overseas. Ensure that you have no major cavities or abscesses that could ruin your trip abroad.

Prescriptions to obtain from your medical provider before departure. If you buy certain prescribed medications while abroad (particularly in a developing country) for debilitating ailments, the quality of prescribed medications is uncertain. Therefore, when you have your physical exam, get a prescription for 500 mg of ciprofloxacin (Cipro) for infectious diarrhea and 250 mg of metronidazole (Flagyl) for giardiasis. Fill the prescriptions before departure, and use them for either affliction per the advice of a local medical provider or the physician who prescribed them. (Contact a physician by phone, if possible.)

Altitude sickness. If you expect that you will be ascending rapidly to a high altitude (10,000 feet or above), obtain a prescription for acetazolamide (Diamox). Take this medication two days before entering a high altitude and for three days after you arrive. (Note that this medication may not be needed on *gradual* ascents to high altitudes.) A rapid ascent might typically involve flying from Miami to La Paz, which is an elevation of 14,000+ feet. See **http://www.traveldoctor. co.uk/altitude**. Another effective remedy, although it tends to agitate Drug Enforcement Agency agents, is *mate de coca*, or coca tea, which is derived from the leaves of the coca plant and contains several alkaloids, including cocaine. Most foreigners use commercially made tea bags of *mate de coca* as a very good solution to altitude sickness. In Peru and Bolivia, I used the tea, and it works. *Mate de coca* bags have a very small percentage of cocaine; however, regular use could produce a positive drug test result for cocaine. Note: *Do not* attempt to bring *mate de coca* bags into the United States, unless the products are "de-cocainized" (much like decaffeinating coffee). After this is done, the tea can be brought into the United States legally.

Get other prescriptions you will need. Obviously, if you believe you will need other prescribed medications, get a script from your doctor, and get it filled before you go abroad. If you are inclined to contract yeast infections or serious jock itch, get a prescription for Fluconzale. Imagine being without it on an ecotour, 100 miles from civilization.

Assembling a first aid kit. If you are traveling to a *developing* country, assemble your own first aid kit. Many commercial kits do not include what you need. Two Web sites that provide first aid kits include **http://www.travmed.com** and **http://www.adventuremedicalkits.com**. To assemble your kit, first purchase a small fanny pack that you can store in your luggage. Next, go to a pharmacy, purchase the items below, and put them in the fanny pack.

- Imodium/Pepto-Bismol tablets (for diarrhea)
- Aspirin
- Momentum (great for back pain)
- Icy Hot medicated patches (for muscle strains, sprains, arthritis, and back pain)
- Motion sickness tablets (if needed)
- Tylenol (for pain, body aches)
- Assorted Band-Aids (cuts)
- Benadryl (for allergies)
- Dramamine (for motion sickness, if needed)
- Adhesive-backed medium-sized bandages (for larger cuts)
- An Ace bandage (for sprains)
- Second Shield (for foot blisters)

- Pepcid Complete (for stomach upset and heartburn)
- Neosporin (antibiotic ointment)
- Hydrocortisone cream 1% (for itching)
- Suphedrine (antihistamine and nasal decongestant)
- Tucks medicated pads (for hemorrhoid and vaginal care)
- Super Glue (for closing up painful calluses and blisters)
- Iodine (for purifying water), or go to **http://www. steripen.com** for one of the easiest methods for having bacteria and virus-free drinking water
- Roll of gauze and adhesive tape
- A Conform Stretch Bandage (very absorbent, best used for bad wound with gauze pads underneath; also works in restricting splints)
- Several small bottles of hand sanitizer
- Small scissors and tweezers
- Package of small sewing needles (for removing slivers, foreign objects)
- Eyedrops for polluted air, dry eyes, and allergies
- A daily multivitamin
- Anything else you might need specific to you

Note: Regardless of the length of your trip, take your prescribed medication (in original containers) with you on the flight in your carry-on luggage.

Don't forget international health and evacuation coverage.

In 1999, two young American men in their early 20s were traveling in Honduras and had been drinking at a local nightclub in the capital, Tegucigalpa. They emerged from the club at about 0200 hours and encountered three young Honduran men who demanded their money. Intoxicated and inexperienced, they made the wrong choice and refused to give up their wallets. Subsequently, one of the Hondurans hit one of the Americans over the wrist with a machete, partially severing his hand from his arm. Suddenly, the Hondurans ran off as the American began bleeding profusely. The two foreigners, who had no international health coverage, went to a local hospital, where the staff demanded payment before treating the robbery victim. With neither man having money to pay for the treatment, the hospital helped the Americans contact the U.S. Embassy, which provided assistance so that the man could be treated. Unfortunately, with the loss of time receiving treatment, he never regained full use of his hand.

In another case, an American attorney traveling to Bangkok on business was critically injured when he stepped off a curb to cross the street. Unfortunately, having just arrived in country, he mistakenly looked right, but Bangkok traffic travels on the left. Consequently, a taxi traveling at a high rate of speed hit the attorney. Although the victim survived, he sustained major head injuries and was later medically evacuated to the United States at a cost of $70,000. The attorney personally paid this cost because he had no international medical and evacuation coverage. Remember to get a physical examination before you go abroad, and **do not** travel without medical and evacuation coverage. Your home-based health insurance is rarely honored abroad, and you may have to pay for your treatment by credit card or in cash. The following are good sources for medical coverage:

- http://www.insuremytrip.com
- http://www.internationalsos.com
- http://www.medexassist.com

Medical data for your wallet. Before you begin your trip, make sure you have the following in your wallet:

- ☐ Authorization card for international medical treatment and evacuation coverage.
- ☐ Names of people who should be called in an emergency (include name, e-mail address, cell phone number, including country code, and relationship).
- ☐ List of prescribed medications, blood type, and allergies you have to certain medications.

Jet lag. Flying across multiple time zones disrupts your body's natural rhythms, which disrupts sleep. This condition is called time zone change syndrome, or jet lag. Jet lag normally happens after crossing three or more time zones and can adversely impact expensive tours, multimillion-dollar business negotiations, and important meetings. It can make you feel awful. Most people require one day of recovery for each time zone crossed, so a trip from New York to Bangkok could take about two weeks of recovery.

Typically, jet lag symptoms can include fatigue, insomnia, irritability, loss of concentration, headaches, upset stomach, and constipation or diarrhea. Do not expect to travel across six time zones and be functional and alert the next day. Regardless of the purpose of your travel, arrange one complete day of rest at your destination before working a full day that requires alertness and energy. Below are some tips for reducing the impact of jet lag:

☐ Get plenty of rest before your trip. Starting out sleep-deprived makes jet lag that much worse.

☐ If you travel east, go to bed one hour earlier each night for a few days before your departure. If travel west, go to bed one hour later for several nights.

☐ Drink plenty of water before, during, and after your flight to counteract the dehydrating effects of bone-dry cabin air.

☐ Avoid alcohol and caffeine; both dehydrate you.

☐ Get up from your seat every hour and walk around and stretch.

☐ Sleep on the plane if it is nighttime at your destination.

☐ Use earplugs, headphones, and sleep masks to help block out noise and light. If it is daytime at your destination, resist the urge to sleep and do not sleep until nighttime.

☐ During an extended layover to your destination, take a shower if the facilities are available. London, Frankfurt, and some other airports provide shower facilities to freshen up and stimulate blood circulation.

☐ Invest in an inexpensive dual-time watch to reduce confusion about home and destination times.

☐ Consider taking a homeopathic tablet called "No-Jet-Lag" (**http://www.nojetlag.com**). It lessened affects of my jet lag. The tablet has been registered with the FDA since 1992 (**http://www.magellans.com/store/jetlag**). Note that some uncertainty exists about the effectiveness of melatonin. Supposedly, if you take it at the wrong time, it can worsen your jet lag. Talk to your medical provider and decide.

Deep vein thrombosis (DVT). Although DVT can be a health risk for airline passengers who are immobile on trips lasting three hours or longer, very few people are affected by it. Travelers at risk are those over 40 and the elderly who have a history of DVT, who have a sedentary lifestyle, who are obese, those who have had recent surgery or childbirth, or who have cancer and are undergoing cancer treatment. DVT involves clotting of the blood in any of the deep veins, usually in the calf. If a clot develops, it usually makes its presence known by an intense pain in the affected calf. If this occurs, seek medical attention immediately. DVT can be fatal if the clot breaks off and travels to the lungs, where it can affect the lungs' ability to take in oxygen. Breathlessness and chest pain can occur hours or days after the clot's formation in the calf. A 2001 clinical study revealed that wearing compression socks while traveling reduces occurrences of DVT; however, if you think you may be at risk, consult your medical provider. Below are some ways to reduce your risk of DVT:

- ☐ Do not take sleeping pills on long flights. Doing so further immobilizes you.
- ☐ Take a short walk before boarding and after deplaning long flights.
- ☐ Bend and flex your feet, ankles, and legs while in your seat.
- ☐ Press the balls of your feet against the foot rest periodically.
- ☐ Walk up the aisle hourly, when it is safe to do so.
- ☐ Drink plenty of water.
- ☐ Do not drink alcohol or overeat.

Traveler's diarrhea (TD). This is the most common illness you will likely experience while traveling. In some countries, as many as five out 10 foreign travelers get TD. Nothing ruins a vacation or business trip quicker than loose stools and abdominal cramps. Do not assume because you are in a developed country that you cannot get sick. Take the risk seriously.

Common TD symptoms include frequent loose stools (usually about four or five daily), abdominal cramps, nausea, vomiting, and/or fever and bloating. Most cases of TD abroad stem from an infectious agent ingested from food or water that is contaminated with organisms in feces. Below are some steps for preventing TD while traveling overseas:

- ☐ Drink bottled water *exclusively*.
- ☐ Avoid ice in drinks; wipe drinking surfaces before using them.

☐ Avoid fruit, raw vegetables, unpasteurized dairy products, and street vendors.

☐ Use hand sanitizers, particularly in developing countries.

☐ Ensure that food is well cooked.

☐ Wash your hands after shaking hands with others and before eating.

☐ Close your mouth while showering; brush teeth with safe water.

If you suddenly develop symptoms of diarrhea, do the following:

☐ Increase intake of clear liquids.

☐ Avoid caffeine and dairy products.

☐ Shift to a bland diet (e.g., bananas, rice, applesauce, toast, cereal, potatoes).

☐ Begin taking a regimen of Imodium (loperamide) or Pepto-Bismol.

☐ Consider Lomotil (diphenoxylate). It does little for the cause but will arrest the symptoms.

☐ If Imodium or Pepto-Bismol does not work, consider using Cipro and/or Flagyl at the directions of a medical provider.

☐ Seek medical attention if you notice blood or mucous in your stool or have a high fever or dehydration.

Sexually transmitted diseases (STDs). Be warned that HIV/AIDS and STDs may be at high levels in nations in which you are traveling. Avoid prostitutes, always use condoms (purchase them at home before departure for quality assurance), and seek medical attention if you develop urethral/vaginal discharge, pain, or genital lesions.

Checked luggage considerations. Before giving tips on luggage and the ramifications of luggage on security screening, the information that follows is on assumptions about luggage and overseas travel:

■ Delayed, lost, and pilfered checked luggage is increasing dramatically.

■ In leaving from and returning to the United States, your checked luggage must be secured but ***unlocked***. If it is locked, the U.S. Transportation Security Administration (TSA) *may* break the locks or locking mechanisms to examine the contents.

■ TSA-approved padlocks (see **http://www.travelsentry. org**) that permit U.S. screeners to open your locked luggage with a special bypass key are available for U.S. travel only. However, foreign aviation security screeners do not possess this bypass key. This means that if you lock your bags with these locks abroad, foreign security screeners may need to inspect your bag and will break the lock.

■ Theft from unlocked bags will rarely result in reimbursement.

■ Airline coverage of lost or stolen luggage may be only 25 percent of the replacement value of the contents of your luggage.

- If scanning of your checked luggage produces an image that cannot be explained, security screeners will open your bag for physical inspection. Normally, they will leave a note inside of the bag that explains that circumstances required a physical inspection.

- In developing nations, the use of soft luggage (compared to sturdy luggage) is discouraged, due to the risk of bags being cut open; however, if you already have soft luggage, see page 146.

- How you pack your bag may determine whether it travels on the next flight.

- Overpacked luggage can snap open during transit.

- Short connections between flights may influence whether your bag travels to your destination as scheduled.

Below are some useful tips to ensure that everything contained in your checked luggage arrives at your destination intact and on schedule:

☐ Know in advance how many bags can be checked without being charged for excess baggage (airlines have different policies).

☐ Do not place breakable bottles, laptop computers, cameras, expensive electronics, computer or cell phone power supplies, or jewelry in your checked luggage.

☐ Some airlines restrict passengers to one carry-on piece of luggage, so visit your airline's Web site to determine its carry-on policies. In such cases, a purse can be placed in a large tote bag, or a laptop can be secured in a larger bag.

☐ More than 70 percent of theft and pilferage from checked luggage involves cutting the bag open. Hence, sturdy luggage is ideally recommended for overseas travel. It is much better protected from the elements and withstands rough handling. The disadvantage of sturdy luggage is that many bags have combination locks that must be left unlocked for travel from and to the United States, which makes them vulnerable to accidental openings during transit. Therefore, if you have a sturdy piece of luggage, ensure that you use a luggage strap to tightly hold it together.

☐ If you do not have sturdy luggage, soft luggage is acceptable if you secure zippered compartments with a device that prevents it from being easily unzipped, such as Travelon Secure-a-Bag cable ties (**http://www. luggageonline.com**). A package contains 60 ties, along with two small nail clippers to cut the ties at your destination. The package costs about $6.95 online, but you can buy it for $4.95 at American Automobile Association stores. Of course, these plastic ties are designed to prevent your belongings from actually coming out of the bag during transit, but will do little to deter a determined criminal. I recommend that travelers not place items in external zippered compartments, unless they secure the compartments with ties. If you are traveling abroad, keyed or combo locks may be cut if screeners need to examine your bag.

☐ Ensure that each bag has a covered-face luggage tag with your name, work address, cell phone number, and e-mail address. Do not use your home address on the tag. This provides personal information about the location of your home while you are traveling.

☐ Place your name, address, cell phone number, and e-mail address in an envelope marked "If My Luggage Is Lost," and place it inside each piece of luggage in the event your luggage tag separates from your luggage.

☐ So that your bag stands out and so that you do not inadvertently claim the wrong bag upon arrival, purchase a brightly colored baggage strap that makes your luggage easily identifiable on the carousel.

☐ Determine in advance whether your homeowner's insurance covers theft of your luggage. If not, consider baggage insurance. Most airlines will cover $650 per bag internationally. These are depreciation rates, not replacement rates. If you purchase medical and emergency evacuation coverage described earlier on pages 137–139, you can usually bundle baggage insurance with the medical coverage through most underwriters.

☐ Theft of luggage in airports is a regular occurrence. Watch your luggage, especially your carry-on bags.

☐ Lock carry-on bags stowed aboard aircraft if unattended or outside your view. Passengers have been known to steal from unlocked bags on aircraft.

Flying international: some considerations. I could write an entire book on what to know about flying internationally, but I will keep it short here and offer these key tips:

☐ Regardless of where you fly to or from, flight delays are more the ***norm*** than the exception. In the United States, this statement is even truer, largely as a result of too few runways, too many flights and an outdated aircraft monitoring and navigational system. Weather is often blamed, but bad weather has been around since the Wright brothers first flew. So, plan your flight to your destination and allow at least two to three hours on the ground at intermediary airports en route to your destination. That way, if your flight is late leaving your point of origin (more likely than not), you have extra time to catch your connecting flight. If you do not do this and you arrive at the next airport after your flight has left, you may end up staying the night at your own expense.

☐ Do not trust travel agents who tell you that an hour on the ground is enough time to make your second flight. Many agents do not travel internationally very much. They do not always know where the terminals are, and they are often unaware that at international terminals, you may have to go through a second security screening when transiting one terminal to another. This obviously increases the time you need on the ground.

☐ In light of the death of a passenger who couldn't breathe on an international American Airlines flight in February 2008, travelers should keep in mind that it is not wise to travel long distances by air with a serious health condition. According to MedAire, an emergency medical support company, in-flight medical emergencies have doubled since 2000, with 83% of those who died in 2006 being over 51 years of age. As said elsewhere in this book, a physical exam is a must before traveling abroad.

☐ Do not take a large piece of luggage as a carry-on. Check the airline's Web site for dimensions and the allowed number of carry-on pieces. After you leave the United States, some foreign carriers permit only one carry-on piece. If you do not check size limitations, your oversize bag may not fit in the scanners, which means a trip back to the ticket counter.

☐ Know the number of bags you can check and the allowable weight. Excess baggage can be expensive, so if you know you are going to be over the weight restrictions, you may save money by sending other effects via UPS, FedEx, or DHL.

☐ Select your seat assignments for your international flight as far in advance as possible, otherwise you're going to be sitting in a center seat cursing yourself for all of eternity. To ease this process, go to: **http://www.seatguru.com**.

☐ Avoid "direct" flights as much as possible and try to book non-stop flights as much as possible. Note: "Direct" flights involve at least one stopover.

☐ Sign up for email alerts that will tell you whether your flights have been delayed. This can be arranged online either with airlines or through **http://www.flightstats.com** and **http://www.flightview.com**.

☐ When possible, book flights that leave earlier in the day, as evening flights run greater chances of being delayed, resulting in a forced overnight.

☐ Visit **http://www.airsafe.com** and check the safety records of airlines on which you will travel. At the site, click on "Fatal events by airline," which will take you to a regional breakdown of the safety record of all airlines. If flying internally in a developing country, check very carefully the safety record of internal carriers. Many are not in compliance with International Civil Aviation Organization (**http://www.icao.org**) safety standards. Also, visit the U.S. Federal Aviation Administration's Web site (**http://www.faa.gov/safety/programs_initiatives/oversight/iasa/media/iasaws.xls**) for a breakdown of Category 1 and Category 2 airlines worldwide. Category 1 includes airlines that are in compliance with ICAO safety standards, while Category 2 includes airlines that are not in compliance.

☐ Avoid flying on Category 2 airlines, if possible.

☐ Avoid start-up airlines abroad that are not well-capitalized or who have a history of aviation accidents.

☐ To check the European Union's list of banned or restricted airlines, go to: **http://www.ec.europa.eu/transport/air-ban**.

☐ When flying *internally* in some developing countries, keep in mind that many governments do not have the sophistication of air and ground navigation infrastructure to which you are accustomed. Hence, internal commercial flights may be VFR (visual flight rules) only versus IFR (instrument flight rules), which means the risk is increased during poor weather conditions. Many air crashes in developing countries occurred because pilots chose to fly in bad weather in the absence of critical ground navigation and ATC (air traffic control).

In September 2007, an MD-82 flown by the budget airline One-Two-Go crashed during very heavy rain on the Thai island of Phuket, thus killing 66 of 123 foreign tourists. In December 1998, a flight flown by Thai Airways also crashed in heavy rain in Surat Thani, thus killing 101. In July 2007, a TAM Airlines A320 ran off the runway and skidded across a major highway in Sao Paulo, thus killing 199.

Just because a pilot is willing to fly in bad weather in a developing country with poor navigational infrastructure doesn't necessarily mean you have to follow his imprudence. Some internal carriers in developing nations are high-risk operations. You do not have to take the same risks; you can take a flight in better weather.

☐ Fly on nonstop flights to your destination if possible. This will cut down on travel time.

☐ In light of an airline passenger recently dying on an American Airlines flight as a result of cardiovascular disease, ensure you are fit enough to fly on long-haul flights.

☐ Fly wide-bodied commercial airliners as much as possible.

☐ Wear your seat belt when an aircraft is flying! Each year, hundreds of passengers are injured by turbulence (sudden flight deviation of often no more than inches) while not wearing seat belts. Two-thirds of turbulence-related accidents occur above 30,000 feet. In January 2008, an Air Canada flight destined from Victoria to Toronto, ten passengers required hospitalization when the Airbus A319 suddenly bucked and rolled, when the aircraft's computer went out, causing dishes to fly, carts to tip over and unbelted passengers to find themselves being hurled upward into luggage compartments.

☐ If you are middle-aged or older, select an aisle seat. You have more legroom, quicker access to the restrooms, easier access to the aisle to stretch your legs on a long flight, and a quicker exit point from the aircraft.

☐ Commercial aircraft *evacuations* occur every 12 days on an airliner somewhere around the world! When you settle into your seat, read the emergency evacuation card, know where the nearest exit is, and count the number of rows from your seat to the exit. You may not be able to see the exit in an emergency. Consider buying an emergency smoke mask, which fits in your carry-on bag and can also be used in hotel fires. In August 2007, 157 passengers and eight crew members were evacuated unhurt from a Taiwanese Boeing 737-800 minutes before the entire fuselage ignited in flames shortly after its arrival in Okinawa from Taipei.

☐ If you are traveling on business, ask your employer to authorize business class travel. It makes a huge difference in the level of fatigue and jet lag. If you are an entrepreneur, freelance journalist, or small businessperson, try to upgrade to business class if you can. The cost is tax deductible. To find reduced costs on international tickets abroad, visit **http://www.cookamerican.com** or e-mail **amex-a@representative.planetamex.com**.

☐ If you travel abroad often (five or more trips per year), consider becoming a member of the airport hospitality club of the airline with which you travel regularly. These clubs offer food; drinks; e-mail, telephone, and fax services; and sometimes even shower facilities. In view of the delays when traveling internationally, using these clubs accommodations ($350–$600 per year) can reduce jet lag and fatigue and allow you work while you are waiting. Another option is to join Priority Pass (**http://www.prioritypass.com**), which offers 500 VIP lounges worldwide in more than 200 cities, regardless of the airline or class you fly ($99–$4000 per year).

☐ The Registered Traveler Program is a program that TSA has instituted in order to help frequent travelers undergo screening much quicker by providing personal information and being subjected to being photographed, fingerprinted and have an image of their iris electronically captured. Although the jury is still out on the effectiveness of this program, participants say that it reduces screening time by roughly 30%. Unfortunately, it has not been implemented in all U.S. ports of departure. It also costs $128. For further information, go to: **http://www.flyclear.com**.

Traveling by bus and hired transportation. Traveling by bus abroad has its advantages: reduced cost, scenic visibility, logistical ease, social interaction (particularly if part of an organized tour), and sharing the experience of traveling.

The disadvantages are that bus travel, particularly in mountainous areas and on icy and poorly maintained roads, can have irreversible results, as refected on pages 37–38. In other cases, bus accidents often occur because vehicles are poorly maintained or do not have seat belts, drivers are not licensed or occasionally are inexperienced and intoxicated, roads do not have barriers or guardrails in mountainous or hilly terrain, or drivers use poor judgment in traveling in very hazardous road conditions.

Other bus trips that ended tragically for tourists include:

- Six Taiwanese tourists were killed and 40 injured because their bus driver was driving too fast and lost control of the bus on the way to Rio de Janeiro.

- In 2001, three Britons were killed and 14 injured when their tour bus plunged down a ravine at Cradle Mountain on the island of Tasmania. The vehicle fell from the road after the earth below it gave way.

- In 2002, nine people, including four Britons, were killed and 12 injured in a bus accident in South Africa while returning to Johannesburg from a game park. The bus company was involved in another accident in 1999 that killed 26 British tourists.

- In 2003, 28 German tourists were killed en route to Spain from Lyon, France. Their bus driver was driving too fast as he attempted to overtake another vehicle in wet weather. A week before this accident, a bus of elderly German tourists drove into the path of an oncoming train in Hungary, thus killing 33.

- In 2006, 12 Turkish tourists were killed and 20 injured in Rome when a bus driver failed to negotiate a curve and caused the bus to plunge down a ravine. The tour was returning to the hotel from a day trip.

- In January 2006, three German tourists were killed on the highly dangerous road between Bangkok and the beach resort of Pattaya, south of the capital. In that case, a Thai driver who had been hired by the Germans fell asleep at the wheel of the van and collided into a tractor trailer at a high rate of speed.

The majority of tour buses get to where they are going without incident. Nevertheless, buses carrying foreign travelers do crash regularly throughout the world. Consequently, the following is suggested to reduce tour bus accidents:

☐ Whenever possible, avoid taking poorly maintained and overworked buses, particularly in rural, mountainous regions.

☐ Avoid traveling by bus at night in developing countries.

☐ Avoid hiring tour buses on your own, unless the reputation of the company, its drivers, and the safety of its vehicles have been well vetted and references checked. Use reputable travel agencies and tour operators that come highly recommended.

☐ Avoid tour buses whenever the weather is particularly hazardous.

☐ Consider the use of a number of 4WD vehicles in convoy rather than a large passenger tour bus, particularly on bad roads and in hazardous driving conditions.

Caution is also suggested in hiring or leasing cars and minivans with drivers. Throughout much of the developing world, the following assumptions should be made:

■ Many drivers who offer transportation for hire do not have valid driving permits.

■ Many for-hire vehicles do not have insurance that covers injuries to occupants.

■ Many drivers have been involved in a number of accidents.

In light of the above, I suggest the following:

☐ On road trips greater than 30 minutes, hire vehicles and licensed drivers through reputable, insured, and bonded transport firms (the hotel concierge can usually make reliable referrals). Cost should never be a primary consideration when your life is at stake.

☐ Always pay attention to what the driver is doing and correct him or her as necessary if he or she is not alert or driving too fast or recklessly.

The Web site I gave you earlier (**http://www.asirt.org**) offers excellent road safety reports.

Natural Disasters

Recall the 2004 Tsunami in Southeast Asia that claimed the lives of more than 200,000; the recent earthquake in northern Japan; the 1985 Mexico City earthquake that killed an estimated 10,000 people; the 1985 volcano eruption in Nevado del Ruiz, Colombia, that killed more than 23,000; Hurricane Katrina in 2005 that killed more than 1,300; and the 1991 cyclone in Bangladesh that killed at least 139,000. All are reminders that regardless of where you are traveling, you should prepare for natural disasters.

Keep in mind that *natural disasters that occur in developing nations usually have much higher rates of casualties* than do those that occur in most developed nations, mainly because of developed nations' improved construction codes, emergency communications, capabilities of first-responder services, mass-casualty hospital management, and interagency coordination. Hurricane Katrina was the exception for a developed nation. The 8.0 earthquake in southern Peru in August of 2007, which claimed the lives of more than 600 people, underlines the high casualty rate that can result in developing nations.

In anticipation of a major natural disaster, always have ready an evacuation bag that contains the following:

- Map of the city and the country
- Contact information for friends, families, and colleagues
- Whistle
- First aid kit
- Rain gear
- Toiletries
- Prescribed medications
- Bottled water and a small blanket for each person in your party
- Portable radio with batteries, preferably shortwave
- Cell phone with two extra batteries
- Change of clothes (including comfortable shoes)
- Passport, credit cards, and at least $300 in small denominations
- Swiss Army knife
- Compass

Because of the resulting higher rate of casualties in developing nations, below are some quick tips on actions to take in the event of the following:

Cyclones (revolving storms in the Southern Hemisphere that blow in a *clockwise* circle).

☐ Fill bathtubs and containers with water to flush toilets and sanitize items if water systems fail.
☐ Fuel your car, and park it under a solid cover.

☐ Close shutters and board up or heavily tape all windows.

☐ Disconnect electrical appliances and turn off the gas.

☐ Stay inside in the most secure part of the building (cellar, internal hallway, or bathroom). Stay clear of windows.

☐ If the building starts to break apart, protect yourself with mattresses, rugs, or blankets or take shelter under a strong table or bench. If necessary, hold on to solid fixtures, such as water pipes.

☐ If you are driving, *stop* away from water, trees, and power lines. Stay in your vehicle.

Earthquakes. Some 1,370 earthquakes occur each day, somewhere around the world. Of those, 275 are felt by humans, and of those, three have sufficient energy to cause damage. If you are living in an earthquake zone, you can take a number of steps to prevent injuries during an earthquake:

☐ Remove anything that could fall or move.

☐ Bolt down shelves, cupboards, bookcases, and china cabinets.

☐ Secure or bolt down appliances. They move during a tremor.

☐ Secure the water heater to wall studs, and bolt it to the floor.

☐ Store water and food to last for five days.

☐ Secure a portable radio with batteries to monitor emergency reports.

☐ Keep fragile or heavy objects on bottom shelves.

During an earthquake:

☐ Stay clear of windows, fireplaces, or appliances.

☐ Turn off gas, electricity, and water.

☐ If you are indoors, drop to the floor and make yourself small with your knees on the floor and your head tucked toward the floor (earthquake position). Place one hand on a table leg to stabilize it and one hand over the back of your neck. Alternatively, get low next to a heavy sofa or armchair, and cover your head and neck with a pillow.

☐ Seek cover on either side of exterior walls of buildings, and away from glass and items that can fall on you.

☐ Stay out of the kitchen and clear of flying objects.

☐ Stay away from items that can fall from overhead.

☐ Do not use staircases or rush outside while a building is shaking, or move around amid flying glass or debris.

☐ If you are outside, get into an open area away from buildings, power lines, chimneys, and falling objects.

☐ If you are driving, quickly but carefully move your car away from traffic and stop. Do not stop on or under bridges or overpasses or under trees, light posts, power lines, or signs. Do not remain in your vehicle after stopping, but rather seek cover next to it.

Hurricanes. In the Northern Hemisphere, cyclones are called hurricanes or typhoons and blow in a *counterclockwise* circle. High wind is not the danger; the danger is flying debris and damage to buildings. The conditions for a hurricane are usually spotted days before one actually develops. If you stay in your house, make sure you have sturdy locked shutters to protect the windows and everyone in the house. If you do not have shutters, use heavy plywood and nail it to the window frame. Below are some safe locations in a hurricane:

- ☐ The safest place to be during any high-wind storm is a basement, away from windows, in the middle rooms or closets of the house, or under a heavy piece of furniture.
- ☐ If you do not have a basement, go to the innermost closet or bathroom without windows and hide under heavy furniture.
- ☐ Listen to the news to determine the hurricane type, and decide whether you should stay home or go to a shelter.
- ☐ If you are in a car and spot oncoming bad winds, leave the car and take shelter in a building or ditch.

Tsunamis. Tsunamis (giant waves) evolve from ocean-generated earthquakes. The Indian Ocean tsunami of December 26, 2004, was the worst tsunami (in terms of loss of life) in *recorded history*. In coastal areas, tsunamis can reach a height of 30 feet or more, although the 2004 tsunami reached 108 feet. They can also move inland for a considerable distance and faster than a person can run. When you can see the wave of a tsunami, you are *too* close to escape.

- ☐ If you are at the beach or near the ocean and you feel the earth shake, move immediately to higher ground.
- ☐ Approaching tsunamis forewarn with the noticeable rise or fall of coastal waters.

☐ Approaching large tsunamis usually emit a loud roar that sounds very much like a train or an aircraft.

☐ High, multistory, reinforced concrete hotels are located in many low-lying coastal areas. The upper floors of these hotels provide a safe place to find refuge should a tsunami warning occur and you cannot move quickly inland to higher ground.

Volcanoes. Volcanic activity comes in many forms, from trickles of lava to violent explosions that spew rocks, ash, and gas many miles into the air. Fortunately, most of Earth's 500 active volcanoes are carefully monitored, and scientists can usually provide some advance warning before an eruption. If you travel, work, or live near a volcano, you are always at risk. Below are some useful tips for surviving volcanic eruptions:

☐ Get a topographical map of the region around the volcano and plan an exit.

☐ Listen for radio or TV advisories when an eruption is anticipated.

☐ Leave the area promptly if told to do so.

☐ Relocate to high ground. Lava flows, mudflows, and flooding are common in a major eruption.

☐ Avoid breathing poisonous gases. They can kill you in minutes.

☐ If you live near an active volcano, purchase a respirator or mask. If neither is available, moisten a piece of cloth and cover your nose—this will protect your lungs from clouds of ash. Quickly get far away from the volcano.

☐ Seek safety in a strong building, and put duct tape around windows and doors.

☐ Driving through heavy ash is dangerous. Visibility is limited, the roads become slippery, and the car radiator can get clogged. Keep your headlights on, proceed slowly, and watch your car for overheating.

You *rarely* can outrun a lava flow, but you may be able to dodge it, especially by climbing to higher ground. Never try to cross a lava flow. Flows that appear to be cooled may simply have formed a thin crust over a core of extremely hot lava. If you attempt to cross a lava flow, you risk being trapped by another suddenly developed flow. Do not attempt to cross geothermal areas. Failure could result in serious burns or death. The best way to ensure surviving a volcanic eruption is to live at least 10 miles away.

For a review of some of the world's worst natural disasters, please visit **http://www.epicdisasters.com** and **http://www.earthquake.usgs.gov/regional**.

Special Topics

Vetting tour operators. As you have seen in case studies in this book, selecting a tour operator or transportation provider "on the cheap" or one that is not reputable can yield unintended consequences.

For example, I took our family to Costa Rica during the late 1980s. We flew to San Jose and arranged through a travel agent to stay at a beach resort on the Pacific coast. There, we arranged a snorkeling trip and selected an expatriate couple as tour guides. This couple dropped us into deep water roughly 200 yards offshore in weather unsuitable for boats, let alone people. My younger daughter, Jennifer, 15, was very apprehensive, but I was naively comfortable with our guides' "expertise." That comfort did not last long. Almost immediately after getting into the water, we were pulled by strong currents. We eventually bounced into sharp lava rock in the shallows. and got scraped up pretty badly on the rocks, but we finally made it safely to shore. Needless to say, we were fortunate, no thanks to our "guides." I learned my lesson well that day: whether you are looking for a tour package abroad, an adventure or ecotour, or a guided sightseeing trip, verify tour operators' bona fides before hiring them. You can do this by following the steps below:

☐ Use nationally or globally reliable travel companies to handle your travel. They know the risks and will connect you with competent providers.

☐ Use tour operators who are members of the U.S. Tour Operators Association, the National Tour Association, the American Society of Travel Agents, and/or the International Association of Internet Tour Operators. For adventure travel, check out *National Geographic*

Adventure magazine's list of 160 rated outfitters (**http://www.ngadventure.com/ratings**).

- **http://www.ustoa.com** (U.S. Tour Operators Association)
- **http://www.ntaonline.com** (National Tour Association)
- **http://www.asta.org** (American Society of Travel Agents)
- **http://www.iaito.org** (International Association of Internet Tour Operators)

☐ Beware of tour and transportation companies with no online contact information.

☐ Pay for trips, even ground transportation, with a credit card, not a debit card. If things go bad, you can potentially get your money back.

Cruise ship security and safety. Most cruise ship lines are reputable and many actually take proactive steps to keep you safe when you are in their charge. That said, passengers should conduct their own assessment of cruise lines and talk to friends who have taken cruises before making a deposit for a trip. They should also go to: **http://www.internationalcruisevictims.org**, (ICV), to get a feel for the criminal threats that confront cruise ship passengers. Currently, cruise lines are facing several challenges, such as new cruise lines entering the market and more competition for potential profits, less scrutiny of crews, larger passenger-to-crew ratios, and increasing security risks as the number of passengers increases.

In March 2007, Salvador Hernandez, deputy assistant director of the FBI, testified before Congress on the FBI's role in investigating crimes against American citizens traveling aboard cruise ships. During his testimony, Hernandez stated that during 2002–2007, the FBI opened 258 cases for crimes on the high seas. (Approximately 50 cases are opened annually.) Of the 258 cases, 184, or 71 percent, occurred on cruise ships. Sexual assaults and physical assaults on cruise ships were the leading crime reported to and investigated by the FBI during the past five years. Approximately 55 percent were sexual assault cases, and 22 percent were physical assault cases. Most of the sexual assaults on cruise ships took place in private cabins, and more than 50 percent involved alcohol. Physical assaults were the second most frequently committed crime. Thirteen death investigations on cruise ships were also opened during this five-year period. Two of the 13 cruise ship deaths were homicides; the remaining 11 deaths were caused by suicides, accidents, or natural causes. *Statistics cited above relate **only** to cruise ships under the jurisdiction of the FBI; actual crime statistics on all cruise ship lines are unknown. There are indications that some cruise ship lines may have as many as 50 rapes per year aboard their vessels, with the majority of them being committed by crew members.*

The U.S. Congress held three hearings in 2007 with cruise industry representatives (**http://www.cruising.org**),

International Cruise Victims (ICV), and federal agencies. At the latest March 2007 hearing with the Cruise Line International Association (CLIA) and ICV, Congress gave CLIA six months to collaborate with ICV to develop a proposal to increase the transparency of the industry and report the safety records of cruise line vessels. ICV developed a plan for additional cruise line safety titled the Cruise Line Law Adherence Monitoring Personnel (CLAMP), which requires an independent security force aboard all cruise ships. According to ICV, cruise lines assert that they are not obligated to investigate crime and that their reporting requirement to law enforcement should be voluntary.

Below are some tips for keeping yourself safe and healthy while traveling on a cruise ship:

- ☐ Visit **http://www.internationalcruisevictims.org** before booking a cruise to see which cruise lines have had major security incidents aboard their vessels.
- ☐ In recent years, many cruise ships have been plagued by increasing outbreaks of stomach flu, gastrointestinal infections, colds, and influenza. Most of these illnesses are brought aboard by passengers. The best countermeasure is to bring with you cold and flu remedies and medications such as Immodium, Cipro, and Flagyl (see pages 135 and 136).
- ☐ Stay hydrated, wash your hands frequently, use hand sanitizers, keep your hands away from your mouth, and report illness to the ship's doctor.

☐ According to a study in the British medical journal *Lancet*, ginger worked better for seasickness than various anti-motion-sickness medications (Antivert, Bonine, or Dramamine). Ginger, incidentially, comes in several forms (powder, tablet, tea or carbonated drink).

☐ Do not drink alcohol to the excessive. Intoxicated passengers are more often vulnerable to crime, sexual assault, accidents, and falls.

☐ Do not take valuable jewelry aboard the ship or ashore.

☐ Always let family and friends know where you are.

☐ Apply the entirety of this book to shore trips when you are on a cruise.

☐ Thoroughly research the security risks that exist at ports of call you will be visiting during your cruise and take appropriate precautions described elsewhere in this book.

☐ Cruise ship travel should be a pleasant, fun and memorable experience. Unfortunately, some cruise ship lines have had far too many security incidents and have responded with far too little empathy and help. In 2004, a federal appellate court in Miami upheld a $1 million jury award to a woman passenger on a cruise ship for sexual battery committed by a ship's waiter while the victim was ashore in Bermuda.

☐ It is not easy to fall from a cruise ship—you have to work at it. Railings in common areas and on balconies are intentionally high and solid. Yet, in the past year, a number of cases have occurred where passengers have fallen from vessels. In most cases, the falls have been attributed to irresponsible pranks and excessive drinking while on medication. In a few cases, those who have fallen from ships are never found; in most cases, they are recovered. In March 2007, a young couple unexplainably fell, or jumped, from a ship and was recovered hours later. Two weeks later, another man fell from a ship after having too much to drink. The Coast Guard found him alive after he drifted some 15 miles. In June, a young man disappeared from a Caribbean cruise and was never found. As I have said repeatedly, drinking excessively makes you vulnerable to crime and accidents.

Foreign study programs: useful information for students and parents. In recent years, incidents against university students abroad in foreign study programs have increased. Students are increasingly becoming victims of vehicular accidents, larceny, armed robbery, rape, and, in some cases, murder.

Consider the following:

■ In May 1997, 12 University of New Mexico (UNM) students and their advisors arrived in Guayaquil and were en route to Cuenca when bandits, claiming to be narcotics officers, forced their bus to a stop. After robbing the group, the gunmen fired indiscriminately at the bus and killed the wife of the group leader. As a result, UNM programs in Ecuador were suspended.

- In January 1998, four gunmen attacked a group of 16 U.S. college students and teachers from St. Mary's College (MD) who were on a regional study tour in southern Guatemala. The gunmen robbed all of them and raped five women in the group between the ages of 18 and 20. The gunmen forced the group's bus off the road with a pickup truck and ordered the 13 students and three teachers into a sugarcane field where the robberies and rapes occurred. The attack occurred while the group was traveling along Guatemala's Pacific Highway, 40 miles southwest of Guatemala City. It happened at the end of a three-week trip for the students to learn about Guatemalan culture. In 2002, St. Mary's awarded three of the victims $195,000, despite a lawsuit for several million dollars. Maryland state law limited the college's liability to $100,000 per plaintiff.

- In October 1998, former Earlham College student Erika Eisenberg settled in a multimillion-dollar lawsuit stemming from Eisenberg's allegation that she was raped by her Japanese host while studying in Japan.

- In March 1999, an anthropology student from the University of Chicago nearly died when Hutu rebels kidnapped and killed eight of her party in Uganda. Ironically, the Peace Corps had withdrawn its volunteers from Uganda years earlier on the basis that it could not ensure their safety.

- In March 2000, Emily Howell, a student at Antioch College who was working on a photography project, and

Emily Eagen, a friend and former student at Antioch, were raped and murdered near Cahuita, some 90 miles east of San Jose. One of the suspects was sentenced to 70 years in prison in 2001.

- In October 2004, a U.S. citizen participating in a semester-abroad program in Ecuador under the auspices of her university arranged a week-long trip in the Galapagos Islands. On the last night of her trip, and on the return to Guayaquil, she was allegedly raped by the tour boat's captain. The incident was subsequently reported to the U.S. embassy.

The majority of university foreign study programs are cognizant of the increasing risks to students while they are abroad, but many are deficient in their risk management efforts to safeguard students while they are abroad. Most universities do not have the expertise to assess and manage the security of the students they send abroad. Universities often spend little funding on such protection and are often naive to the many threats. Universities that have foreign study programs should:

☐ Have stated university policy that foreign study programs will not be conducted in countries where the U.S. State Department posts a travel advisory and/or discourages travel.

☐ Have written delineation of the university's responsibilities and the student's responsibilities as far as safety and security are concerned in the foreign study program.

☐ Have detailed reports on the security threats that exist in countries in which students will live and guidance for countering such threats.

☐ Provide online predeparture security/safety foreign travel briefings on the destination country. These briefings should include pre- and posttesting that documents the students' comprehension.

☐ Obtain a signed statement by each student verifying that he/she has read university policies and procedures on security abroad and understands information and briefing content.

☐ Thoroughly vet host families, residential facilities, and travel arrangements and have written policies on the vetting process.

☐ Send a letter to the parents of each student that identifies the university's foreign study security representative and provides contact information during work hours and after hours. This letter additionally should advise parents on how they can help keep their son or daughter safe while abroad and provide parents a copy of the university's contingency plan for handling security emergencies that students might confront abroad. Additionally, this letter should advise parents on how to access U.S. State Department travel advisories, consular information sheets, public announcements, and reports at **http://www.osac.gov**.

☐ Hire independent security consultants with experience in keeping travelers and expatriates safe while abroad and in managing all aspects of security for foreign study programs.

☐ Debrief students after they return home to identify security concerns they experienced while abroad that were not addressed by the university or university policy.

Unfortunately, many universities are ill equipped to deal with threats in the developing world. Although many have published guidelines, they often lack substance and are too generic for specific threat situations. Telling young adults to be careful is not enough; in violent environments abroad, it is essential to give students a security infrastructure and policies that significantly help reduce risks.

Celebrities, very important people and political figures.
Having spent a good part of my State Department career as an armed protective agent, where I was responsible for accompanying foreign dignitaries, American ambassadors, cabinet secretaries and legislators, I continue to be puzzled by the proclivity of many celebrities, VIPs and political figures to ignore best practices that can keep them alive and safe.

One merely has to examine a number of case studies in point that have occurred in the last few years to fully understand how well-known figures ignore the threat and make very bad choices. The most obvious example is the assassination of former Pakistanti Prime Minister Benazir Bhutto, who was killed in December 2007, when, after surviving an earlier assassination attempt, stood up through an open portal in a limousine and was killed by an assassin because of her vulnerability. Interestingly, those that remained in the protected vehicle, were not harmed. Bhutto's failure to adhere to basic security practices in VIP protection resulted in her unnecessary death.

In another case, Russian tennis star Anna Chakvetadze (seeded #6) was robbed and tied up when six armed men broke into her home on the outskirts of Moscow. During the home invasion, the gunmen stole $106,000 in cash and $200,000 in jewelry, but the lingering question is, how did the intruders know she had such a large amount of cash and jewelry in the home, and why was it not properly safeguarded?

Two other high-profile assassinations of political figures include billionaire and former Lebanese prime minister Rafik Hariri, and Amine Gemayel, an anti-Syrian member of the Lebanese Parliament and minister of industry, both Christians. Hariri was assassinated in February 2005 as his motorcade passed by a 1,000kg truck-bomb near Beirut's St. George Hotel that was detonated as the motorcade passed the bomb. Twenty people died in the attack and 220 others were injured. As for Gemayel, he was assassinated by gunmen in November 2006, when his assailants rammed the front of his vehicle with another car and sprayed the vehicle with 9mm automatic weapons. Gemayel later died in a hospital. Hariri's death was caused by poor advance work, inadequate security on his movements, a massive bomb that rendered an armored vehicle useless . . . and because Hariri himself was driving his vehicle, rather than using a

trained security driver. Ironically, though, Hariri had traveled past the St. George only six times in a three-month
period, giving credibility to the notion that there may have
been multiple car bombs on several routes. Gemayel's death
was caused by his not traveling in a fully armored vehicle
and using predictable routes. Syrian extremists were blamed
for both attacks.

Finally, in February 2008, Anna Loginova, a former
model-turned CEO of a security firm specializing in providing
female bodyguards to wealthy Russians, was killed in Moscow
when a carjacker pulled her out of a luxury Porsche Cayenne.
Unfortunately, rather than do the prudent thing and give up
the car to the carjacker, Loginova held onto the door handle
and was dragged some distance before letting go. Ironically,
Loginova months earlier fought off another carjacker, but
never quite learned that property is not worth your life.

Clearly, political figures, celebrities, CEOs and other targets of means should ensure that their protection is assessed
and managed by experienced professionals who understand
how to:

☐ Assess the security threats they face;
☐ Evaluate home, office, vehicular, family and travel security, with an eye toward reducing physical and procedural vulnerabilities;
☐ Adhere to route variance and tight security on daily
schedules and movements;
☐ Effectively use armored vehicles and use trained security
drivers;

☐ Institute emergency procedures in the event of a threat;

☐ How to train the principal (i.e., the person being protected) in avoidance, non-resistance and evacuation/escape from the scene of the threat; and

☐ Recruit, train and supervise protective operatives (as appropriate) who will evacuate the principal from the scene of a threat, rather than engaging in a gunfight or altercation with the assailant(s).

The risks that diplomats and military personnel and their families face abroad.   The risks that diplomats and military personnel face in Iraq and Afghanistan are well known. In war zones, inhabitants anticipate a threat every moment.

Even more difficult is maintaining security awareness for staff and travelers in conventional countries that are not at war, but where violent crime and the threat of terrorism are foreseeable events. Admittedly, foreign diplomats and military personnel working and living abroad often fall into a lapse of security awareness where incidents and attacks are not occurring regularly, which is why vigilance must be a part of everyone's daily routine. As such, this section is designed to make diplomats and military staff aware of the threat and action to be take: American, British, and Canadian government personnel abroad (approximately 50,000) cannot maintain around-the-clock vigilance. As such, this section addresses foreign governments' security abroad.

The greatest risks are not at embassies or military installations, where diplomats and military personnel typically work. Rather, the risks are at "soft targets" that they frequent: restaurants, bars, hotels, tourist attractions, shopping areas, airports, and other gathering places.

To review how diplomats and military personnel have been attacked at "soft target" locations in the past, consider the following:

- January 1982: LtCol Charles Ray, USA, assistant defense attaché, is shot and killed outside his apartment in Paris by the Lebanese Armed Revolutionary Faction (LARF).

- May 1983: Lieutenant Commander Albert Schaufelberger, USN, deputy of the embassy's U.S. military group, is shot and killed by three gunmen of the Central American Revolutionary Workers' Party (PRTC), a sub-group of the Farabundo Marti National Libertation Front (FMLN). Unfortunately, Schaufelberger had been dating a woman who worked at the Central American University in San Salvador for some months. As a result, the Navy SEAL made a bad habit of picking his girl friend up at the same time and honkling when he arrived. Although he was driving an armored vehicle, the air conditioning of the vehicle was broken, which forced him to remove the ballistic-resistant panel from the driver's window. When his girl friend came out of her office, three gunmen stopped her, walked up to Schaufelberger and shot him in the head several times with a .22 cal. pistol through the open window.

- February 1984: Ray Hunt, a retired Foreign Service officer who was head of the 10-nation Sinai Field Mission force that monitored the Egyptian-Israeli peace treaty, is assassinated by the Red Brigades outside his home in Rome.

- November 1983: Captain George Tsantes, USN, head of the U.S. military group, is shot and killed by the terrorist group November 17 while being driven to work. His chauffeur was also killed.

- March 1984: U.S. Consul Robert Homme is shot by a gunman on a motorcycle in Strasbourg.

- April 1984: 18 U.S. servicemen are killed in a bomb attack near a U.S. Air Force base in Spain.

- June 1985: Four Marine Security Guards assigned to the U.S. Embassy are assassinated by the Farabundo Marti National Liberation Front (FMLN) while seated at a sidewalk café in San Salvador. Nine Salvadorans are also killed.

- June 1988: The U.S. Defense Attaché in Athens, Captain William Noorden USN, is killed outside his home when a car bomb detonates.

- April 1989: The New People's Army (NPA) assassinates Col. Jim Rowe, USA, in Manila as he traveled in a light-armored vehicle.

- June 1996: 19 U.S. servicemen are killed when a truck bomb detonates at the Khobar Towers housing complex in Dhaharan.

- December 1996: Several U.S. diplomats are held hostage at a reception at the Japanese ambassador's residence in Lima, when members of the Tupac Amaru Revolutionary Front (MRTA) seized several hundred hostages.

- August 1998: 12 U.S. citizens and hundreds of Kenyan and Tanzanian citizens are killed during the simultaneous car bomb attacks on the U.S. embassies in Nairobi and Dar es Salaam. Al-Qaeda was linked to both attacks.

- June 2000: November 17 claims responsibility for the assassination of British defense attaché Stephen Saunders in Athens.

- March 2002: Evacuated from the U.S. Embassy in Islamabad after the events of 9/11, State Department employee Barbara Green and her daughter, Kristen, 17, returned to Pakistan just weeks before they were killed in the Protestant International Church, 400 yards from the U.S. Embassy. Both were killed when extremists ran through the church and threw hand grenades into the crowd of worshippers.

- October 2002: USAID executive officer Laurence Foley is assassinated by two al-Qaeda gunmen outside his home in Amman.

- November 2003: The British consul and three other consulate employees are killed in a car bomb attack that causes major damage to the British Consulate and HSBC, the world's second-largest bank, in Istanbul. The attack is linked to al-Qaeda. Twenty-seven people are killed, and 450 are wounded.

- January 2008: John Granville, employed by the U.S. Agency for International Development at the U.S. Embassy in Khartoum, was assassinated, along with his Sudanese driver, while the driver was taking Granville home after a New Year's Eve party. The diplomat's vehicle was cut off by the assailants' vehicle, after which gunmen opened fire on the two and left. Nothing was taken from Granville or the vehicle, suggesting a political motive. Granville died at the hospital after surgery.

The following information provides guidance on how foreign diplomats and military personnel can reduce their risk while assigned abroad, particularly if they are not living on diplomatic or military premises.

☐ If living in an apartment or residence in a foreign city, be cautious of telling others where you work. Depending upon who your neighbors are, you may want to be vague as to your specific duties.

☐ Do not place your diplomatic or military business card on your door or mailbox or gratuitously hand it out to strangers.

☐ In selecting a residence, avoid homes that force you to park on the street, where you may be vulnerable to acts of crime, terrorism and surveillance, and rather seek a residence that includes underground or protected parking not visible to the public. Consider residences that allow you to park your vehicle in a garage with controlled access.

☐ Advise your spouse and older children that they should be cautious of sharing personal information, such as where you work and live. Encourage them to be aware of abnormal or suspicious behavior.

☐ If your embassy or military security officer has instructed you not to patronize certain hotels, restaurants, bars, and discos, comply. This warning could be based upon reliable intelligence information.

☐ Do not wear apparel, such as baseball caps, sweatshirts, or T-shirts, or carry a briefcase emblazoned with a flag of your nation or other government logos that could disclose your government affiliation.

☐ Be predictably unpredictable in departure and arrival times from your home and office and locations of other scheduled activities (golf, tennis, children's practices).

The risk of being an aid worker. Twenty-plus years ago, being an aid worker was respectable and appreciated work. The choices were many: UN peacekeeper, Peace Corps volunteer, a foreign assistance agency, World Health Organization, Doctors without Borders, the International Committee of the Red Cross (ICRC), Save the Children, United Nations relief organizations, foreign governments, and NGOs. However, in recent years, with the rise of rebel and extremist groups, Islamic terrorism, suicide bombings, and indiscriminate violent crime, being an aid worker offers little protection. The result has been a steep rise in aid worker injuries and deaths, evacuation of staff after lethal attacks, and insufficient funding to protect the workers themselves. Clearly, *aid workers have one of the highest rates of injury and death when compared to any other foreign occupational category.*

Unfortunately, the number of attacks is difficult to track. Many aid organizations maintain statistics only on foreigners they deploy to so-called trouble spots. Sadly, the injuries and deaths of local aid workers are often not recorded. As dedicated as aid workers are, their employers generally provide inadequate security support. The rising number of victims is attributed to more aid workers being hired and deployed and the deterioration of security in their work environments.

Before agreeing to being deployed to a high-risk country in a developing country, first consider the following:

☐ Have a clear and detailed understanding of the personal risks you will face.

☐ Ask your prospective employer (a) how many employees have been injured or killed while working for the organization in your country of choice, (b) why these incidents occurred, and (c) what action could have been taken to prevent them.

☐ Confirm that you will be evacuated from the country at your employer's expense when your government authorizes evacuation and when it is impossible for you to safely work there.

☐ Determine the type of security training you will receive that helps you manage your personal risk while in the country.

☐ Determine the specifics of the life insurance, medical coverage, and medical and political/evacuation support your employer will provide.

☐ Determine specific actions your employer will take if you are kidnapped or held hostage.

☐ Ask for a copy of the organization's security guide for aid workers. It should include policies and procedures governing staff security and how to reduce risk while in the country. If it does not exist, proceed cautiously before accepting employment. That organization may not make staff security a top priority.

Personal security for journalists abroad. According to the Committee to Protect Journalists (CPJ) (**http://www. cpj.org**), 661 journalists have been killed worldwide since 1992; most of these deaths occurred in developing countries. This mortality rate puts journalists in one of the highest-risk occupational categories. Depending upon the risk index used, journalists could have a higher risk of being injured or killed than aid workers. The risks of being an international journalist are well documented at the CPJ Web site. The kidnapping of *Christian Science Monitor* journalist Jill Carroll and the kidnapping/beheading of *Wall Street Journal* correspondent Daniel Pearl are two cases that were prominently covered in the media. If you are a journalist working in developing countries, ask yourself the following questions:

☐ Has my employer briefed and informed me of the threats I will encounter?

☐ Have I been honest with my family about the severity of these threats?

☐ Are my personal affairs in order? If something happens to me, would my family know what to do in my absence, and would they have the financial resources to do it?

☐ What actions will my employer take if I am kidnapped, held hostage, disabled, or killed, and what financial and humanitarian support will they provide my family?

☐ If I am working in a war zone, do I have reliable communications equipment, credentials, protective equipment, and, if necessary, a protected vehicle to minimize the risks?

☐ Do I fully trust the interpreters, stringers, and local journalists I work with, or are they communicating to others what I am doing?

☐ Have I properly corroborated the reliability of my sources, or am I getting myself into a dangerous situation?

☐ Am I cognizant of the threats I will face if I am working on a story that may prompt physical retaliation from government officials or criminal or terrorist organizations?

☐ Do I keep trusted associates informed of what I am doing and where I am going?

Maritime piracy. This section is for ocean-going luxury yacht captains and owners who may encounter modern-day pirates who prey on blue-water yachts and commercial ships, including large tankers.

In December 2001, Sir Peter Blake, 53, who led New Zealand to winning the America's Cup sailing championship in 1995 and 2000, was shot and killed aboard his 119-foot yacht, the *Seamaster*, while it was moored on the Amazon River near Macapa, Brazil. The incident happened when armed and hooded river pirates climbed aboard the *Seamaster* at night and demanded money. As the gunmen were stealing a spare engine from the ship and watches from the crew on deck, Blake emerged from below deck with a rifle, which jammed when he attempted to fire at the pirates. The pirates who shot and killed Blake were later arrested and convicted. Remember that material goods are not worth your life.

In 2007, global pirate attacks increased 10 percent when compared to 2006, with Somalia and Nigeria showing the biggest increases according to the International Maritime Bureau (**http://www.imb.org**). In 2007, 198 attacks on ships were reported between January and September, up from 174 in the same period in 2006. Indonesia remains the world's worst piracy hot spot, with 37 reported attacks. Attacks rose rapidly in Somalia to 26 reported cases, up from only eight a year earlier. Nigeria experienced 26 attacks, up from nine in 2006. While Africa remains problematic, Southeast Asia's Malacca Strait, one of the world's busiest waterways, has been relatively quiet, with only four attacks compared to eight a year earlier. This is because of increased cooperation among neighboring states.

In November 2005, pirates attacked the *Seabourne Spirit*, a luxury cruise liner carrying 150 passengers and a crew of 160. Pirates in two small boats suddenly appeared and fired machine guns and an RPG (rocket-propelled grenade) at the ship in an attempt to overtake the vessel. However, the vessel's captain acted quickly and eluded the pirates. Given that Somalian waters are notorious for pirate attacks, the cruise company ceased operations there.

Below are some thoughts for yacht and ship owners and travelers:

☐ Decide whether traveling in pirate-active waters is necessary.

☐ Do not navigate in pirate-active waters without (a) a marine radio capable of making emergency calls to police and Coast Guard units and (b) radar technology capable of identifying other vessels in your proximity.

☐ Yachts and ships should always file a navigational plan and maintain constant radio contact when traveling in pirate-active waters.

☐ Cruise ship passengers should ensure that friends and family know the route of the ship on which they are traveling.

☐ For vessels traveling in high-risk, pirate-active waters, external surveillance cameras, crew vigilance, and communications with local Coast Guard and maritime police are essential.

☐ If aboard a ship or yacht that is attacked by pirates, go below deck (passengers and nonessential crew).

☐ Carrying firearms aboard a yacht or ship can result in impoundment of the vessel and arrest of the crew. *Note: In an emergency, flare guns can be useful in repelling pirates and criminals.*

☐ When traveling in pirate-active waters, yachts and ships should approach Coast Guard and police units and request escort assistance, where possible.

☐ Cruise ship enthusiasts should examine carefully the prudence of taking a cruise in Nigerian, Somalian, and Indonesian waters.

☐ Cruise ship passengers should follow crew directions in the event that pirates are encountered. In the case of the *Spirit*, the captain ordered passengers to their cabins when the ship began taking fire; one passenger was injured, and the ship was damaged.

General aviation air travel. General aviation (GA) comprises worldwide air travel, other than military and scheduled service. Since the events of 9/11, GA travel has increased because of airport delays and time-consuming passenger screening. Given the less stringent regulatory levels afforded GA, less capable aircraft, and less experienced pilots, accident statistics for GA are often higher than those for scheduled carriers.

In November 2006, a Learjet 35 owned by a Brazilian air taxi company crashed into several houses after taking off in Sao Paulo, killing the pilot and copilot. In the same year and country, a New York–based Legacy owned by ExcelAire Service, Inc., bound for Manaus, crashed into a Gol Airlines 737 airliner while both aircraft were in flight, killing 154 people onboard. The Legacy, piloted by two U.S. pilots, landed safely with all seven passengers unharmed.

Outside the United States and other developed nations, GA accidents are higher because of a number of factors: (1) inadequate pilot experience, (2) poor pilot judgment in adverse weather conditions, (3) absence of real-time meteorological/weather information, (4) inadequate ground navigational infrastructure, and (5) having to fly under visual flight regulations (VFR) in many situations.

When considering the use of GA air travel abroad, do your homework. Contact the aviation officer or commercial attaché at your embassy, the chamber of commerce, or colleagues you trust who live or have worked in the country. Or you can e-mail me, and I can provide contact information for some vetted air charter services working in the country in which you operate.

If you fly GA aircraft abroad, below are some pretrip planning tips to consider:

☐ Do not underestimate the subliminal effect of jet lag and fatigue on long flights.

☐ Prevent health problems by ensuring that you have international medical and evacuation coverage. Thoroughly read the health sections of this book and do not assume you can "tough it out" and work through an illness. This could put your passengers at risk.

☐ Remember that good nutrition and a well-balanced diet are critical on long flights, especially with the added stress of jet lag.

☐ Keep abreast of new developments in providing pilots graphic images of thunderstorm formations; in-flight icing; and ceiling, visibility, and winds-aloft forecasts.

☐ Keep abreast of the threat conditions in countries you are flying to and from. Your underwriter may have restrictions on where you can stay overnight and where you cannot stay because of security deficiencies or the potential for political unrest and/or terrorism. Know intimately the exclusions in your aircraft's policy.

☐ Realize that you and the pilot may be solely responsible for the aircraft on the ground. Some smaller airports may not have a perimeter fence, roving patrols, visual surveillance, or tarmac security. Consider the following to enhance security:

- If necessary, use LLE Language Services' 24-7 telephone interpretation (see page 112) to call the airport to which you are destined to determine any security support you can expect for your aircraft. If security protection is inadequate or you get an inadequate response to your call, go to the next point below.

- Speak to your embassy's security representative and aviation officer before arrival, and get their assessment of aircraft security at the airport(s) you will use. Also, ask which guard forces in the country are reliable and how to hire one to provide 24-hour security around your aircraft.

- Where necessary, use instrument panel barrier locks, portable perimeter alarm systems, or wheel locks to prevent the theft of your aircraft.

- If you must take your aircraft into isolated, rural areas, purchase a portable perimeter alarm system to detect unwanted visitors. Consider alarming doors and hatches, and purchase a handheld remote enunciator to detect unauthorized entry.

☐ Ensure that crew members have unlocked quad-band cell phones (**see page 101**) with extra batteries so that they can stay in touch.

☐ Arrange for a vetted English-speaking driver and reliable vehicle capable of accommodating crew and luggage.

☐ Check with your embassy to obtain the names of hotels known to have effective security for guests.

SECTION THREE

Getting from the Airport to Your Destination and Home

Despite the media frenzy that unfolded following September 11, 2001, and the continued preoccupation with terrorism in print and broadcast media, six years later, crime is still the most disruptive event that might confront an air traveler while en route to a foreign destination. A writer friend of mine had his trip sabotaged in Spain when his carry-on luggage (including laptop and return ticket) was stolen while he was waiting for the arrival of his checked luggage.

Crime is still the major threat in airports. Even though only ticketed passengers can gain access to departure gates in most countries, many airports, particularly in developing countries, continue to experience larceny (of carry-on luggage), armed robbery, carjacking, and rape in public-access sections of passenger terminals. These crimes often occur after passengers rent cars or use unauthorized taxi services. Remember that jet lag, fatigue, and poor judgment contribute to crimes in airports.

Before departing for the airport. Ensure that your flight is on time, and dress comfortably for the trip, preferably wearing shoes you can easily take off and put on when you go through security. Once outside the United States, you rarely have to remove your shoes. Wear belts with little or no metal and a cheap athletic watch with a nonmetallic band. Consider a Casio with a dual-time feature. Ensure that each piece of checked luggage has a covered luggage tag with your name, business address, cell phone number, and e-mail address. If traveling with children, remind them that jokes about bombs and terrorists can get them in trouble and delay flights.

Since August 10, 2006, passengers and flights originating in the United States and abroad may take liquids and gels (shampoo, lotions, creams, and toothpaste) into airline cabins *only* if they fit into a clear plastic food storage bag that does not exceed a quart. Each container in the bag cannot exceed three ounces and passengers are permitted to have only only one storage bag of liquid containers, that must be placed on the X-ray conveyor during pre-boarding screening.

Before leaving for the airport, go through your carry-on luggage and make sure it does not contain prohibited items, such as knives, mace, or weaponlike items.

Arrival at the airport. For an international flight, arrive at the airport at least two hours before the flight is scheduled to depart. Do not forget your passport and your ticket. When you arrive at the airport, DO NOT leave your carry-on luggage unattended or ask a stranger to watch it for you.

Checking in. Being a member of an airline frequent flyer (FF) program is a great benefit: depending upon your account, you can check in through the business class line, even if you fly economy class. Do not assume that your bag will be routed properly to the final destination; ask the ticket agent to ***show you*** the baggage routing information before he or she tags your bag(s). Before leaving the ticket counter, ensure that the agent places your baggage claim receipts on your ticket envelope and that you have boarding passes for the flights.

Security screening. If leaving from the United States, visit the TSA Web site (**http://www.tsa.dhs.gov/travelers/airtravel**) so that you know what is permissible to store in your carry-on luggage. The following suggestions should help you quickly get through the airport screening area:

☐ Place everything ***except your ticket, boarding passes, and passport*** in your carry-on luggage before arrival at the x-ray unit.

☐ Arrive at the screening area with nothing in your pockets except your passport, ticket, and boarding passes and present them to the prescreener before you approach the screening equipment. You may consider placing your passport and ticket in a cloth wallet around your neck so you do not lose them.

☐ Remove outer coats; they must go through the x-ray unit.

☐ When you approach the table situated before the x-ray unit conveyor, remove your shoes and place them and your laptop and the quart-size bag of liquids and gels (if applicable) in the plastic bin to be scanned. Ensure that your laptop is in sleep mode in the event screeners want to inspect it.

☐ Lay your luggage flat on the conveyor.

☐ Proceed through the magnetometer when instructed, and show the screener your boarding pass and passport.

☐ Collect your belongings, and enter the secure flight departure area.

Once aboard your flight. Be mindful that U.S. and foreign international flights have armed government agents aboard them to discourage acts of in-flight terrorism and disorderly conduct. A final note: do not assume that passengers sitting near you are trustworthy. Many passengers have wallets and valuables stolen from carry-on totes stored under the seats in front of them, even in business/first class. If you have a purse, place it inside a tote bag, and use a small padlock to secure your bag for times when you leave your seat.

In the event of a disorderly person or terrorist on an aircraft. Many people recall the events of 9/11 with anger and insist that they would never let a group of extremists take over a U.S. airliner again. Before you abruptly stand up in the aisle of an aircraft to physically challenge extremists or disorderly persons, remember that the aircrew and an armed air marshal are responsible for security in flight. You *cannot* and *should not* act unless the crew or an air marshal (whose identity is known only to the crew) asks for your help. If you observe suspicious or potentially dangerous activity, activate your call button or go forward or aft and privately talk to a flight attendant. If you mistakenly engage in physical action against a suspicious person, you could be sued for wrongful injury or death.

What to do in the event of an aircraft hijacking. Statistics show that aircraft hijackings are rare. Hijacked passengers have a 98 percent chance of surviving the ordeal. Even so, travelers should prepare for the possible occurrence of an airline hijacking. Unfortunately, many travelers who have been hijacked were not prepared for such an incident. Their experience was more traumatic simply because they had never anticipated such a reality. The following suggestions can help prepare you:

☐ If hijackers order passengers to surrender their passports to determine the nationalities of passengers, comply immediately. Keep in mind that you don't want a passport wallet with U.S. or Israeli seals, particularly if the hijackers are Islamic extremists.

☐ Remain calm and cooperate with hijackers.

☐ If you are wearing or carrying an item (Christian cross or the Star of David) that could provoke or irritate the hijackers, discreetly remove and conceal it.

☐ If hijackers question you, respond directly. Avoid saying or doing anything that might provoke them.

☐ Do not resist or aggravate the hijackers.

☐ Lessons learned indicate that individuals who react aggressively to hijackers, challenge them, or cause them to lose face incur dangerous risks.

☐ Fears of death or injury are natural. Do not dwell on them. In the Kuwaiti Airways hijacking, a U.S. auditor was killed because he was unresponsive to the hijackers because of intense fear.

☐ Regain your composure quickly after the hijacking occurs. Pause, take a deep breath, and organize your thoughts.

☐ Make mental notes of the physical qualities of the hijackers as well as their mannerisms, the types of weapons they display, their conversations, and their names. This information is important to law enforcement agencies after the incident is over.

☐ If you speak the hijackers' language, conceal it. Lessons learned indicate that the traveler is better off speaking his/her native tongue and acquiring knowledge by listening to the hijackers' conversation. This strategy could provide you with important insight into the hijackers' plans.

☐ During the incident, attempt to seem disinterested. Read a book or sleep. Do not attract attention. Hijackers tend to leave passengers who are not a threat to them alone.

☐ If the hijacking lasts beyond a day, attempt to do isometric exercises in your seat to enhance your circulation and occupy your mind.

☐ If you detect that a rescue attempt is imminent, slide down in your seat as far as possible. Cover your head using your arms and a pillow to protect yourself if gunfire is exchanged. If a weapon is dropped by one of the hijackers or rescuers, do **not** pick it up. You could be mistaken for one of the hijackers.

Clearing local customs and ground transportation. To expedite customs clearance and get out of the destination airport quickly, do the following:

☐ Fill out customs forms *before* you exit the plane. If you are a short-term traveler versus a resident, declare nothing.

☐ Some airports in developing countries require a surety bond on laptops. The concern is that they will be sold in country. Consequently, carry your laptop in a padded knapsack, which is less conspicuous.

☐ Watch your hand-carried luggage at all times.

☐ After you clear customs, do not allow anyone to handle your ***carry-on*** luggage!

☐ Decide in advance how you will get from the airport to town. First determine whether your hotel or employer can provide transportation. If not, get a good travel guide of the country, which will list transportation companies that will take you into town. Also, visit **http://www. worldtravels.com/airports**, which lists airport and ground transportation service Web sites worldwide. This site will provide information on departure taxes, which can be as much as $50. Another excellent source is **http:// www.transitionsabroad.com/besttransportation**.

☐ Many airports in developing countries have poor security; therefore, arrive during daylight hours and ensure that you have scheduled transportation to town or back to the airport with a reputable service. Ideally, have your hotel send a car to pick you up rather than risk unsafe vehicles and unlicensed drivers. Nevertheless, many airports are working to provide safe transportation services. Since the robbery in November 2006 of a group of elderly British tourists as they were leaving the Rio de Janeiro airport (described earlier), Infraero (which runs 68 airports in Brazil) established a restricted arrival zone to protect arriving passengers. Occupants of the zone must possess an Infraero-issued permit.

☐ If you are going to be picked up at the airport by an unfamiliar person, e-mail him/her your photo. Have him/her give the photo to the driver, so he/she can identify you in the crowd. This reduces the risk of a crime. Criminals with cars frequent airports and offer inexpensive rides to new arrivals. Also, criminals have been known to steal names from other drivers holding up signs or make their own signs and move to the head of the line to meet passengers, who unwittingly leave the airport with them, only to be victimized.

Departing your destination and entering customs back home. Regardless of your nationality, upon returning home, customs officials will inspect the validity of your travel document and your personal effects to ensure that you have not exceeded your personal customs exemption and that you are not bringing prohibited items into the country. In most cases, individuals returning to the United States are allowed an $800 personal exemption. If they travel abroad twice in 30 days, they can use the one $800 exemption only. For further information, visit the U.S. Customs and Border Protection (CBP) Web site (**http://www.cbp.gov**). Below are some useful suggestions for clearing customs:

Before departure from your destination:
- [ ] Do not export antiques without a permit, and do not export banned products.
- [ ] Exchange local currency before departing.
- [ ] Pay your departure tax (if there is one).
- [ ] Claim value-added tax (VAT) reimbursement, if available.
- [ ] Fill out your departure form.
- [ ] Proceed through immigration control for your flight.

Prior to arrival at home:

☐ Itemize purchases in a notebook.

☐ Do not export prohibited items, and declare all items. The CBP Web site defines prohibited and restricted items.

☐ Do not export fruits or vegetables.

☐ Items purchased in duty-free shops may be subject to a tax upon your return home. One liter of alcohol per individual can enter the United States duty-free.

☐ Carry purchase receipts for expensive non-U.S.-made equipment (e.g., laptop computers). You could be taxed upon your arrival on equipment you took abroad.

☐ Have available in your carry-on luggage receipts of purchased goods.

☐ Cuban products can be exported only if you are authorized to travel to and from Cuba. If not, Cuban products are prohibited.

☐ Counterfeit products (pirated CDs, DVDs, apparel, and luggage) may be seized and the traveler fined. Generally, customs officers will permit one such pirated or counterfeit product.

☐ When preparing to return to the United States, place acquired items in easily accessible locations in your luggage.

If you are not a U.S. citizen, visit the Web site of your home office or ministry of interior for customs clearance guidance.

SECTION FOUR

Staying Safe
While Abroad

Emergency Evacuation

Governments, including that of the Unites States, have comprehensive emergency and evacuation (E&E) plans that enable them to notify, advise, and assist in the evacuation of their citizens from countries undergoing political unrest, natural disasters or major turbulence. The world witnessed this in the summer of 2006, when 60,000 foreigners were stranded in Lebanon after hostilities broke out between Israel and Hezbollah (the Iran-supported Party of God).

If you are employed abroad, familiarize yourself with how your employer/embassy will contact and assist you in getting out of the country when governments recommend or mandate that their citizens leave the country. The Web site **http://www.sendwordnow.com** is a useful service that employers can use to simultaneously contact a select number of or all employees abroad. The site is also excellent for sending threat information and instructions to employees.

If you are abroad alone, register your travel with the State Department or your government's foreign ministry, and check the Web sites of those organizations for emergency evacuations. Registering ensures that you are not left behind in the evacuation.

If you are in a volatile country where emergency evacuation is always a possibility, follow these guidelines:

Always carry your:
- [ ] Passport
- [ ] Credit cards
- [ ] Medical coverage and evacuation information
- [ ] Cellular phone, charger, and an extra battery
- [ ] Phone numbers of critical family members, friends, and embassy personnel
- [ ] Prescribed medication
- [ ] A small FM/SW radio with extra batteries
- [ ] A satellite-based Personal Locator Beacon (PLB), which can notify friends and family where you are. For a list of vendors, please contact me.

Always have a "get out" bag packed and ready. This bag is a small piece of luggage that is packed in the event that an evacuation is ordered. Have one small bag for each adult and one for young children, if you are accompanied by children. The children's bag should include necessary items for the appropriate age group, such as disposable diapers, formula, games, baby food, and packaged food. A "get out" bag should contain:

- ☐ Important documents (inventory of household and personal items, medical treatment card, vehicle documentation, and contact information for those who have keys to your home)
- ☐ Cell phone, charger, and battery
- ☐ Passport
- ☐ Clothing and toiletries for at least three days and appropriate for the country to which you may be evacuated
- ☐ Portable FM/SW radio with extra batteries
- ☐ Credit cards and $1,000–$2,000 in a hard currency
- ☐ Bottled water and protein energy bars
- ☐ Prescribed medication

Depending upon your status, you may require an exit visa from the country, which should be processed by your employer or through your embassy.

If you have pets, they generally must be left behind with local friends, depending upon whether the evacuation is hostile or permissive. You may be unable to take them with you when evacuated by your employer or government.

High-Threat Destinations Require Special Security Arrangements

If you are traveling to a country described on pages 21–22, despite the likely travel advisories of your government, you should determine steps necessary to remain safe while in the country. Consider the following:

- ☐ Rigorously research the threats you will face in areas you plan to visit.
- ☐ Register with your embassy.
- ☐ Being young, naive, reckless, or thinking that you're immortal does not give you a "do-over" bonus card for being in the wrong place at the wrong time, nor does it give you protection from injury or death.
- ☐ Determine whether traveling in dangerous areas is worth your life.
- ☐ Arrange for protected vehicles and/or armed security escorts.
- ☐ Ensure that you have reliable voice communications, and know how to get help and/or report your situation to embassy officials and your in-country support mechanism.
- ☐ Do not carry firearms unless you are authorized to do so.
- ☐ Know how to safely get out of a high-risk situation. If you do not know how, you should not be there.
- ☐ Read this book *very* carefully in its entirety.

Hotel Security

Theft, violent crime, and the potential of a fire in and near hotels abroad are common risks for international travelers. These risks are prevalent even in upscale international hotel chains. Luxury hotels are a magnet for criminals and con artists, but so are quaint, smaller, local hotels. Better hotels attract criminals because the guests are perceived as wealthy; small hotels also attract criminals because they have marginal security, are easy to gain access to, have limited or no surveillance cameras or security personnel, and may have inferior guest room locks. Choose reputable hotels that cater to foreign visitors and that have sprinkler systems and smoke detectors.

Hotels in both developed and developing countries have, since the events of 9/11, been the targets of bombings. One only has to reflect on the case of the suicide bombings at the 2005 Hyatt Regency, Radisson and Best Western hotels in Amman, Jordan; the 2002 bombing at the Marriott hotel in Jakarta; the bombing of another Marriott hotel in Pakistan in 2006; and the 2008 bombing of the five-star Serena Hotel in Kabul (in which eight people died, including an American and a Norwegian journalist) to understand the magnitude of the risk. The attack on the Serena, incidentally, involved both a small arms attack and a suicide bombing.

Fires in hotels abroad are *very* common. Fire safety-conscious hotels generally have effective fire safety mechanisms (i.e., automatic fire detection systems, monitoring service, proximity to a fire department, smoke-retardant stairwells, emergency lighting, sprinkler systems, and trained staff to evacuate guests), while other hotels, even high-rise properties, rarely have effective fire deterrents and preparedness.

Moreover, regardless of the hotel, in developing countries, firefighters invariably arrive at a fire scene in rubber raincoats and have no self-contained oxygen units. Their truck ladders often can reach no farther than the sixth floor. If you stay in a hotel in Eastern Europe, Latin America, or Sub-Saharan Africa and you are staying on the fifteenth floor and there is a serious fire, your risks are very high. Why? If you attempt to evacuate the building by using the nearest internal stairwell, you will likely encounter many panicky guests who are all screaming, yelling, and trying to reach the ground floor. The stairwell may be filled with smoke, which means you may not have enough time to get from the fifteenth floor to the ground level on one gulp of air.

Having experienced a hotel fire many years ago, I never stay in a room above the sixth floor unless I can reach the ground floor on one deep breath and I have my escape hood (**http://www.safehomeproducts.com** or **http://www.magellans.com/store/safety**). Although a room higher up provides great views of the city, play it safe; try to get a room between the third and the sixth floors. That way, you are above levels convenient for criminals and you are reachable by most fire ladders. Can you imagine being on the twenty-third floor of a hotel in Mexico City during a major earthquake?

Below are some tips for staying safe in a hotel:

☐ The bombings at the three luxury hotels in Amman by three suicide bombers and the car bombing at the Marriott in Jakarta convince me to select a room on the inside of the hotel, preferably not above the lobby, where most bombings are directed. Try to get a room fairly close to the emergency stairwell.

☐ If possible, select a hotel room in or near the place you will be spending most of your time, providing it is not in a high-crime area or near governmental buildings in a politically unstable country where demonstrations are likely.

☐ When registering at the hotel, omit cell, home, and office phone numbers on the registration card, and use your business address, not your home address.

☐ Instruct the desk clerk not to give out your name and room number and to notify you of any inquires.

☐ Before leaving on your trip, always pack a small flashlight with extra batteries, which will become priceless if the power goes off, or if you must evacuate the hotel.

☐ Leave a tip for the housekeeping staff. Place the money in an envelope and mark it "housekeeping." This reduces the risk of theft of your personal items.

☐ Inform the housekeeping staff in person that your room is free to be cleaned. Note that placing the "please clean room" sign on the door handle advertises that you are not in the room to unwanted people.

☐ When you are in your room or are absent for brief periods, leave the "do not disturb" sign out, and leave the television or radio on. No one will know whether you are in or out.

☐ Do not deposit your key at the front desk when you leave the hotel. Not doing so creates an uncertainty about when you might return.

☐ Always carry a copy of the hotel's business card with you, particularly if you are in a country that does not use your language. Invariably, hotel cards include the address in the local language. If it isn't on the card, ask the concierge to write it down for you in the language.

☐ Use the hotel lobby safe-deposit box and not the in-room safe. The latter has a "back door" entry. Also, do not use locked drawers in your room. Duplicate keys exist.

☐ After you check in, locate the nearest stairwell exit, fire extinguishers, and hand-activated fire alarms.

☐ If you hear fire alarms, do not call the front desk. In the event of a fire, front desk employees will be unable to speak to guests individually. Evacuate the building via stairwells; do not use the elevators. Most good hotels have a hotel-wide public address system that enables communication with guests.

☐ When in a hotel fire, feel your room exit door before opening it. If it is cool, open it slowly, and proceed to the nearest exit. If your door is hot, do not open it; notify anyone that you can by phone that your room door is hot. Your room may be the safest place to be. Fill the bathtub with water, and seal door cracks with wet towels, blankets, curtains, or clothing. If you have duct tape, seal the cracks around the door frame. Open a window only if it can be closed. An open window may draw smoke into your room.

☐ When in your guest room, keep the door bolted. This will prevent hotel staff from walking into your room at an inopportune time. Before leaving for your trip abroad, purchase a couple of **rubber doorstops** that you can trim with a knife. Use them in hotel room doors that have faulty lock hardware.

☐ Never open your guest room door to knocks until you look through the optical viewer and determine who is knocking. (If there is no optical viewer, you are probably not in a very secure hotel.) Absent a viewer and if you are not expecting anyone, ask the person to slide his or her ID under the door.

☐ If you have a car at the hotel, do not leave any valuables in it, and park it in the hotel parking area or garage. Do not park it on the street.

☐ Do not disgard documents that may be sensitive in the wastebasket. Rather, use the shredder in the business center, or have a trusted colleague destroy them.

☐ If you do not speak the local language, use the hotel's business cards or matchbooks to communicate with and direct taxi drivers to your hotel.

Residential Security Abroad

In cases where readers are assigned short-term or long-term to a foreign country, note that economic crime and political violence have changed the way in which the international business community must live. Criminal threats have significantly reduced a foreigner's ability to lease or buy a single-family home (SFH). In the past, this was considered one of the luxuries of living abroad. Consequently, where violent residential threats are a serious problem, an apartment, a condominium, or a gated community with active physical security is strongly recommended. If available, such residential options offer a greater level of security (controlled parking, access control, lobby security, guard patrols, etc.) and usually are less expensive than the security expenditures normally required to effectively secure SFHs.

Apartments and condominiums. The advantages of an apartment, a condo, or a protected community over a SFH include (1) adequate lobby security (intercom, key or card access, a 24-hour-a-day guard or receptionist); (2) protected parking; and (3) often being in an urban area close to one's office, thus eliminating the need for long commutes. Before selecting an apartment or apartment building, consider the following:

☐ Avoid residences located near universities, host government offices, radio/ TV stations, stadiums, or embassies. These attract crowds, and local dissident groups target them.

☐ The residence should have at least two entry/exit points. Do not live in a residence that is accessible from only one road; avoid chokepoints.

☐ Determine who else lives in or near the property. Residences that house diplomats, business executives, and/or respected members of the local business community tend to have built-in security features.

☐ Residences with controlled parking are desirable. Parking your car on the street invites vandalism, car theft, carjacking, and/or abduction.

☐ Access to the building lobby or elevator should be controlled around the clock by a guard or a key bypass/intercom-controlled door release system. Ideally, it will have both. Avoid any apartment building that has neither.

☐ Do not consider apartments or condos below the third-floor level, unless you are considering a ground-level property inside a gated community (see page 212). The agility and persistence of burglars in some countries is amazing, especially when aided by parking garage awnings, adjacent fences, and trees. Regardless of the floor level, secure balcony sliding glass doors with a lock.

☐ The residence should have smoke detectors and fire extinguishers. If the residence does not have an exterior stairwell or fire escape, occupying the building on an upper floor could be risky.

☐ Ensure that the building has a key-controlled distribution system for delivered mail; otherwise, have your personal mail sent to your office, or rent a post office or commercial box.

☐ In developing countries where the potential exists for violent residential crime and where burglars are often armed, ensure that entry doors to your apartment are equipped with solid or grilled doors, optical viewers ("peepholes"), and double-cylinder dead bolt locks to protect against forcible entry.

☐ In high-risk countries (Mexico, Venezuela, Guatemala, Jamaica, South Africa, and Kenya), heavy steel-gauge gates (or "rape gates") are installed outside apartment entry doors or in hallways leading to bedrooms. The gates are equipped with high-security locks to prevent criminals from breaking through wooden entry doors.

☐ Alarm systems can further enhance security. Those opposed to electronic alarms may wish to purchase a "four-legged alarm"—a dog. In developing countries, dogs housed outside are often poisoned to defeat security. Dogs should be kept indoors for their protection.

Gated communities. Protected complexes are desirable and offer the space and environment of a SFH. However, many do not permit pets and multiple vehicles, nor do they always have tennis courts and club facilities, but they do have attractive walls or fences that are at least nine feet tall and a 24-hour guard service to screen pedestrians and vehicles entering the complex.

If apartments, condos, and gated communities are unavailable. In countries where secure apartments or gated communities are unavailable, SFHs pose a considerable risk for crime if they are not adequately protected. If you are located in a developing country, the SFH should *have a 360-degree wall or perimeter fence at least nine feet high.* Of the two, the wall is preferable, as it conceals activity inside the perimeter. The top of the wall, depending on the threat level, should have a *top guard* (strands of razor ribbon or concertina wire). In addition, the residence should have the following security features:

☐ Ground-level windows in SFHs should be grilled to discourage burglars. In high-risk developing countries, second-floor windows should be grilled also. At least one window with a locking device for egress in the event of a fire should be grilled on each floor.

☐ Exterior entry doors should be constructed of solid wood or steel and equipped with double-cylinder dead bolt locks.

☐ Avoid entry doors with glass, particularly if the door lock is a single-cylinder dead bolt lock. This configuration allows burglars to break the glass, reach in, and unlock the door with a thumb knob.

☐ Wooden entry doors should be equipped with chain locks and optical viewers.

☐ Lock SFH garage doors to protect the occupants' vehicle(s). If the occupant is a target of bombers, take special precautions to protect the vehicle.

☐ Consider installing a central alarm station and/or purchasing an inside-housed dog.

Preventing burglaries abroad. For clarification, a burglary is defined as the unauthorized breaking and entering into an unoccupied or occupied residence where property is stolen by burglars who may be unarmed or armed but who do not confront or threaten the occupants.

Home invasions abroad. In contrast to a burglary, a home invasion is defined as a situation whereby well-armed criminals enter a residence for the purpose of armed robbery of residents, ATM abduction, vehicle theft, and/or rape. Home invasions may be associated with the criminals holding the occupants hostage while they methodically search for valuables. Home invasions also occur after criminals conduct mobile surveillance against targets at work, recreation facilities, or restaurants, particularly if targets drive luxury vehicles. Home invasions occur often in Latin America and Sub-Saharan Africa, although they occur in developed countries as well. One problem in developing countries is the slow response time to crimes by police and medical emergency technicians. Below are a few examples of recent home invasions abroad:

- February 2004: Three American citizens were the victims of a home invasion/armed robbery in Cameroon. A knock sounded on the front door of the apartment, and before the victims could react, a man armed with a pistol opened the unlocked entry door. Two other men followed him, one of whom was armed with a large knife. The three robbed the victims and left. No one was physically harmed.

- April 2005: An American living in Maseru returned home late at night and was attacked and slashed with a knife when he surprised two burglars. The victim sustained multiple slashes and bruises and lost a quantity of blood. A month earlier, the victim's home was broken into because he did not activate his alarm system because of his pets interfering with the system.

- March 2006: A U.S. family with an American missionary organization living just outside Nairobi was the victim of a home invasion. Some 20 armed men broke through windows and entered their home. The gunmen attacked the husband/father, leaving him with serious head and chest wounds. His wife was severely beaten with a club and molested in the kitchen. A teenaged daughter was hit in the jaw with a metal pipe and received glass cuts to her hip and hands. The family's three other children hid from the attackers and were unharmed. The gunmen stole roughly $2,000 in personal property.

- October 2006: A French expatriate living in Cameroon and working for a U.S. organization returned home at about 1830 hours. There, he encountered several armed men who bound and gagged him while they went through the house, gathered valuables, and placed them into the victim's vehicle. As the intruders left in the expatriate's car, they told him that he was lucky he was French; if he had been an American, they would have killed him.

- December 2006: A young Canadian family from Calgary, Mark and Mona Keffer and their two young sons, was celebrating Christmas in a Bangkok apartment. A gunman entered the apartment through an open balcony door just above the ground level. After taking $400 in cash and a digital camera from the family and four other guests, Mona Keffer unwisely attacked the gunman with her purse. During the struggle, Mark was shot and killed, and Mona was wounded when the robber fired his handgun. As I have stated, material goods are not worth your life. Moreover, resisting an armed person is simply unwise.

- December 2007: A U.S. woman, 37, was shot and killed in her husband's family's third-floor apartment in Bucaramanga, Colombia, when two gunmen broke into the residence, after believing that the occupants had just visited an ATM. The American was shot in the neck during the robbery, after which $200 and a laptop were stolen. This case points to the need for effective physical security and entry doors.

Below are some tips for countering home invasions if you live in a private residence (an apartment or a condo):

☐ Install a central alarm station, and use it **24-7**. The alarm can prevent intruders surprising you when you get home. A barking dog can also be a part of your home invasion prevention program.

☐ If you are living in a country where armed intruders are known to break into occupied homes, do the following:

- At exterior entry doors, install grilled gates made of heavy steel and equipped with double-cylinder dead bolt locks. For condo and apartment dwellers, install these high-security gates outside the normal entry door.

- Configure a "safe haven" in your home (an area in where you can seek refuge in the event people attempt to break into your home, particularly armed criminals). A master bedroom, bathroom, or large walk-in closet is suitable as a safe haven. The entry door to the safe haven should ideally be reinforced steel with internal horizontal barricade bars on the top and bottom or alternatively, solid wood. This safe haven should also have a grilled and lockable window that permits safe escape from the home. Additionally, the safe haven should be configured with a rollable fire escape ladder and equipped with a fully charged cell phone, water, food, and a firearm if you can legally possess one. The firearm protects you if the intruders attempt to break down the door of your safe haven (see pages 290 and 291).

☐ If you have a SFH, upon arriving home, carefully approach the house and check for suspicious persons or vehicles. If anything looks suspicious, drive on and call the police.

☐ If you have domestic staff in your home (cook, nanny, driver, housekeeper), inform them that they are not to open the door of your home to anyone unless you advise them otherwise beforehand.

☐ Practice good countersurveillance techniques: know who is driving behind you; use your rearview and side mirrors. Many home invasions begin with criminals following targets to their homes.

☐ If living in a SFH, ensure that you have good exterior lighting, effective perimeter security, and an armed guard inside the perimeter 24-7 (if the threat warrants).

☐ If you are abducted outside your home, do not resist; cooperate fully with the intruders. Resistance will likely result in injury.

☐ Although the use of a firearm will be discussed later, I will mention that the best home protection weapon is a shotgun, preferably a 20-gauge. It can be easily handled by men and women alike. I advocate complying with the demands of criminals in a street robbery; however, if their plan during a home invasion is to hurt you or those close to you, living or dying may be determined by your ability to use a firearm, if legally authorized.

Finally, below are three steps you can take to protect yourself if you live in a private residence:

☐ Purchase a dog with a *good* bark, and keep it indoors.
☐ Install a central alarm station, and activate it daily.
☐ Use a home safe that is bolted to the closet floor and that has a single-cylinder dead bolt lock for safeguarding passports, credit cards, jewelry, at least $2,000 in U.S. currency for emergencies, local currency, and important documents.

Countering Threats While Driving

General principles. Experience tells us that 80 percent of crime and political violence abroad occurs while the target is in or in proximity to his or her car. Regardless of whether you are driving a vehicle, being chauffeured, or taking a taxi, there are some prudent precautions you should take:

☐ Even as a passenger, know the routes; obtain a good map of the city.

☐ Always fasten your seat belt and keep doors and windows locked.

☐ Do not permit drivers to pick up unknown passengers or hitchhikers.

☐ When getting into a vehicle, remain aware of your surroundings.

☐ Establish rapport with your driver.

☐ When the vehicle is stopped, do not buy merchandise from street vendors, offer money to the poor, or pay to have the car's windows washed. These situations can increase risk. Very often "washing windows" is a pretense for determining whether there are valuables in the vehicle or whether the car is a good target for a carjacking. In Latin America, it is common for carjackers to use young children to offer car wash services at one traffic light to collect information about valuables (watches, laptops) inside the car. If they see worthwhile items, one of the children places a piece of red bubblegum high on the driver's side of the windshield to alert carjackers at the next light to steal your car at gunpoint.

- [ ] Advise drivers of your destination only after the car is in motion.
- [ ] Do not give drivers your daily schedule. If you must give advance notice of the destination, describe it only in the vaguest of terms.
- [ ] Be alert to motorcyclists or bicyclists who stop next to your vehicle, particularly if there are two riders.
- [ ] Although an armed attack against a vehicle you may be riding in is remote, riding with foreign government officials or local businesspersons who may be targets can increase your risk.
- [ ] Ensure that drivers do not leave the vehicle unattended. If they must leave the vehicle, it should be locked.
- [ ] If you have an armed bodyguard, have him/her keep a low profile. Have him/her conceal firearms. Normally, the bodyguard sits next to the driver and accompanies you at all times. Do not change your schedule without coordinating with the bodyguard.
- [ ] Avoid flight arrivals/departures at approximately the same time each day.

If driving your own vehicle:

- [ ] Drive with doors locked and windows up.
- [ ] Never leave valuables or personal items in the vehicle. Car thieves are very skilled at breaking into locked cars and trunks.

☐ Whenever possible, park in open lots with attendants. Underground parking garages, though often managed by attendants, are rarely patrolled or monitored. The lack of security gives thieves and violent criminals uninterrupted opportunities.

☐ If you drive a car on a regular basis, consider the use of a steering wheel lock, an alarm system, or an electronic tracking system to counter a car theft.

☐ Install shatter-resistant film on the inside of your car windows to prevent criminals from entering your car through a broken window.

Carjackings. As we have seen in carjackings in developing countries such as Kenya and others, victims must make the right decision the first time. Carjackers invariably target individuals driving late-model automobiles, particularly luxury or sports-utility vehicles. Security professionals urge foreign travelers not to rent cars in countries with high rates of carjacking. Criminals target foreign drivers who rent cars. The alternative is to use reputable taxis. If confronted by a carjacking, the following is suggested:

☐ If an individual points a firearm at you in your car while you are at a stoplight, at a stop sign, or while parked, **do not** attempt to step on the gas and escape; you could be shot.

☐ Keep your hands visible, keep still, and make it clear to the carjacker that you will surrender your car without resistance. Then, quickly exit your car. If the criminal directs you to give him/her your watch, necklace, purse, wallet, or money, comply quickly.

☐ If a potentially dangerous yet *unarmed* person approaches your car while you are parked or temporarily stopped, use emergency escape and evasion measures to leave the scene.

☐ If an armed carjacker wants your car and attempts to abduct you, be prepared to react if you feel that your abduction could be a life-threatening situation.

☐ Use tinted and/or shatter-resistant auto glass to conceal the vehicle's occupants and their identities from potential criminals and to protect the occupants from physical harm.

☐ Install an automobile alarm system to prevent others from tampering with your car.

☐ If you drive in a foreign country, remove emblems, flags, decals, or stickers that identify you or help political extremists target you.

☐ In a high-threat environment, executives and drivers should know vehicle escape and evasion techniques to counter vehicular kidnappings and other car attacks. If you live in a high-risk country, get specialized executive driver training to respond to vehicular threats abroad. Two vehicular training Web sites are **http://www.vehicledynamicsinstitute.com** and **http://www.bondurant.com**.

Convoys in a high-threat environment. Particularly in rural areas in high-threat developing countries, convoys are good for safely moving people. Admittedly, convoys can attract rebels and criminals, so the convoy's organization and use are important. Ideally, the following should be considered in organizing a convoy that travels in high-risk environments:

☐ Determine whether the vehicles should be modified with ballistic-resistant transparent/opaque materials to prevent injury.

☐ Determine whether any members of the convoy should be armed and determine the rules of engagement.

☐ Assume that an armed attack on the convoy is possible and prepare for emergencies.

☐ Carefully plan the road trip so that alternative routes can be used.

☐ Determine whether government or commercial armed security escorts can be used to accompany the convoy or whether they can travel as an advance party.

☐ Ensure that vehicles in the convoy can communicate, preferably through VHF/UHF encrypted two-way radios.

☐ Identify a convoy leader in the event that problems arise or that the convoy has to stop. The convoy leader and the unit leaders will decide on stops.

☐ Identify a unit leader for each vehicle to communicate with the convoy leader.

☐ Inform trusted persons not in the convoy of the route of travel.

Protecting Financial Instruments

Phone card and credit/debit card fraud are two of the fastest-growing crimes against international travelers. These are enabled by acts of larceny, pickpockets, purse snatchings, armed robbery, and lost wallets and purses. Although fraud can and does occur when a traveler discards a transaction slip, large-scale fraud usually occurs when criminals obtain wallets, purses, electronic organizers, and daily planners containing a great deal of personal financial information. To reduce the risk of phone and credit card fraud:

- ☐ Use credit cards with the highest levels of encryption issued by major financial institutions. Credit card criminals can transfer funds from one credit card account to another when targeting banks with poor security protection.
- ☐ Carry as few credit cards as possible, and do not display cards in a wallet.
- ☐ Do not discard written records of credit card transactions.
- ☐ Always carry one credit card that is not used internationally. That way, if a primary card is declined because of fraud, the traveler has a "clean" card that can be used to satisfy financial obligations (payment of hotel bills, access to cash, etc.).
- ☐ Do not use ATMs located on the street, particularly at night. Criminals surveil customers using the machines.

Rather, use ATMs in banks and buildings with visible security.

☐ Do not maintain large balances in debit card accounts. Debit cards do not have the same degree of protection as do credit cards. You may not get reimbursed for the losses after a specified period.

☐ A common act against expatriates occurs when a domestic employee (or person with access to checks and financial statements) removes a blank check and a canceled copy of a check with the expatriate's signature and sends these documents to a confederate in the expatriate's home country. The confederate, using fraudulent identification and the expatriate's personal information, transfers a large sum of money to a bogus account. The money is later withdrawn and the account canceled.

☐ When living abroad, always safeguard canceled and blank checks and financial records under lock and key.

☐ While it is convenient to use a long-distance phone card (issued by your local provider), the risk is considerable when one realizes how easy it is to charge $10,000–$20,000 onto a phone card in a matter of a day or so. I strongly recommend that travelers and expatriates purchase local phone cards sold in kiosks and convenience stores, thereby reducing the risk of phone fraud.

☐ My personal favorite: don't tape your PIN on any phone, debit, or credit card!

Dealing with Street Crime

Although many cities are exotic and exciting to explore, nonviolent and violent street crimes are realities where unemployment, poverty, inflation, overpopulation, and/or political instability exist. Be cautious, anticipate what might happen next, and have a plan to respond to threats. Obtain a good pedestrian map and know the area. Locate the police stations and high-crime areas in the city.

Watches and jewelry. Before traveling, look at your wrist, your neck, and your fingers. If you are wearing a watch, how much is it worth? If it is worth more than $40, leave it at home. In general, wearing inexpensive wrist, neck, and finger jewelry lowers your value assessment profile in the eyes of criminals.

Your wallet. Remove credit, gas, department store, and phone cards from your wallet. Purchase an in-county phone card. A stolen wallet usually results in roughly $20,000 in card charges before it can be reported. Ideally, purchase an inexpensive wallet and carry your driver's license, international driving permit, two or three credit cards (including an ATM or check card), medical identification card, business card, emergency contact card, and a few significant photos.

The art of being clueless. I'm always intrigued by some foreign travelers. Regardless of how educated and sophisticated they may be, they often arrive in a country unfamiliar to them with little or no information on the threat situation. They check into a luxury hotel, get up early the next morning, don their jogging clothes, walk through the hotel lobby, activate the time-lapse feature of their sports watch, and jog out the front door of the hotel. All the while, they are poorly informed on their destination and the existing threat level in the area. In a similar situation, ask the doorperson whether running is safe within a couple miles of the hotel. If it is not, use the hotel fitness center.

Below are some tips on dealing with street crime and how to avoid being a victim:

☐ As stressed throughout this book, your money, wallet and property is *never* worth your life. So do not resist a street robber, as you never know whether an a criminal is armed, or in the company of other confederates.

☐ Maintain focus. Avoid being distracted or talking on the phone while walking down the street in high-crime countries, as it can make you more vulnerable to crime.

☐ Do not carry mace, pepper spray, or similar devices. They are illegal in most countries and it is also illegal to take such devices aboard an aircraft (even in checked luggage). More important, improper use can cause self-injury, or you can unexpectedly have it used against you.

☐ If you are a long-term resident in country, do not carry a concealed weapon without a permit. In some countries, you can be imprisoned for illegally carrying a firearm.

☐ Carry a whistle. This applies to both men and women, as it is an excellent way to attract attention and assistance when you are in danger.

☐ Do not carry large sums of cash. Do carry about $50–$75 so that if you are confronted by a robber, he or she will go away satisfied. If you tell robbers that you do not have money, they become frustrated and may react harshly.

☐ Do not walk alone at night; take safe taxis.

☐ Do not carry your passport in a purse, fanny pack, or back pocket. Thieves can snatch purses, cut the fanny pack from your waist, and remove your passport from your back pocket. Instead, carry your passport in an under-the-shirt wallet or under your undergarments.

☐ Consider a zippered sock or a money belt that can safe-guard at least $500, but carry a small amount of cash in your pocket or wallet (**http://www.letravelstore.com**).

☐ Leave your passport, extra money, and credit cards in the hotel safe-deposit box, and carry a photocopy (unless local law dictates otherwise). Remember: do not use in-room safes.

☐ Walk in foreign cities with confidence, and know the local scene. Walking around looking lost signals vulner-ability. Learn enough of the language to give yourself the confidence to ask the locals questions.

☐ When possible, walk in the middle of the sidewalk. Walking too close to buildings or curbs leaves you vul-nerable to a would-be thief.

☐ Stand several feet back from curbs when waiting to cross the street. Motorcyclists can grab purses or briefcases while pedestrians wait for the light to change.

☐ In one pocket, carry small-denomination bills for small purchases such as newspapers and coffee, and in another pocket, place large-denomination bills that are not needed frequently, so as not to disclose larger bills to observant criminals. Still, don't carry more than $75.

☐ For women, be careful with your purse. Carry it close to your body with the latch side facing in or the zipper closed. Carry money and identification in a small pocket-size purse. If necessary, carry a bag for sunglasses, cosmetics, and inexpensive items.

☐ If you are approached or followed by a suspicious person, cross the street or change direction. Find areas where the presence of others will discourage personal threats.

☐ Avoidance and nonresistance may not always work. Thus, be prepared to fight back if no other options are available.

☐ Self-service elevators can be dangerous. In one case, a robbery victim erred in getting into an elevator with three intoxicated men already in it. The result: a jostling that resulted in the loss of $600 and several credit cards. Inasmuch as elevators are a fertile ground for robbery and assault, some simple precautions are suggested.

   ■ If you suspect danger, use the stairway instead. At least on the stairs or in hallways, you have room to run, and someone is more likely to hear you if you need help. Better yet, use elevators with a friend. Criminals are less likely to confront two people at a time.

■ If the elevator stops at a floor on which a suspicious person gets on, simply get off.

A final thought. For both men and women, please do not walk or jog *alone*, during daylight or nighttime, in *high-risk* countries. In May 2005, a young American woman, jogging alone at 0600 hours, was stopped by three Namibian men who severely beat her. Two of the muggers held her down on the ground and struck her repeatedly, as they removed her rings and took her house keys. There were no verbal demands for her valuables; the muggers simply beat her up.

Sexual Assault: Understanding, Preventing, and Responding

This section is for both women and men, as MEN should understand:

1. What traveling abroad is like through a woman's eyes
2. The emotional and physical challenges women face in contemplating what to do if confronted by sexual assault or rape
3. How to support a friend, family member, or colleague who has been sexually assaulted or raped in a foreign country

Before you begin this chapter, know that I shared the contents of it with a number of woman friends who offered several suggestions and revisions. For readers who have been raped in the past, rape in any form is never justified. If you have been raped, you did *nothing* wrong; your rapist did. Clearly, in cases of rape, it is natural and understandable for victims to "freeze" or be unable to resist for a number of reasons (life experience, age, physical condition, multiple assailants, emotional frame of mind, etc.). You should never feel guilty about the way you handled yourself at the time of a rape. I do hope, though, that the perspective described in this chapter will enable you to look at the options available to you in the future. Like rape victims, those who are victimized by armed robbery, burglary, armed carjacking, or abduction often are in shock or panic at the time of the crime. These victims often later wonder whether the outcome might have been different if they had made different choices. The bottom line is that one will never know. What is important is that we become better informed and hopefully empowered to act differently in the future.

No one truly knows how he or she will react if faced with a life-or-death decision. Some people have a rush of adrenalin that could well work in their favor; others are more prone to panic and become incapable of action. However you think you would react to such a horrible prospect, I do hope that you'll find this chapter and the information and options it offers helpful.

In most countries, sexual assault and rape are frequently committed crimes. However, incident analysis suggests that in developing countries, the motives for such crimes are often exclusive of simply dominating the victim. As was the case of the American woman in Bolivia (see pages 14–15) who was raped because of U.S. policies, some women are attacked simply because of their nationality. In other cases, Western women are raped and sexually assaulted because their "provocative dress" is seen as a violation of local religious or moral standards. Many Western women are often viewed as promiscuous or "loose," as in the case of a dramatic rise in the rape of Danish women by Somalian immigrants in Denmark.

In this chapter, we will discuss definitions, sexual harassment, the influence of dress in certain cultures, and three approaches to dealing with sexual assault and rape: *understanding*, *avoiding*, and *responding*. I would also like for readers who have been sexually assaulted or raped to know that the choices a woman makes when confronted with an assailant are personal ones. Hence, her decision to resist or not to resist should be respected, given the victim's perception of the threat, frame of mind, physical abilities, and life experience. Nevertheless, I would ask that all women who read this section reserve their decision on whether to resist or not to resist until they have read the chapter in its entirety.

Understanding

Definitions. For clarification purposes, criminal codes worldwide vary in terms of defining *sexual assault* and *rape*, but for the sake of discussion of these subjects in this chapter, we will define sexual assault as "behavior that involves any unwanted sexual contact, such as touching, fondling, or groping of intimate parts of the body." Sexual assaults can be committed by threats or by force or when someone takes advantage of circumstances that render a person incapable of giving consent, such as intoxication. *Rape*, conversely, is "any kind of sexual intercourse (vaginal, oral, or anal) committed against a person's will, with physical force or with a threat to hurt the victim or another person." If the victim is intoxicated or unconscious and unable to give consent, any sexual intercourse is considered rape. Rape generally involves penile sexual intercourse, or it can involve inanimate objects.

Prevalence of rape. According to the seventh and latest edition of the United Nations' **Survey of Criminal Trends** (1998–2000), the following are the top-20 countries in the world insofar as the frequency of rape:

1.	South Africa	11.	Papua New Guinea
2.	Seychelles	12.	New Zealand
3.	Australia	13.	United Kingdom
4.	Montserrat	14.	Spain
5.	Canada	15.	France
6.	Jamaica	16.	South Korea
7.	Zimbabwe	17.	Mexico
8.	Dominica	18.	Norway
9.	United States	19.	Costa Rica
10.	Iceland	20.	Venezuela

The U.S. State Department and the foreign ministries of most developed nations (with the exception of Canada and England) do not release reliable data on how many of their citizens are sexually assaulted abroad. According to the data released by the British government, 127 British nationals were raped in Greece, Spain, and Turkey alone during 2005 and 2006. This figure suggests that the total number of foreign travelers raped abroad in all countries could be significant. Note that only Spain is in the top 20 of the United Nations' list above.

Case Study: South Africa

A British tourist was blindfolded, threatened with a pistol, and repeatedly raped during a 14-hour ordeal after being abducted on a mountain road in South Africa in 2002. The 29-year-old woman and her South African boyfriend were driving near Kruger National Park when they stopped at a popular picnic spot.

As the couple got out of the car, five men suddenly emerged from the bushes and waved a pistol, as if they had been waiting for victims. The men pushed the couple into the back of the car and blindfolded and beat them. The men drove hundreds of miles across South Africa, during which time they repeatedly raped the woman.

The ordeal ended when one of the assailants lost control of the couple's car and caused it to careen off the road and roll over. Two passing motorists stopped on the side of the road because they thought they had happened upon a road accident. One of the kidnappers opened fire on one of the motorists and killed him instantly. In the chaos, the British woman and her boyfriend managed to run away into the darkness and hide. Some time later, they were able to flag down a car and call for help. Police arrested two of the five assailants. Considering that South Africa has the highest level of HIV/AIDS in the world, the woman in this case was administered a series of drugs designed to suppress her exposure to the disease.

Lessons learned:

☐ Visit picnic, recreational, and sightseeing areas **only** when other people are gathered (an absence of people may suggest that locals know something you do not).

☐ Research the type of violent crimes that occur at your destination.

☐ Find out tactics the local criminals use (e.g., hiding in bushes and lying in wait for victims) and areas you should avoid.

☐ Consider carrying condoms in rural areas and locations where criminals actively operate and where police patrols are in short supply (even if you are accompanied by a significant other or friends).

Case Study: Kenya

A rape that took place in Nairobi several years ago occurred largely because of a clash of cultures. The victim was a female AID worker who was working closely with a male Kenyan employee of her organization. They had been in the field working when the AID worker realized she had forgotten something in her hotel room that she needed for a report. When they got to her hotel, the woman felt uncomfortable leaving her Kenyan colleague waiting in the lobby of the hotel. She feared he would interpret this as a lack of trust or recognition that he was a coequal, so she naively asked the man to come up with her while she retrieved the documents. The Kenyan perceived her behavior as a romantic overture and ignored her rejections. He raped the woman, later telling authorities that he thought the invitation to her room was for sex.

Lesson learned:

☐ Western women are perceived in many parts of the world as being promiscuous and immoral—in this case, it is much better to err on the side of offending the man than to give him any reason to believe that those perceptions are correct.

☐ Eye contact from foreign women is often perceived by locals as romantic interest (wearing sunglasses often solves this problem).

☐ What Western women perceive as being "friendly" men of other nationalities perceive as invitations for sex.

☐ Never invite people you do not know well to your hotel room or residence.

☐ Dress conservatively.

☐ Do not discuss your personal life with local men.

Sexual harassment. Apart from the risks of sexual assault and rape, you should keep in mind that sexual harassment in developing countries is pervasive with few legal protections. Even where laws exist, there are few prosecutions or administrative remedies. Nevertheless, that does not mean that foreign women should not take action. Here are some thoughts to consider:

☐ Ask local women whether the country has sexual harassment laws and whether they are enforced.

☐ Save voice mails and e-mails that you consider sexual harassment and keep a memo as to the circumstances of harassment—note in the memo whether you have a witness.

☐ Wear a wedding band to dissuade harassment.

☐ Avoid eye contact with men or staring at men (as previously stated, one option is to wear sunglasses).

☐ Never invite people you do not trust to your hotel room or residence.

☐ Avoid one-on-one meetings with harassers.

☐ Eat lunch with other female colleagues to discourage a harasser from sitting down with you.

☐ If you are forced into a meeting, bring a female colleague.

Provocative dress. As we all know, women in the United States, Canada, Australia, and much of Europe commonly wear halters and midriff tops. However, such apparel—even running tops and shorts—in other countries would be in very poor taste, and the woman would be considered uncultured and insulting. In other countries, she would be seen as being in major violation of religious mores, which could provoke attacks that could lead to death or severe injury. Also, if you are representing your government or employer abroad, the success of your trip may be dependent upon your adhering to local dress protocols. When in doubt, always err on the side of overdressing and you will never go wrong. Probably one of the best guides on dress for women in foreign countries can be found at **http://www.journeywoman.com**.

A couple of years ago, I was member of a foreign assistance delegation that was sent to a Middle Eastern country. One of our delegates was a young American woman who showed up at the airport wearing a midriff shirt and never changed into appropriate dress before landing in the capital city. Of course, our police counterparts met us at the airport upon our arrival. I felt embarrassed for the woman's poor taste and concerned that she would offend our foreign hosts. The generals were too diplomatic to say anything, but I read what their eyes were saying. Nonetheless, the woman's provocative dress (in the Middle East) reflected poorly not only on her but also on the entire group. When you travel to foreign countries, you owe it to yourself and to the host government to learn what is appropriate and inappropriate for that country. It is common courtesy.

One suggestion I can offer to women traveling to Saudi Arabia and more conservative Islamic countries is to consider purchasing a black *abaya*, which covers the body but not the face, hands, or feet. It will make you feel more comfortable and less self-conscious. Some of these countries have so-called religious police, called the **mutawa**, *whose job it is to ensure that women and men comply with that country's dress code. If they do not, they are caned on the legs. Foreign women whose legs and arms have been exposed have also been subjected to caning.* Interestingly, this is the same group that in March 2002 prevented firefighters from putting out a fire and evacuating students of a girl's school in Mecca. The *mutawa* was also observed beating girls who were not dressed properly and preventing students from escaping from the burning school. Fourteen girls died because they were not fully covered as required by Saudi law.

Date rape drugs. One tactic that women should be very aware of abroad is the use of date rape drugs, such as GHB (gamma hydroxbutyric acid), Rohypnol (flunitrazepam), and ketamine (ketamine hydrochloride), which come in various forms:

- **Rohypnol:** A pill that dissolves in liquids
- **GHB:** Liquid with no odor or color, white powder, and pill form
- **Ketamine:** White powder

These drugs are regularly used in roughly half of the countries of the world in nightspots, restaurants, and wherever people gather. In October 2006, a young American tourist, aged 20, was at a nightclub in Bermuda with friends. While she was preoccupied by two suspicious men, her drink was spiked with Rohypnol. Noticing she was in a risky situation, her friends took her from the club, and by the time they got her home, she could not control her muscles, walk, move her limbs, or use the bathroom without assistance. Date rape drugs often render victims helpless and unable to refuse sex, with little memory of what has happened to them. These drugs are also used by criminals to facilitate theft and robbery. Here are some tips to avoid being drugged:

☐ Do not leave your beverage unattended.

☐ When drinking alcoholic beverages, always go out with friends.

☐ Avoid drinking in excess, as the alcohol increases the potency of the drugs, making you even more vulnerable.

☐ Ask hotel concierge staff and locals which night spots to avoid.

☐ Be wary around new acquaintances.

Men, take note. The use of date rape drugs is a frequent occurrence in both Latin America and Sub-Saharan Africa, although they are also used elsewhere, against both men and women. In one case, an American tourist was robbed in his hotel room in Sea Point (not far from Cape Town) after a woman he had casually met drugged him. He awoke 12 hours later to discover that his passport, jewelry, and money had been stolen. In another Cape Town case, a foreign tourist died from a combination of a date rape drug and excessive drinking.

Prevention

There are ways to avoid being sexually assaulted or raped. Please consider the following:

- ☐ Keep in mind that the potential for rape is significantly reduced when you are among trusted friends and colleagues; however, keep in mind that date rape is the most common form of sexual assault.
- ☐ Always carry a cell phone, a whistle (to solicit help if you're in trouble), and a list of people who can help you in an emergency.
- ☐ Dress conservatively.
- ☐ Forget the stiletto heels; always wear comfortable shoes you can run in.
- ☐ Don't hail taxis on the street—order a taxi by cell phone from a hotel stand.
- ☐ Avoid public transportation in high-threat countries.
- ☐ Don't use open-air *samlors*, jeepneys, cyclos, pedicabs, rickshaws, or auto-rickshaws because these forms of transportation render you vulnerable to robbery and rape. A German woman, an employee of Lufthansa, was raped and robbed of her cell phone and purse by an auto-rickshaw driver and his accomplice in India in 2005.
- ☐ Don't walk or jog alone in isolated areas, particularly at night.

☐ Always let friends know where you are and when you'll be back.

☐ Don't jog or walk in a high-risk country *alone*.

☐ Don't go out at night alone in countries where Western women are held in low regard by local men.

Keep in mind that sexual assault and rape often happen in countries you would never expect. Below are some examples:

Case Study: Greece

In 1998, a British tourist, age 46, was walking alone near Aristotle's school (50 miles west of Thessaloniki) when she was grabbed by three unarmed Albanians who robbed, beat her, and repeatedly raped her in a nearby cave. They also punched her until she gave up her PIN for her ATM card. Fortunately, she was able to escape when one of the men fell asleep while the other two were gone emptying her ATM account. She was hospitalized for several days after the incident.

Lessons learned. Sightseeing by yourself in foreign countries can be extremely risky in that criminals gravitate to tourist attractions and actually wait for tourists who are alone and vulnerable. An organized tour not only gives you greater information on the attraction but also gives you the built-in security of being with other people. Another point to consider in this case is that the victim suffered a severe beating because she refused to give up her PIN. Although she may not have been able to avoid being raped, she might have avoided the severe beating had she given up her PIN readily.

Case Study: Cyprus

In 2002, a young British woman, age 22, was waiting for a friend outside an Ayia Napa disco when a Greek Cypriot diver abducted her without a weapon and raped her. When found in a field the next day, she had been severely beaten and will have disabilities for the rest of her life. To make matters worse, her identity was revealed in the local media, which outraged President Glafcos Clerides. Fortunately, her assailant was arrested, tried, convicted, and given a lengthy prison term. Subsequently, the Cypriot government paid the victim's hospital costs and provided the victim's parents with round-trip airline tickets between the United Kingdom and Cyprus. Following the rape, local talk shows complained about the overbearing machismo of Greek Cypriot men toward women and emphasized that worse, rape victims are often laughed out of police stations by officers who feel that sex is what they came to the island for. Sadly, country culture is slow to change.

Lesson learned. Women traveling alone must recognize first and foremost that they are at much greater risk. Be circumspect in dealing with local men, as they may have their own negative perceptions and values of women. Don't accept rides from men you don't know well, avoid one-on-one contact in isolated areas with such men, and try to stick with mixed groups of men and women in social settings. Always stay sober—this will help you remain cautious. Always carry a cell phone and have the numbers of your hotel, your embassy, and the local police on your speed dial.

Traveling alone in rural areas. Traveling *alone* in rural areas of developing countries is never a good way of managing your risk or being prudent. A case in point involved the rape/murder of a U.S. citizen, 20, a California native who was murdered in the Belizean village of Toledo in November 2005. The victim entered Belize through the western border with Guatemala with a group of friends, but after arriving in Belize, she broke off from her companions and remained in Toledo alone, where she joined up with a group of Belizeans at a village bar. One of the group members subsequently raped and murdered the young American. Her knapsack and passport were found a few feet from her battered body.

Response

Assumptions. Before getting into specifics about the safest way to respond to a sexual assault or rape, I want to cover some basic assumptions about how rape differs from one region of the world to another:

- In a developed country, sexual crimes will generally be handled promptly and professionally.
- In some developing countries, sexual assault and rape are not seriously investigated by the police.
- Many hospitals in developing nations are not staffed to provide compassionate care and forensic collection of evidence (i.e., use of a rape kit, which collects physical evidence).

- Police in developing countries often do not have rape investigative training and have primitive forensic labs; if DNA is analyzed, it is usually in another city or country.

- If you call local police on your cell phone for emergency assistance, they may not respond for hours, particularly if a language barrier exists.

- The local police may often be less than helpful to rape victims.

Having worked abroad as both a U.S. Embassy RSO and a security consultant for multinational companies, I have handled a number of rapes of both expatriates and diplomats. The one thing I have learned from these cases is how important it is for a woman to seriously think about—*before the fact*—how she can:

1. Reduce vulnerabilities to these crimes (much of which we've talked about and demonstrated through the examination of case studies).

2. Take action if she finds herself in a situation where she potentially could be assaulted or raped.

Below are some thoughts about resistance to rape:

- Many women have been socialized to believe that they are no match in a confrontation with a man.

- Many women believe that if they submit to rape, they will not be injured or killed.

- Many women believe that they must have self-defense or martial arts training to successfully resist a rape.

The reality is that all three of these assumptions have little foundation in fact. Nevertheless, let me stress that self-defense or martial arts training will give you the agility, practice, discipline, confidence, and physical strategies for defending yourself and getting away. Here are some statistics to consider:

- 70 percent of women who fought back during a sexual assault *avoided* rape (Bart/O'Brien, 1985), regardless of the presence of a weapon.

- 9 percent of women who were raped *did not* resist (Sanders, 1980).

- Four out of five rape attempts were *not completed* when the target fought back (McDermott, 1979).

Pauline Bart and Patricia O'Brien, coauthors of an excellent book on resistance, *Stopping Rape* (Teachers College Press, 1993), have conducted empirical research on rape. Their research, supported by several other credible studies, demonstrates that resistance is effective for a number of reasons.

Bart and O'Brien's research into resistance has demonstrated that women's resistance to sexual assault is more likely to succeed when it is active, multiple strategies are used, the woman is determined and outraged, and the resistance includes a physical component. These findings are supported by seven independent studies, and they contradict decades of advice given to women to "not resist—it'll only make him angry." In another study that Bart managed ("Avoiding Rape:

A Study of Victims and Avoiders: Final Report," National Institute of Mental Health, 1980, pp. 18–19), the results produced the following data:

- 81 percent who tried running were able to escape rape.
- 62.5 percent who screamed or yelled escaped successfully.
- 68 percent who used physical force of any kind avoided rape.

Another interesting point is that according to the Statistical Analysis Center of the Illinois Crime Report Data for Chicago (1981), less than 1 percent of women assaulted in rapes or attempted rapes are killed. Another excellent study conducted by Robbie Burnett, Donald I. Templer, and Patrick C. Barker ("Personality Variables and Circumstances of Sexual Assault Predictive of a Woman's Resistance," *Archives of Sexual Behavior*, Vol. 14, No. 2, 1985) found that women who strongly resisted assault were less anxious about dying as a result of the assault, were assertive, and perceived themselves as being in control of their destiny. Unfortunately, women have often been discouraged from resisting assault because of beliefs that resistance will escalate the assault and result in greater injury. Researchers, however, find that most women who resist rape are not seriously injured (*Queens Bench Foundation Study*, 1976). Deciding not to resist does not guarantee fewer injuries. In this regard, Bart found that women who did not resist or who pleaded with their attacker were more likely to be raped. She commented that although there was a "somewhat higher possibility of non-serious injuries for women who resisted," these women also had a "substantially higher probability of avoiding the rape."

The rape/murder of an American artist in Mexico.

Despite the research supporting the benefits of resisting a rape attack, every case of rape is different and has very unique dynamics, particularly when you factor in the impact of foreign cultures. This is why every woman needs to be prepared to make a choice of whether to resist based on the facts available in a given threat situation. Making a decision theoretically is impossible.

One of the most tragic cases I've examined is the rape and murder of an American artist, 40, a well-known Connecticut artist and former Yale professor, who on March 29, 1998, decided to go on a Sunday walk on Zicatela Beach (one of the top-10 beaches in the world), near Puerto Escondido, in the state of Oaxaca. While walking the beach in broad daylight, the victim encountered two Mexican men who raped, severely beat, and drowned her. Later, it was discovered that these men were career criminals recently released from prison. Incriminating scratches on their faces indicated that the American vehemently resisted her assailants. In 1999, the defendants were convicted of rape and murder and sentenced to 40 years in prison on the basis that the many bite marks on the victim's body matched dental records of one of the defendants.

One thing we will never know in this case is whether her resistance played a role in her rape and murder. Given the fact that her assailants were hardened criminals who had a history of violence, she was very likely doomed whether she had resisted or not.

Being careful and not resisting may not always be the best choice. Many women who travel abroad have simply been told to "be careful," avoid situations where they could be sexually assaulted, and not resist when rape is inevitable. Admittedly, there is a place for common sense and avoidance. However, when that is not enough, I would like to offer you some strategies on resistance for consideration

☐ Wherever you are, be observant. Reread some of the tips in the chapter on surveillance. Be cognizant of who is around you at all times. If you see a man who seems to be following you, increase the distance between you as you observe his behavior. This will give you the edge if you have to run. (Don't forget: avoid the stiletto heels.) Make sure he knows that you know he is there. Many would-be rapists have broken off when they lose the element of surprise.

☐ Walk with confidence at all times. Your body language will convey how vulnerable you may or may not be.

☐ Always carry a whistle. It will attract attention as you're running away from your assailant.

☐ If you are confronted by a rapist, use all of your skills (verbal, nonverbal, and physical), depending upon the situation.

☐ If confronted, immediately think back to a time when you felt the strongest or most in charge (e.g., working out at the gym, running a marathon, saving a life, achieving goals you never thought you could, etc.). This will give you psychological empowerment, confidence, and energy to resist.

☐ Remember that men who don't respect women have two *huge* weaknesses: they assume you will be intimidated and submit to them and they are not expecting you to resist.

☐ Recognize that if you choose to resist, you must resist fully, with no holdbacks and no hesitation. Recognize that you have two compelling strengths: the element of surprise and your motivation to get away being greater than your assailant's. He, on the other hand, also needs to be preoccupied with noise, Good Samaritans, witnesses, and the police.

☐ If the assailant is unarmed, resistance will be simplified. If he is armed (with a knife or handgun), you still need to stay focused on getting away and escaping. Don't be dissuaded by the presence of a weapon, as most rapists use one only as a means of threatening a victim into submission. Remember that less than 1 percent of rape victims are killed. Having minor physical injuries is far less problematic than the emotional trauma of rape.

☐ Consider that many women have verbally dissuaded assailants from raping them by telling the assailant they have herpes or that they are having a particularly high blood flow from their period. One would-be victim even convinced her assailant that she wanted to get to know him better before they had sex and talked the assailant into going to a restaurant first, at which point the victim was able to escape.

☐ If verbal efforts fail, remember that you need to do two things: (1) **surprise** your assailant with one or more neutralizing blows and (2) **run** as fast as you can for help. Don't try to win a street fight with a 200-pound man, as you'll very likely lose. Your only objective is to **get away.**

☐ Before we go on, a word of caution about resisting any crime abroad. If you seriously hurt, incapacitate, disable, or kill an assailant in what you believe is a life-or-death situation and there are no witnesses to support your assertion, you could potentially face civil or criminal proceedings. Obviously, you are going to protect yourself or those close to you, regardless. Just keep in mind that you could possibly become a defendant in a foreign criminal court where there is no jury or bail and where foreigners, particularly Americans, are often held in low regard by judges. Remember that your only objective is to get away—not to kill your would-be assailant.

☐ Below are a few scenarios with suggestions of how you can potentially escape:

- Being grabbed from behind. Your assailant has grabbed you from behind with his arm across your chest and neck as he drags you in a direction he wants you to go. What you really want to do in this situation is let him draw you closer to him so you have room to hurt him. There are actually a number of choices. If you let your assailant pull you closer to his body, you can powerfully swing a fist in reverse as hard as possible into his scrotum, which should cause him to bend over in severe pain—and let you go. Other options are to suddenly throw your head backward forcefully into his face, hopefully breaking his nose, or stomp very, very, very hard on his toes, which may stop him from chasing you. Then, twist out of his grasp so that you can maneuver yourself into another blow while he is crippled by whatever damage you've already inflicted. If he's down, kick him in the head and RUN. If he's still standing yet in pain, take the heel of your hand and forcefully hit him as hard as you can in the ribs or face or stomp his ankle.

- Being grabbed in a frontal hug (with your assailant holding you close to him). Your arms and fists are probably against his body and on an equal level with his groin. You could knee or strike him with force in the groin, but you can also bring your hands up quickly toward your chest; if his hold on you is not tight, slowly bring your hands to your chest, strike his nose hard with your forehead and, squeeze his windpipe tightly or forcefully bring the heel of either hand under his chin, any of which should divert his attention from holding you. If you can accomplish any of these moves, he should drop to his knees. Then, using the heel of your hand in an upward position, strike his nose and scrape your nails across his eyes. Of course, a very nice add-on if he is no longer on his feet is to kick him in the ribs, stomp his knee, or kick him in the head so that he cannot chase you.

■ Being pulled into an alley or toward a car and your assailant is holding both of your arms. If you are being pulled in his direction, let him think that you are complying. While he is holding both of your wrists with both of his hands, a snap-kick into a kneecap, raking your nails across his eyes, poking and gouging an eye very hard, squeezing his windpipe, or kicking him hard in the ribs when he's down will give you time to escape.

These are just a few examples of tactics you can use to get away. But, once you've intellectually decided in your mind that you will resist a sexual crime, take a self-defense course or learn one of the many martial arts that will give you the skills you need to successfully hurt your assailant and *escape*.

Note: We talked about pepper spray and other repellant agents earlier when we addressed street crime, but let me reiterate again: Do not carry repellant sprays on a key chain or permit it to be visible to would-be assailants. It should be carried concealed in a place where it can be put into use quickly and those who carry spray dispensers should not carry them unless they've actually practiced in how to use such devices, are fully committed in using it on an assailant until he is on the ground, giving the targeted victim an opportunity to eacape to safety. Finally, users of sprays should be cognizant that assailants can and have taken dispensers away from and used them against victims, causing major injury.

Another issue to think about while abroad is the risk of HIV/AIDS exposure. Even if you intend to resist and escape if confronted by a rapist, many women who travel frequently or live in high-risk HIV/AIDS countries often carry a couple of condoms in their purses, just in case. Although few rapists are likely to stop to use a condom, they might if the victim is convincing that she has an STD or she is menstruating.

If you have been sexually assaulted abroad:

☐ Call your embassy duty officer, consul, RSO, security representative, and/or employer.

☐ Contact your family and friends.

☐ If in a developing country, go to local police or a local hospital **only** after conferring with your embassy or employer. Ask them to accompany you to the police station or hospital.

☐ Do not shower or brush your teeth (in the event you contemplate prosecution).

☐ Ensure that you get copies of all police and medical reports and photographs as this may have an impact on insurance issues at home.

☐ Don't decide on whether you intend to file charges against suspect(s) until conferring with those in your support network.

☐ Make no major decisions until you've recovered.

☐ Seek reputable medical and counseling support as needed.

If a family member, friend, or colleague has been raped abroad:

☐ Assist in dealing with embassies, police, hospitals, etc., to give the victim time to recover.

☐ Reinforce that the attack was not the victim's fault.

☐ Do everything possible to make the victim feel more comfortable.

☐ Serve as a sounding board to the victim in making required decisions (whether to pursue prosecution, whether to leave the country immediately, when to go back to work, etc.).

☐ Help her in any way you can, and reassure her that you will stay by her.

In the event a woman is raped in a country with a high incidence of HIV/AIDS, please note that a regimen of treatment is available, known as Non-Occupational Antiretroviral Post-Exposure Prophylaxis, and involves commencing a number of antiretroviral medications as soon as possible (no later than 72 hours) after exposure to a known HIV/AIDS-positive contact. The evaluation of the patient as well as the initiation of the medications is done by a physician, usually in an emergency room or public health clinic setting (most primary care offices would not keep these on hand or be familiar with using them). The medications would have to be taken for 28 days and, during that time, the patient would likely be followed by an infectious disease specialist. The medications are likely to cause a number of side effects and the decision to start the treatment would be made by the clinician after weighing the risks and benefits. A lot of factors must be taken into consideration before a patient would be considered for the prophylaxis and not every exposure would be eligible, even in the case of rape.

One last thought for women employed by U.S. Government contractors in Iraq and Afghanistan. The U.S. media has prominently covered several cases of women employees of such contractors being raped, sexually assaulted and sexually harassed while working in countries where there is no functioning criminal justice system. Consequently, some Federal contractor have been less than cooperative in terms of the manner their complaints have been handled by their employers and how difficult it can be to file charges in a U.S. court for offenses that have occurred in military theaters. In such environments, sexual harassment is commonplace. To underline this statement, the U.S. Army's Criminal Investigation Command investigatged 124 cases of alleged sexual assault in Iraq in one three-year period.

Those considering employment in military theaters should be cognizant of the challenges they may face and query prospective employers as to how they will be be protected abroad from sexual assault and harassment and the legal remedies available to them.

As a wrap-up on this chapter, please review some of the following Web sites that provide excellent information for women who will be traveling abroad:

- http://www.travel.state.gov
- http://www.voyage.gc.ca/main/pubs/her_own_way-en.asp (Her Own Way)
- http://www.transitionsabroad.com
- http://www.fco.gov.uk
- http://www.womankind.org.uk
- http://www.4women.gov/faq/rohypnol

Traveling in Rural Areas and Transiting Checkpoints

Before you travel into rural areas in developing countries, check with Transparency International's CPI (**http://www.transparency.org**) for the country you are traveling in to ascertain the likelihood of being "shaken down" for money or other valuables should you encounter the inevitable checkpoint. These checkpoints may be manned by police or, sometimes, by criminals or rebels. Before traveling in rural areas, also ask credible colleagues or locals who know the countryside and solicit their advice as to how you should conduct yourself at checkpoints (ensure that you ask what you should give those at the checkpoints if they solicit you).

If you are working in rural areas in a high-risk country where armed carjacking is commonplace or where foreigners may be subjected to abduction, kidnapping, extortion, rape, etc., discuss the possibility of using a convoy (whereby all vehicles can communicate with one another), hiring competent and reputable armed security escorts, or using ballistic-resistant vehicles, if they are not provided to you. Conversely, if you are traveling on your own and do not have those types of resources available, I strongly suggest that you reread some of the cases earlier in the book that spoke of murder and abduction of people who made road trips in dangerous areas (e.g., Tom Hargrove and the American birdwatchers, who were abducted and held by the FARC for over a year and a month, respectively, and the Mormon missionary who was shot and killed while on a bus bound for Mexico).

Before traveling by road in any high-risk developing country, do the following:

☐ Obtain road and topographical maps of the area in which you will be traveling.

☐ Contact your embassy, and request security advice on the threats you may face; if you are told that diplomats are prohibited from traveling in that area, follow that advice.

☐ Register with your embassy, and advise the officials there where you will be staying and how they can reach you.

- ☐ Make sure you have your vehicle's registration and proof of insurance.
- ☐ Carry a cell phone that will work in your area and an extra battery.
- ☐ Carry a pair of binoculars so you can observe the legitimacy of checkpoints before you get so close to them that you have no options.
- ☐ Talk to the tourist police or other police agencies, and get the phone numbers of their stations in the area that you will be visiting.
- ☐ Know where the hospitals are and have their numbers—mark them on a map.
- ☐ Ensure that you will be able to refill your gas tank before you leave.
- ☐ Carry extra water, food, and flashlights with batteries.
- ☐ Learn what police and military uniforms look like and how foreigners are treated at government checkpoints.
- ☐ Ask credible locals whether bribes are solicited at checkpoints and whether you should pay them.
- ☐ Carry photocopies of your passport and entry visa.
- ☐ Carry cash to cover emergencies, and hide most of it (in your shoe, a zippered ankle sock, a money belt, etc.).

Roadblocks and checkpoints fall into four categories:

- ■ Police or military checkpoints that legitimately check your travel documents, the purpose of your travel, and your destination; search your vehicle; and then wave you on.

- Police checkpoints that legitimately check your travel documents, the purpose of travel, and destination; occasionally search your vehicle; and solicit a bribe or a "fee" for a multitude of infractions, real or imagined.

- An impromptu checkpoint set up by rebels who solicit "transit fees," money, or anything you have that they want and then wave you on.

- An impromptu checkpoint set up by criminals to steal your money, passports, possessions, or vehicle.

Case Study: Guatemala

In 1998, a U.S. expatriate family that lived in Guatemala City was driving north of the capital in a Jeep Cherokee to do some weekend hiking. As they came around a curve on a rural road, they looked ahead and saw what appeared to be a fallen tree blocking the middle of the road and several men standing in front of it. Rather than scrutinizing the situation more carefully, the woman proceeded toward the men because she thought it might be a police checkpoint. As she approached the men, she soon realized that they had cut the tree down as a means of stopping and robbing motorists who might be driving by. The criminals began waving guns at the SUV. Rather than stop, the driver drove through the barricade, with the gunmen firing at the vehicle as it sped away. The driver was shot in the back but received medical treatment in the next town. The entire group could have been killed. The gunmen in that case had no vehicle, so the Americans would have been able to turn around their vehicle and take another road.

Lessons learned:

☐ Always carry binoculars in your vehicle when in rural areas so that you can examine a situation ahead to determine whether you should proceed or promptly turn around and take another road.

☐ Learn how to back up quickly or make a U-turn so that you can get out of a situation.

☐ Do not resist an armed robbery or a carjacking. Nothing is worth your life.

If a demand for money is made at a police checkpoint, ask what the purpose of it is and ask for a receipt and the name and badge number of the officer. Another option is to say that you do not have the money and need to call a friend who can bring it to you. Yet another approach is to ask to call the U.S. Embassy or another point of contact. An officer conducting a legitimate police stop should have no qualms with such a request, while an officer or impostor conducting an illegal stop will often rescind any "fines" or fees requested. Never leave your vehicle without taking your cell phone with you; it may be your only connection to the outside world if a criminal absconds with your vehicle. Always have the phone number of your embassy or consulate, as well as numbers of local police, so you can report shakedowns after you have left the roadblock.

Office Security

Regardless of whether you are assigned abroad long-term or whether you are simply visiting on a short-term business trip, you should keep in mind that since the events of 9/11, criminals and terrorist groups are far more likely to target "soft targets" (e.g., office complexes, hotels, tourist sites, universities, shopping malls, etc.) instead of "hard targets" (i.e., those that have formidable physical security, guards, protected perimeters, etc.). Consequently, here are some features that security-conscious employers will have in place to protect employees and visitors:

- Effective external physical security of the building or the space, aimed at preventing criminal and terrorist attacks.
- Written policies and procedures on all aspects of organizational security.
- A means of screening incoming mail and couriered packages for potentially harmful materials (including IEDs and anthrax).
- Shatter-resistant film on all exterior windows of automobiles to minimize injury and death to occupants as a result of bomb incidents and earthquakes.
- Issuances of displayed identification cards to all employees.
- Written organizational emergency plans explaining to staff the actions to take in the event of emergencies (e.g., explosions, political unrest, bomb threat, natural disasters, fire, etc.).

- An emergency public-address system that permits building management to advise staff and visitors on all floors of emergencies and what action to take.
- Lobby areas protected with electrical, remotely controlled locks, card access systems for employees, a walk-through metal detector, and hand search of briefcases and purses. Visitor passes will be issued before visitors are afforded access to interior offices.
- A warden system on each floor that mandates action that employees and visitors should take in the event of an emergency. In the event your employer shares space with other tenants, preincident coordination must be in place for all tenants on emergencies and evacuation.
- Well-trained, uniformed security guards capable of taking action in the event of a threat or emergency. Such guards should be capable of immediately soliciting local police.

Further, here are some key tips while working in offices abroad:

☐ Request guidance or a security briefing from your local office.

☐ Discuss your travel plans and movements with as few people as possible.

☐ If the press must know about your visit, do not disclose where you are staying or your arrival or departure times.

☐ Ensure that your office (both at home and abroad) has the following information:

- Passport number
- Hotel and room number
- Cell number
- Instruction on whom to notify in an emergency
- Blood type and allergies

☐ Avoid sitting by windows close to the street in countries where bombings or violent protests are likely.

☐ Avoid large demonstrations.

☐ Be careful discussing sensitive matters on the telephone, particularly over international communication lines.

☐ Do not reveal personal information about staff members to unknown callers.

Handling Personal Threats

Infrequently, international travelers, expatriates, journalists, aid workers, diplomats, multinational executives, and consultants have been the recipients of threatening letters, telephone calls, faxes, e-mails, and even verbal and physical threats. Often, such threats stem from "downsizing" operations, disgruntled local or third-country national employees, criminal activity, those terminated for cause, those employed by a state-owned company that is undergoing privatization, or labor strife.

An example of this type of violence occurred in February 2007, when three French aid workers working for the French-Brazilian NGO, Terr'Ativa, were stabbed to death by three hit men hired by the organization's treasurer who had embezzled $38,000 from the NGO financial accounts. The treasurer paid his accomplices $500 each to kill the aid workers and gave them knives and carnival clown masks to use in the crime. He was arrested shortly after the murders.

Experience has shown that anyone who perceives that an action taken by his or her employer will cause a loss of money, status, or benefits may pose a potential threat. While the majority of these international human resources actions generally occur without any retribution, the employees may occasionally threaten those they feel are responsible for their plight.

In an international environment, local police are often ineffective in preventing potentially threatening situations initiated by disgruntled employees or former employees. What happens after announced layoffs or downsizing? Non-threatening letters and telephone calls protesting the action are often received. Such letters are normally handled by human resources specialists and the organization's legal advisor. Occasionally, those affected by a downsizing program discover that they often have no administrative recourse and may take their case to media organizations, unions, and others who may support their position. It is normal during downsizing operations for angered staff scheduled for separation to make verbal, written, or telephonic threats. Sometimes such threats occur before the formal announcement is made or because those involved believe that threats will change the course of the downsizing operation. Generally, though, the threats occur after the fact, once reality has set in.

Even though threats of violence can be very upsetting, experience has shown that few people who make such threats actually carry them out. Nevertheless, occasionally they do, which is one reason all verbal, written, and telephonic threats must be handled carefully, assessed, and investigated. In an international setting, and primarily in developing countries, any response should be handled by in-house or independent security professionals or HR executives. When the threat is deemed serious, the organization must take appropriate action to protect the threatened staff member. Threats can take many forms:

- Face-to-face verbal threats
- Telephonic threats
- Written threats
- Assault (including sexual assault)

General advice for those who may be threatened:

☐ Realize you may be targeted.

☐ Seek out the company of others while at work and at home. It is easier to target those who are alone.

☐ Vary the times you arrive at and leave work and home.

☐ Realize that predictable behavior at work, home, or a hotel will inform those wishing to express their anger of where you are likely to be at a particular time.

☐ Be aware of what is going on around you. If you suspect you are being followed, report it to top management, either at the subsidiary abroad or to the home office.

☐ Be suspicious of anything that is not normal.

☐ Consider having a colleague walk you to your to car or taxi if you suspect you are being targeted or followed.

☐ Avoid parking your car in isolated areas.

☐ Reduce nighttime activities at work.

☐ Carry emergency numbers of people who can help you 24-7.

☐ Carry a cell phone.

☐ Realize that carrying a firearm or nonlethal weapon can often increase your risk rather than decrease it.

☐ Do not drive home if you suspect you are being followed, as this could very well intensify the threat.

☐ Drive to your embassy, hospital, or other place where large numbers of people are present and where reliable assistance can be obtained.

Face-to-face verbal confrontations. Individuals who may be threatened should advise the disgruntled person that they are sorry for the outcome but that the decision was not made by them. Then they should walk away confidently rather than permit the encounter to escalate.

Telephonic threats:

☐ Consider using caller ID (if available) and recording devices on telephones on which you may receive potentially threatening calls. Such approaches may lead to the identification of the caller.

☐ Listen carefully to what the caller is saying, and try to recall exactly what is said. Immediately afterward, notify

top management, your diplomatic representative, or
local police.

☐ If you receive a threatening voice mail message, save it
as possible evidence.

Written threats:

☐ Realize that you may receive potentially threatening letters from disgruntled staff through your office mail, at
your hotel, at your home (in the case of an expatriate),
or by fax or e-mail. A note may simply be left on the
windshield of your vehicle.

☐ Save all such communications (including envelopes)
and give them to top management or your embassy for
appropriate investigation.

Verbal altercations and assault:

☐ Realize that people who have displayed anger or aggressive behavior at work in the past are more likely to resort
to physical violence than are those who have not.

☐ Keep in mind that angry people may approach you, verbally taunt you, call you names, and try to pick a fight.

☐ Realize that if efforts to defuse the situation are unpro-
ductive, you should say, "I'm sorry you feel the way you
do" and walk away, preferably to safety.

☐ If threatened physically, take the necessary measures to
protect yourself, and call for help. If you have a whistle

(and I recommend that everyone carry one), use it to alert bystanders. Try to leave the scene of an altercation before it occurs.

☐ Report the incident immediately to appropriate officials.

☐ Realizing that rape has a great deal more to do with power and control than sex, female managers should not rule out sexual assault by potentially violent persons who may blame them for employment-related adverse actions.

Molotov Cocktails, Small Arms and Grenade Attacks, and Mines

Unquestionably, our world has gotten smaller as a result of air travel that can get us half a world away in less than a day. This chapter will examine actions you should take if confronted with Molotov cocktails, small arms and grenade attacks, and mines.

Clearly, the potential for encountering these types of threats is slim, but it does occur, as evidenced by the hand-gun attack on foreign tourists at the Roman ruins outside Amman (see pages 29–33). Also, several years ago, a young couple from Colorado and the husband's father visited Mexico for a couple of days. While there, the three Americans were caught in the middle of a shoot-out between competing drug gangs. When the firing began, the husband and his father instinctively dropped to the ground, but the wife did not. She was killed instantly.

Molotov cocktails. The term *Molotov cocktail* is mockingly named after Vyacheslav Molotov, a Soviet premier, following the Russian invasion of Finland in WWII, when the Finns refused to surrender ports to the Soviet Union. To combat Russian tanks, the Finnish Army borrowed an improvised incendiary device (IID) from the tactics of the Spanish Civil War. Hence, the term *Molotov cocktail* began to be used throughout the world. The use of these IIDs continues today, including in demonstrations in France, Denmark, Greece, the United Kingdom, and the United States. The students responsible for the Columbine High School massacre used Molotov cocktails, but the devices failed to ignite. Below are some tips on minimizing risk from these devices:

☐ The use of Molotov cocktails can be countered by installing shatter-resistant film on residential or office windows or iron grills to deflect them.

☐ When riding in vehicles, always keep the windows up to deflect Molotov cocktails and hand grenades.

☐ If a Molotov cocktail is thrown at your vehicle and breaks, continue to drive away from the scene of the attack even if flames engulf the vehicle. If the cocktail is thrown against the front windshield, the flames may impair your vision, but eventually they will burn out. So, simply try to drive to a safe area.

Small arms attacks. As we saw in the handgun attack on European tourists at the Roman ruins in Jordan (see page 29), being caught up in small arms attacks or a cross fire can occur anywhere in the world. If you hear gunfire while on foot, do the following:

☐ Fall to the ground quickly, lie flat on your stomach, and cover your face.

☐ Quickly determine the direction in which the rounds are being fired so you can take defensive action.

☐ Depending on from where the hostile fire is coming, you may be able to seek cover behind natural barriers (e.g., cars, columns, buildings, a turned-over table, etc.).

☐ Stand up only after you are sure the small arms fire has ceased and the danger has passed.

If you hear gunfire while you are in a building:

☐ Stay clear of windows and doors.

☐ Seek shelter in bathrooms and closets, behind a solid wall, or under a stairwell, etc.

If you hear gunfire while in a motor vehicle:

☐ Keep windows down about an inch so you can hear outside activity (better to hear the first shot and be able to take evasive action than to be clueless of the attack and be injured or killed).

☐ If the gunfire is coming from the direction in which you are driving, stop and quickly reverse the vehicle; this shows that you pose no threat.

☐ If surrounded by gunfire, stop and take cover wherever you can; do not seek cover directly outside or under your vehicle, as continued firing could ignite it.

☐ If you can safely leave the vehicle and seek cover in a nearby ditch or in a wooded area, do so.

☐ Leave the area once the firing has ceased.

If you encounter an armed roadblock or barricade designed to halt your vehicle and injure/kill you, and in addition to wishing that you had obtained the hands-on emergency driving training that I suggested on page 222, the following is suggested:

☐ Ensure that those attempting to stop you are not genuine cops or soldiers of the host government. If they are not, read the point below. If they are, proceed cautiously and determine what they want, as running a legitimate police or military roadblock is asking for trouble and extremely dangerous.

☐ Determine whether the gunmen at the roadblock have vehicles on-site (that they could use to give chase). If not, make a hasty reverse turn, leave the area, and put as much road between them and you as humanly possible.

☐ If they have vehicles from which they could give chase, determine whether they have two vehicles blocking the road head-to-head or whether they are using only one vehicle. If they have two vehicles, do the following:

■ Approach the roadblock slowly, stopping approximately 10 to 20 feet away, keeping your engine running, and appearing as if you are going to comply with the gunmen's instructions.

- As they appear ready to approach your vehicle, step on the gas, get your vehicle up to about 15–25 mph, ignore the gunmen (who by now are running for cover), and aim your vehicle at the center of the two vehicles that are head-to-head so that you are hitting them at an angle and can push them away from each other with the least possible resistance. The intent is to damage their vehicles so that you can drive away and the gunmen will be unable to give chase. Your vehicle should not shut down as long as you are determined and keep moving.

☐ If the gunmen have only one vehicle blocking the road, you want to repeat the tactic described above. The exception is that you want to direct your vehicle at one end of the vehicle so that you can spin it around as you drive through the roadblock. Again, the intent is to damage their vehicle and give you enough time to get away.

Hand grenades/rocket-propelled grenade (RPG) attacks.

Fragmentation grenades come in two forms: those that are thrown and those that are fired from a purpose-designed grenade launcher. Most hand grenades are an antipersonnel weapon, while grenades fired from a launcher can be designed to inure and kill people, neutralize vehicles, or cause major damage to and casualties in buildings. Most hand grenades that are used by political extremists originate in the old

Soviet Union. Most RPGs are also Soviet-made and can be found in an assortment of models ranging from the RPG-2 to the RPG-29. The RPG-7 version is the favorite of most terrorists because it can be reloaded with a new rocket. The effective range of the RPG-7 is about 50 meters, although a skilled operator can easily hit a target at 100 meters.

When the pin holding the safety lever on a hand grenade is pulled, the thrower must hold the safety level in place while preparing to throw the grenade. Variations in grenade design influence how many seconds will pass before a thrown grenade detonates, but most grenades will detonate within five to eight seconds. Some throwers may "cook off" a grenade, which means that they wait a couple of seconds after releasing the safety lever before throwing the grenade to ensure it is not thrown back. This, however, is very much a "living on the edge" strategy for the thrower. A much safer technique is to bounce the grenade on its way to its target to reduce the time it can be thrown back. Casualties usually occur within 10 meters, although fragments can reach 200 meters.

In March 2002, two U.S. citizens were killed in a grenade attack during a Christian church service only 400 yards from the U.S. Embassy in Islamabad. Although the media tend to focus on suicide bombers and more dramatic terrorist attacks, the reality is that fragmentation grenades are one of the most often used terrorist tactics.

In January 2007, an RPG was fired at the U.S. Embassy in Athens and caused minor damage but no injuries. The attack was claimed by the radical group Revolutionary

Struggle, which emerged following the neutralization of the November 17 group. The group opposes the U.S. intervention in Iraq and Afghanistan as well as the policies of the conservative Greek government.

If your destination is a country where terrorist attacks have occurred and particularly where thrown grenades and RPGs have been used in the past, exercise security awareness at all times. Be vigilant in areas where grenade attacks have been used, such as sidewalk cafes; churches, mosques, and synagogues; theaters; hotel lobbies; etc. If a hand grenade is thrown in your direction, do not try to throw it back. You have no idea when it is going to detonate, and you definitely do not want that happening in your hand. Instead, do the following:

- ☐ Try to get as far away from the grenade as possible as quickly as possible.
- ☐ Seek cover if you can.
- ☐ Fall to the ground, face down.
- ☐ Cover your head and face.

If you see an RPG being fired in your direction, remember that it will detonate when it hits something, so get low on the floor and cover your head. Another good option is to get behind a wall and crouch down on the floor in a closet or bathroom.

Land mines. Land mines have been placed all over countries that have been at war. They can detonate decades afterward if someone walks over them. Mines come in two styles: anti-tank and anti-personnel. An antitank device usually requires 100 kg of weight, while an antipersonnel requires only 3 kg, which is why so many children have been killed by them. Consider the following:

- [ ] Never touch a mine or suspicious object.
- [ ] Talk to locals to find out whether there may be mines in the area and what areas should be avoided.
- [ ] Use binoculars to scan areas that may be mined.
- [ ] Avoid dirty-yellow, green metallic, or plastic objects that look like they do not belong.
- [ ] Mines can often be found in areas where battles have occurred.
- [ ] Be cautious around abandoned buildings, destroyed vehicles, remnants of dead animals, footwear, human bones, etc.
- [ ] Do not touch and do avoid wires protruding from the ground.

Special Situations

If you are arrested. Even though international travelers rarely encounter problems that might result in their arrest, they can and do happen. Frequently, such arrests are the result of cultural misunderstandings, excessive drinking, drug possession, not having a visa, currency violations, disorderly conduct, and a multitude of other offenses. This is why I put so much emphasis in this book on knowing the local laws and finding out what can get you into big trouble. Regardless of the cause, the experience of being arrested or detained in another country can be far different from what occurs in your home country. If you are arrested, ask permission to notify your employer and/or embassy. If you are denied, keep asking. Be polite but persistent. In many cases, arrest means you are jailed until arraigned and the case adjudicated, as many countries do not have bail systems. Also keep in mind that many developing countries do not plea-bargain cases, which means you could be in jail for some time. My best advice is to do *nothing* that would give a local law enforcement agency reason to have an interest in you.

If you are detained for questioning. This would mean short of being arrested but not free to go. It could also mean being jailed without being charged. Unlike in the United States, Canada, the United Kingdom, and many other developed nations, saying "either charge me or release me" could be an antagonizing statement in developing countries. Prudence is suggested. If you are detained longer than brief questioning on the street and are taken "downtown," consider yourself *not* free to go. If detained, do not admit to any wrongdoing or sign any document. I repeat: do not admit to any wrongdoing or sign any document, even if it is in English. Persist in your requests for the ability to call your embassy and/or your employer.

If you are caught up in disruptive political unrest or a major natural disaster. Disruptive political unrest or a major natural disaster would mean that normal commerce and day-to-day activities cease, martial law is declared, the airport is closed, a bloody coup is under way, or an incident of mass destruction or catastrophic natural disaster has occurred. Suggested actions include:

☐ If you are at your hotel, stay there. If not, try to get there safely.

☐ Do not try to go to your embassy; it will be very chaotic and you'll have a better chance of communicating with it by email.

☐ If you have a cell phone that works and has e-mail capability, go to your embassy's Web site, register, and tell officials where you are. Give them your cell number.

☐ Try to hire someone to take a note to your employer and/or your embassy; if everything else fails, try to contact other friendly embassies or the United Nations by telephone or by delivered note.

☐ Make sure you have your passport and hard currency.

☐ If e-mail is working, get a message to your employer and/or family with information about how to reach you.

☐ If at the hotel, fill your bathroom with water, as you may need it later.

☐ If possible, order lots of room service, as food could run out in a day or less.

☐ Stock up on bottled water, and buy food you can carry with you.

☐ If there is gunfire near your hotel, stay away from windows.

☐ Seek out other guests to create an emotional support base.

☐ Do not try to impress anyone with how important you are. This could raise your visibility and vulnerability.

☐ Know your escape routes in the event you must leave the hotel.

☐ If a natural disaster, read 157–163 again.

Surviving as a Hostage or Kidnap Victim

Pages 61–66 covered the various forms of hostage taking, including express kidnapping. This chapter will provide specific guidance on actions to take if you are held hostage in a number of situations. Action to take in the event of an aircraft hijacking is covered in on pages 195–197.

Every hostage or kidnap situation is different. There are no strict rules of behavior. However, as gleaned from debriefings of a number of single-hostage, mass-hostage, air hijacking, and carjacking victims suggest, there are successful strategies in minimizing the adverse effects of several types of detention. If you are going to travel abroad, particularly in countries where hostage taking and kidnapping occur, talk to your family, friends, and significant other about the possibility *before* something happens. Not doing so will compound problems if your family and close friends do not know whom to call for support and if your family cannot get access to your finances. If you are working abroad, ask you employer what action will be taken if you are abducted or held hostage and who in the company your family should call in the remote chance that it occurs.

The single-hostage experience:

☐ Be certain that you can explain everything you have on your person.

☐ At the time of your seizure, do not fight back or attempt to aggravate the hostage taker or kidnapper. The worst time to resist is during your abduction or seizure, as guns are often used, adrenaline flow on the part of your captors is usually at its highest, and resisting may get you killed—it did Sydney J. Reso, one-time president of Exxon International, who was shot by kidnappers at the time he was seized outside his Morristown, New Jersey, home.

☐ Expect to be drugged or blindfolded.

☐ Fear can sometimes be overwhelming and paralyzing. Although fear of death may be realistic, recognizing your reactions may help you adapt more effectively.

☐ Immediately after detention has begun, pause, take a deep breath, and try to organize your thoughts. Try to determine where you are being taken or what the situation is.

☐ If you are on critical prescribed medication, ask the abductors to get it for you, as they need to keep you healthy during captivity.

☐ Make mental notes of your abductors and their mannerisms, conversations, and apparent rank structure. This may help police after your release.

☐ Be prepared to be accused of being a spy if held by political extremists. When I was director of security of the U.S. Agency for International Development in the mid-1980s, three of our USAID auditors were on the hijacked Kuwaiti Airways flight (KE221). They were repeatedly beaten and accused of working for the CIA.

☐ Anticipate isolation and efforts by the hostage takers to disorient you.

☐ Exercise daily. Develop a physical fitness program and stick with it.

☐ Be prepared for a loss of appetite and weight.

☐ Be as mentally active as possible. Write, read books, study languages, and even consider solutions to problems at your work.

☐ Ask for anything you need or want (e.g., medicine, books, etc.). All they can do is say no.

☐ If you speak your captors' language, use it, as it will enhance communication with those who are holding you. Note: In a hijacking, you want to conceal that you know the hijackers' language, but in a single-hostage situation, building rapport with your captors is key.

☐ Attempt to build rapport with your captors.

☐ Find mutual areas of interest that emphasize personal rather than political interests.

☐ Eat what they give you.

☐ At all times, maintain your dignity and self respect.

☐ Former hostages and kidnap victims report that three types of faith contributed to their survival—faith in self, faith in those who are attempting to secure their release, and faith in a supreme being. Faith in yourself is critical, but if you can have faith in all *three*, so much the better.

Express Kidnapping

In the majority of cases, an express kidnapping involves you being abducted by a criminal off the street, while in a taxi, or while you are driving or riding as a motorist. With few exceptions, you will be threatened with a weapon.

- [ ] Resisting over property is foolish. You do not want to die over money or things. Criminals in developing countries will not hesitate to shoot you because they have little risk of being arrested or sent to prison.
- [ ] Always carry a financial instrument that enables you to get cash from ATMs, but do not take cards abroad with huge balances or credit lines.
- [ ] Do not argue, display anger, or glare at your captor.
- [ ] Do not be surprised if you are held overnight so that another maximum withdrawal from your card can be made.
- [ ] Make mental notes of vehicle numbers, physical descriptions, names, types of weapons used, etc.
- [ ] Always carry a small amount of cash in a security sock (to safeguard small amounts of cash) or a money belt so that you will have cash to get back to your hotel or home after being released.

☐ Call your embassy for assistance.
☐ Report the crime to the police.

Armed Carjacking Abduction

Few carjackings involve abduction of the occupants, although there have been cases of children being driven away in child safety seats and adults being driven away when they do not exit the vehicle quickly. If you have a child or children in the car, strongly appeal to the carjacker that he can have everything, just let you get your child out of the car.

☐ Do not resist an armed carjacking. Doing so can result in serious injury or death.

☐ To avoid being abducted in conjunction with a carjacking, get out of the car quickly. This will also reduce your risk of being shot because you are exiting the vehicle too slowly.

☐ If the car being carjacked is your car, consider electronic monitoring of the vehicle, resources permitting, as not all criminals think of this possibility.

SECTION FIVE

Special Topics for Expatriates

Family and school security. Living abroad with my family was probably one of the best experiences of my life. Our family became closer because of the experience, and my daughters became each other's best friend for life because in many places we lived, they often had only each other. So I am pleased that today, as women in their thirties, they take a sisters trip abroad every year. For those of you who may be overseas-bound with children for a long-term assignment, I would suggest the following:

☐ Include your children in all planning and details in the process of moving and living abroad; it will make them more self-sufficient and the experience richer.

☐ Thoroughly talk to expatriates who have lived in the country of your destination, particularly insofar as school selection, school security, medical providers, libraries,

and cultural and language opportunities are concerned.
Good places to start include:

- **http://www.expatexpert.com** (*Raising Global Nomads*, by Robin Pascoe)
- **http://www.expatexchange.com**
- **http://www.expatforum.com**
- **http://www.state.gov/m/a/os/cl1684** (a list of major international schools abroad)
- **http://www.osid.co.uk**
- **http://www.transitionsabroad.com**

☐ The more you learn about the security threats that exist in the country in which you will be living, the better able you will be to protect your children.

☐ If your children are abroad with you, know that a cell phone in the hands of responsible children or teenagers will enable them to stay in touch with you and vice versa. Considering that emergency services are often inadequate in developing countries, it is key that your children know how to reach you in an emergency.

☐ Do not be reluctant to brief your children on violent threats and the risks of child molestation that exist where you will be living. You cannot protect them if you are afraid of alarming them. You need to empower them with the knowledge of what steps to take if they are threatened.

☐ Before enrolling your children in an overseas school, talk to your embassy security representative about the school's preparedness for emergency situations (fire, political unrest, emergency evacuation, school violence, natural disasters, etc.). Also find out how the school will inform you in the event of an emergency and any actions you should take to get to your children in the event of a national emergency.

How to hire and manage domestic staff. Many expatriates find that living abroad provides an opportunity to hire domestic staff (e.g., cooks, maids, nannies, gardeners, drivers, etc.), particularly in developing countries where such staff can be hired very reasonably. Before rushing to hire someone, though, please consider the following:

☐ Contact your embassy to learn your legal and financial responsibilities in hiring a local national. You may be responsible for additional costs/withholding to be in compliance with the local labor code. In some countries, regardless of how long you employ someone, you may be responsible for severance pay if you discharge him or her.

☐ Do not hire people because they look nice and speak your language. Many criminal gangs prey on expatriates by trying to get someone on the "inside." Also, ***do not accept letters of recommendation at face value***. You'd be surprised by the number of expatriates who hire domestics on the basis of such letters, only to have their house cleared out while away for a weekend. So, before you hire anyone, do the following:

- Determine whether the person you are looking for must speak your language and at what level for the arrangement to work.

- Interview potential employees in great detail and ask them for their address and a copy of their national identity card or passport. Also ask them how they can be reached by phone.

- Ask for the names of three credible employment references, including full names, addresses, phone numbers, and/or e-mail addresses. Contact them so you can discuss the candidate's work habits and whether they would recommend the candidate for employment. *If you cannot obtain the names of three references to talk to, keep looking for other candidates.*

- Ask your embassy how you can have a police check conducted on the person you intend to hire. Normally, you pay a fee, and then you and the prospective employee go to the police ID unit, where prints are taken and an indexes search is conducted, with the results going to you.

- Determine whether you can hire a domestic on a trial basis to ensure that he or she will adapt well to your home and family situation.

How to hire a local driver. Of the categories of domestic staff, this is the one you want to be very careful with, particularly if the driver is going to be driving your spouse and/or your children around town. Some expatriates and diplomats hire personal drivers in a developing country who have never had a driver's license. Keep in mind that in many countries, traffic enforcement is nonexistent and people can get a taxi license by simply buying one. As in the case of other domestics, do not hire a driver until you have spoken to at least three credible individuals for whom the applicant has driven. Do not accept letters of recommendation because they could be fraudulent. Below are some issues you need to consider before hiring a driver:

☐ Make a copy of the applicant's national identity card or passport and his/her driver's license (make sure it is valid).

☐ Send the applicant to a credible physician for a physical and eye exam, and have the doctor send you a letter of his or her findings. (You should pay for the exam.)

☐ Have a bilingual trusted national determine whether your applicant understands your language well enough to follow directions. Have this person write a chronology of the applicant's employment history and the names and phone numbers of former employers. Ask him or her to verify the applicant's work history (if different from those three described earlier).

☐ Determine how you can conduct a police check on the applicant, and get the results before offering employment.

☐ Determine whether your applicant can drive your car without you having to place his or her name on your auto insurance policy. If so, have him or her drive your car with you as a passenger, and ask him or her to take you to those places that you would normally want to go (office, home, school, golf/tennis club, gym, social venues, etc.). If you arrive back where you started and all is well, go to the next point below.

☐ Ensure you are comfortable with the labor code requirements and offer a position to the applicant.

☐ Add the driver to your insurance policy and have maximum coverage for both liability and property damage.

☐ A final note, particularly for expatriates. Rarely will a multinational employer reimburse you for the cost of a driver if you reside in a high-crime or high-terrorism nation, unless you have been specifically threatened, in which case you are likely to either be sent home for your own safety, or provided an armed security escort and an armored vehicle. Few companies pay for expatriate drivers simply because of local threats.

Using firearms as a self-defense tool. First of all, there are three types of people in the world: (1) those who know how to use firearms proficiently, (2) those who do not know how to use firearms proficiently, and (3) those who do not want to know.

Many countries ban residents from possessing firearms, which means that the bad guys usually have most of the guns. That also means that you are going to have to make sure that your home has extremely formidable physical security and a safe haven. Some nations permit you to possess a firearm for home use, but the firearm must be registered with the police. Very few countries allow you to carry a concealed weapon.

A couple of other key points: if you shoot someone *outside* your home and a foreign judge determines that you are not justified in doing so, you could face a lengthy prison term in a rustic local prison. On the other hand, if someone has broken into your home and is trying to hurt you or others and you have a legally registered firearm, you have every right to protect yourself.

If you plan to live long-term (longer than six months) in a developing country where the police are generally ineffective and slow to respond, where incidents of violent crime (including burglaries and home invasions) are frequent, and where foreigners are on everyone's hit list, a firearm may be the only thing that will keep you alive. Consequently, if you can legally possess a firearm in your home in the country in which you are living, you have two choices:

☐ Learn how to use a firearm proficiently before you go abroad, and check with the embassy of the country where you will be living to determine whether and how you can import a firearm or purchase one in the country.

☐ Ensure that the physical security in your home will effectively deter intruders because that could well be the difference between life and death if you are living in a developing country that has rampant violent crime and unresponsive police.

If you choose to have a firearm in your home for self-protection, I recommend a 20-gauge pump shotgun. A 20-gauge does not have nearly the recoil of a 12-gauge, is easy to operate, and has a large pattern that will severely neutralize an armed intruder. Keep in mind that if you intend to use a firearm on an armed intruder, you must know that you are shooting at an actual intruder. In other words, it is more important to know when *not* to shoot than to know when to shoot. Taping a flashlight to the barrel of the shotgun allows you to identify your target before you fire, if the break-in occurs at night. In low light, the flashlight will also startle and temporarily distract the intruder, thus giving you a tactical advantage.

If you are not able to legally possess a firearm in the country you are living in, your only option is to hire competent, well-trained and experienced armed security guards and retain competent security advisors to help you fortify your residence and office premises. If you cannot legally possess a firearm, seek out the advice from the security advisor at your embassy for the names of suggested security companies (if you are a U.S. citizen, this would be the RSO).

Purchasing a vehicle abroad.   Most expatriates who either work abroad or live abroad find the need to have a personal vehicle, unless, of course, the mass-transit system is safe and efficient. Unfortunately, not many countries fall into both categories. Obviously, if you work for an embassy, a military organization or some international organizations, you may be able to import a vehicle (either the one you own or a new vehicle) into the country of your assignment without having to pay import duties on the vehicle. Here are some suggestions on how to select and protect your vehicle:

☐ Before purchasing a vehicle for overseas use, determine in advance what types of vehicles are being stolen or carjacked in the country. Generally speaking, luxury vehicles and Japanese, Korean and European SUVs are at the top of most car thieves' shopping list. Toyota Land Cruisers are particularly desired, although American vehicles are not, as they are so easily identified and because getting parts and maintaining them is difficult. Please note, though, that taking a U.S.-made vehicle abroad is not a good idea, as it often identifies the driver as an American.

☐ Ensure the vehicle has remote locking control on the driver's side for security purposes.

☐ Compact vehicles are not recommended for developing countries, given the high risk of death in the event of a serious accident and the slowness of medical services to respond. Mid-size vehicles with heavy-duty suspension and four-wheel drive is strongly suggested.

☐ Where legal, tinted windows are suggested in order to conceal the identiies of the occupants.

☐ Drivers should never leave home without a cellular phone or a mobile radio.

☐ In a high-crime country, installing shatter-resistant film on vehicular windows will prevent break-ins and attacks on occupants.

☐ If available, "run-flat" tires are recommended so as to enable occupants of a vehicle to drive to safety in a high-threat situation.

☐ All vehicles should have a fire extinguisher and a comprehensive first aid kit.

☐ Flag decals of one's country should not be affixed to your vehicle, nor any decals that would place you at greater risk.

SECTION SIX

Solutions for the Future

This book has covered a lot of ground in terms of how to keep you, your friends, family, and colleagues safe while traveling abroad. I'm sure you also recognize that if government policies were not flawed or nonexistent and if companies; universities; cruise ship lines; airlines; and international, aid, and news organizations established a rigid security programs, your risks abroad would be greatly reduced.

It was my intention that after you read this book, you would become more deliberate, conscious, and prudent in terms of your personal security (i.e., knowing what can happen to you while traveling). And, if you could not prevent a problem from happening, I wanted you, at least, to know the choices and solutions you would have to minimize risk.

I also hope that you'll let me know how you liked the book, particularly if I can answer any questions that were not addressed to your satisfaction. I would be particularly interested in knowing whether this book helped you avoid a problem, deal effectively with a threat, cope with a disruption, or maybe even prevent injury or death.

I would like to share with you a number of thoughts I have in terms of how we, as a global community, can make our unpredictable, uncertain, and turbulent world a bit safer for all of us. Global terrorism and crime are problems that the entire world faces. Consequently, we will confront these challenges and find solutions to them only by working collectively together—not unilaterally in a vacuum.

No one can agree on a definition of terrorism. I have used the word "terrorism" many times in this book, yet the global community cannot even agree on a definition of terrorism. In fact, I've found more than 50 definitions of the word, with many of them crafted with political innuendos or rhetoric that renders terrorism exceptional to a particular country. I continue to be puzzled by the international community's inability to agree on a definition so that every nation can draft and enact similar legislation to prosecute acts of extremism, regardless of where they occur. Given the extent of ambiguity in defining "terrorism," I have crafted my own definition, which I believe can be used by ALL nations with relative applicability.

A suggested definition for terrorism. *Violent criminal behavior against civilians, public and private property, using a variety of tactics designed to instill fear and cause injury and/or death to the citizenry, to include causing mass casualties. The motivation for political terrorism is to use the threat of violence* *or violence itself as a means of political change. Tactics used by terrorists include small arms attacks, bombings, hijackings, kidnappings, extortion, assassination, facility attacks, incendiary attacks, weapons of mass destruction (radiological, nuclear, biological, chemical and explosive/incendiary attacks), and using transportation conveyances (e.g., directing an aircraft, vessel, train or other vehicle into a structure containing people) as an instrument for the purpose of causing mass casualties. Political terrorists can be domestic, foreign or transnational.*

Terrorism is a law enforcement problem, not a political problem. Terrorism is a felonious crime, pure and simple. You can politicize it, spin it, and turn it inside out as much as you want, but you still have a serious crime: threat of violence, arson, criminally motivated injury or death, bombing, kidnapping/hostage taking, assassination, armed attacks, and the like.

All crimes should be investigated. Where probable cause exists, offenders should be charged, tried, and either convicted or acquitted. If probable cause does not exist, suspects should be released and not held for years without being charged and prosecuted. Torture should never be used on criminals—and this is precisely what political extremists are.

If any government uses torture as a matter of public policy, it encourages its adversaries to use torture on a *quid pro quo* basis. It further lowers a government to the level of the extremists for which it has such disdain. When we politicize extremism, we place ideological obstacles in our path that inhibit the prosecution of criminals for acts of extremism.

Countering extremism is a civilian responsibility. State and local law enforcement agencies should be tasked with preventing acts of terrorism through the reduction of security vulnerabilities by using federal funding to fulfill this role. National governmental investigative agencies and courts should have the sole responsibility of investigating and prosecuting acts of terrorism. National governmental intelligence agencies should collect, analyze, and provide investigative leads to investigative agencies only. Military and intelligence organizations should *not* have an investigative role in terrorism because they are generally untrained and ill-equipped to investigate crime. Further, they are not trained to work in a civilian world fraught with legal restrictions.

Governmental responses should not *be based on emotion, anger, or haste.* Governments have procedural law for a reason. It is designed to minimize misconduct and blunders on the part of governmental agencies and reduce sloppy and hasty investigations and prosecutions. Indeed, one of the best examples of professional intergovernmental cooperation was the joint efforts in 2006 of U.S. and British authorities to neutralize the threat originating in the United Kingdom to use liquid-based improvised explosives to down aircraft bound for the United States.

Conversely, two excellent examples of hasty, overzealous law enforcement work are the arrest of a U.S. lawyer who was misidentified as a suspect in the March 2004 Madrid railway attacks and the killing of a Brazilian citizen in London following the 2005 transit attacks when the victim was mistaken for a Muslim extremist.

In the U.S. case, the U.S. government agreed to pay $2 million to settle a lawsuit filed by an Oregon lawyer who was arrested and jailed for two weeks in 2004 after the FBI mishandled a fingerprint match and mistakenly linked him to a terrorist attack in Spain. Under the terms of the settlement, the government issued an apology to Brandon Mayfield for the "suffering" caused by his wrongful arrest and imprisonment.

In October 2007, a British jury found the Metropolitan Police in London guilty of endangering public safety during a tense antiterrorist operation that led to the 2005 shooting death of Brazilian national, Jean Charles de Menezes, 27, who was mistaken for a suicide bomber. In the verdict, the jury fined the police department more than $360,000 and ordered it to pay court costs of nearly $800,000.

Whenever a government uses fear, anger, or "saber rattling" as an extension of its public policy in countering terrorism or extremism, it supports the erosion of its jurisprudence system. Counterterrorism can be achieved only through the adherence to careful investigative and judicial mandates that do not break laws or tread on constitutional and legal statutes and case law.

Governments need an effective system of alerting citizens to terrorist threats. Most observers can agree that the U.S. Department of Homeland Security's color-coded threat system serves no useful purpose. Few people in the U.S. are attentive to the announced threat level (which, incidentally, is heard only in domestic airports). Perhaps a new system needs to be developed that makes more sense. Otherwise, why have it? Many governments have no system at all, which perhaps works as well as the U.S. system. In any event, it is clear that governments need to work together to design a system that can work on an international level, considering that terrorism is a transnational threat. It seems logical, then, that there should be uniformity in how all governments handle the same transnational threat.

Anti-terrorism and law enforcement training provided to foreign governments needs to be better coordinated. During my State Department career, where I directed the design and delivery of anti-terrorism courses provided to foreign governments, I learned only too well that developed nations and international organizations rarely collaborate on the types of training they provide nations in need of anti-terrorism and law enforcement skills. Invariably, a number of nations are repeatedly teaching many countries the same types of training. The result is that foreign police are being overtrained in many subjects and undertrained in skills they vitally need. The end result is that tens of millions of training dollars are wasted.

There is a critical need for a credible statistical database of global acts of terrorism. From 1983 until 2003, the State Department's Bureau of Diplomatic Security issued a very credible and objective annual report entitled ***Patterns of Global Terrorism***, which included analyses of significant terrorist acts as well as statistics of terrorist incidents that were relied on by everyone outside the government. Then, in 2004, it became clear that the State Department and other federal agencies were reporting different numbers on acts of international terrorism. This resulted in the elimination of *Patterns*. Governments around the world are maintaining different numbers for transnational terrorist acts. What they should do is work together to generate one credible report that stems from a threat common to us all.

Customer service is critically important for passenger screening agencies. According to a 2007 AP-Ipsos poll, only the U.S. Federal Emergency Management Agency (FEMA) ranks below the U.S. Transportation Security Administration (TSA) among the least-liked agencies by some 10,000 respondents. TSA ranked right along tax collectors in a favorability ranking of Federal agencies. TSA's parent agency, the Department of Homeland Security, also ranked at the bottom of agencies in terms of favorability. Ironically, filed complaints against TSA amount to only 2% of air travelers, yet travelers indirectly blame TSA for having to get to the airport hours before flights, occasionally missing flights due to long screening lines, inconsistency of TSA regulations and having items stolen from checked luggage that must remain unlocked. Unfortunately, theft is rarely attributed to screeners, but to the hundreds of others who have access to the bags during transit. High attrition amongst screeners also is attributed to long screening lines and the volume of travelers causes frustration for both passengers and screeners.

The criteria used to determine what personal effects can be brought into an airliner cabin needs to be based on sound principals of threat analysis and/or science. Since the events of 9/11, TSA appears to have used a knee-jerk approach to forming public policy on what can and cannot be taken into an airliner's cabin. Although the list of what you cannot take aboard a flight is voluminous, a broken wine glass in the first class cabin, a pencil, or any countless other instruments not on the prohibited list could be used as a weapon. As for the 3-1-1 rule (carrying liquids and gels up to 3 oz. containers in a one quart plastic ziplock bag), what is to stop someone from carrying one of many substances that are not detected by dual-energy scanners? Then there is the requirement that all passengers remove their shoes during screening. Surprisingly, the U.S. is about the only nation that has such a requirement, yet there have been no shoe-bomb incidents in the air since Richard Reid, with a one-day ticket and no luggage, smuggled a shoe-bomb aboard an American Airlines flight in Paris. Further, as we have learned since August 2006, when the binary liquid-bomb conspiracy was disclosed, we have since learned that liquid-based explosives had not actually been produced by the would-be U.K. conspirators. Another concern is that while billions of dollars in lost productivity have been lost to many of these screening requirements, many airports in both the U.S. as well as abroad, have not conducted thorough background checks on airport workers who have access to tarmacs and aircraft on the ground. So, the question is, in the absence of a truly comprehensive program, is global aviation safer that it was prior to 9/11? The answer is yes, we are, largely because all checked and hand-carried luggage is being screened for explosives, and because many, but not all flights have armed air marshals. Unfortunately, though, there are vulnerability gaps that will never be addressed no matter how inconvenienced we make passengers or how much money we throw at anti-terrorism.

Torture should never be permitted as a public policy. Even though in the wake of the events of 9/11, the Bush Administration decided to use interrogation techniques which can only be described as "torture"—techniques we have scene practiced in Iraq's Abu Grraib and the U.S. Marine base at Guantanamo Bay. One would hope that no government, American or otherwise, will ever again use torture as a means of eliciting information from terrorist suspects. Now, the U.S. Government is attempting to prosecute terrorist suspects in a U.S. court proceedings on the basis of confessions that were elicited during torture. Not only does doing so violate the very fabric of American jurisprudence, but it subjects Americans abroad to similar acts of torture abroad if they are ever captured or held by terrorist organizations. Rightfully so, the U.S. Congress is now endeavoring to require that all U.S. intelligence agencies abide by the U.S. Army Field Manual, which prohibits "waterboarding," a means of torture used on al-Qaeda terrorists.

The media should try not to instill fear in the minds of their audiences. After news reports in June 2007, following the discovery of a parked Mercedes near Trafalgar Square that contained an improvised incendiary device constructed of fuel and gas canisters, one international news organization carried a headline of the story that said, "Two Explosive-Laden Cars in London Linked." Yet, interestingly, the narrative of the article that followed the headline made no reference to the discovery of explosives; the device was simply an incendiary bomb that in no way posed the risk of an "explosive-laden" car bomb. More specifically, why is it that a media organization would report that a car contained explosives when it did not, other than to hype the story? Surely, filing such a report tends to instill fear rather than accurately report the facts.

Public reporting of foreign travelers victimized abroad. As noted on pages 24 and 25, few foreign affairs agencies of governments publicly report the number of citizens who are victimized by crime, with the exceptions of the British and Canadian governments. Considering that crime statistics of foreign travelers are not accurately reported by most governments, it seems logical that the foreign affairs agencies should maintain and release such statistics by country and criminal category of citizens victimized abroad. Otherwise, travelers may go abroad without knowing the true nature of the threat.

International organizations should do more to educate travelers abroad. Given the realities that we've seen in the aftermath of 9/11, with terrorism continuing abroad and with violent crime on the rise virtually everywhere, the United Nations World Tourism Organization (**http://www. unwto.org**) should devote more of its resources to helping the international community better educate travelers and the tourism industry of governments to enhance travel safety. Ironically, the last report issued by the UNWTO was entitled *Tourist Safety and Security: Practical Measures for Destinations*, which was published well over a decade ago, when the world was much, much different.

National tourism ministries should take a proactive role in keeping foreign travelers safe. For sure, few governmental tourism ministries publicly acknowledge crime to foreign travelers because they fear it will prevent tourists from coming to their countries. The reality is that travelers know there is crime in every country. They just want guidance on areas to avoid, how to report crime, how to get help and support in the event of a serious incident, and how to understand the criminal tactics. By putting their heads in the sand, tourism ministries make the situation worse.

Can 2.3 million lives be saved? In 2020, 2.3 million people will die annually from automobile fatalities, 70% of them in developing countries. Since 1975, some 6,200 Americans have died in roadway accidents abroad, double the number lost on 9/11. Yet the United States does very little to help developing countries build safer roads, train police in traffic management and enforcement, or improve emergency medical services through its foreign assistance efforts.

Despite the efforts of ASIRT and the Global Road Safety Steering Committee (**http://www.globalroadsafety.org**), which is sponsored by ASIRT, the World Bank, UNICEF, and UNDP, automobile deaths are rising dramatically. Currently, road deaths are the highest in Asia, with Latin America coming in second. The two countries with the highest number of fatalities include China and India. With such carnage and threats to foreign travelers, it is time for international organizations and developed nations to develop a strategy on how to reduce this significant loss of life that renders deaths from terrorism virtually miniscule.

The media and governments contribute to continuing acts of terrorism. If I were a member of al-Qaeda or one of the many homegrown or splinter groups that embrace al-Qaeda's belief systems, I would be spending most of my time learning English and having my eyes glued to American broadcast networks. It's like having one's own personal intelligence service. Everything that the United States, Canada, the European Union, Australia, and our collective allies who are concerned with the threats from Islamic extremists are doing to counter terrorism is on the television every night. As a former government agent, I'm appalled by the amount of useful information that the U.S. government releases to the media every day about what we are doing, thinking, and planning to do in the effort to counter the threat of terrorism. No wonder the threat of terrorism is just as much of a clear and present danger today as it was six years ago. If we were truly prudent, we would be assessing what intelligence benefit everything the media reports on terrorism is having on transnational terrorists.

Foreign students need better support from their universities. As discussed on pages 169–173, institutions of higher learning (IHE) have a legal responsibility to ensure that students and faculty are not placed in high-risk situations abroad in conjunction with university programs. Although many IHEs and foreign exchange associations have disseminated guidelines, the reality is that a large number of universities fail to take adequate steps to protect students and faculty sent abroad. Therefore, they have a legal responsibility when things go wrong. All universities should adopt the recommended actions that I've outlined in the section on foreign study programs. If not, students will continue to be placed in high-risk situations. Further, IHEs should be required to publish crime statistics involving their students while abroad, considering that the U.S. Campus Security Policy and Campus Crime Statistics Act does not mandate reporting of incidents against students abroad.

Cruise ship lines need to seriously address passenger security. It is understandable why the U.S. Congress has been holding hearings to increase the transparency of reporting criminal incidents that take place aboard cruise ships. As mentioned on pages 165 through 169, the CLIA and ICV have been directed by Congress to develop a proposal aimed at achieving better reporting and security onboard cruise ship vessels. That being said, all cruise ships, regardless of registry, need to improve their security awareness and the transparency of reporting incidents to police and Coast Guard organizations.

All organizations that send people abroad need to provide them pre-departure security training. Whether we're talking about airlines, cruise ships, news organizations, aid organizations, international organizations, multinational companies, or those managing international conferences and governments, all organizations that send staff abroad, for the short-term or the long-term, need to establish formal training programs that sensitize travelers to risks abroad and give them the resources to help them when avoidance and prevention do not work. Failure to adequately train staff for which you are responsible could result in large claims or litigation for wrongful injury or death.

Additional Web Sites

Air Ambulance Services
- http://www.airassi.com
- http://www.airmed.com

Auto/Personal Effects Insurance
- http://www.jannetteintl.com
- http://www.clements.com
- http://www.usaa.com

Attacks on Journalists
- http://www.freemedia.at (International Press Institute)
- http://www.cpj.org (Committee for Protecting Journalists)

Automobile Theft
- http://www.autolock.com (excellent site for auto theft prevention information, source for ordering brake and steering wheel locks that come with guarantees)
- http://www.windowarmor.com (reducing risk of thieves breaking through an auto window)

Business Resources

- **http://www.worldinformation.com** (resource to obtain World Bank, IMF, UN, and USG economic trends reports, as well as country business intelligence analyses)

- **http://www.doingbusiness.org** (site where world economies are ranked according to the ease of doing business by foreign companies)

- **http://www.export.gov** (an incredible portal on doing business abroad through the U.S. Department of Commerce)

- **http://www.internationalist.com** (an excellent Web site that includes global business country reports, translator/interpreter referrals, exchange rates, travel advisories, maps, and links to all of the world's newspapers)

- **http://www.uschamber.org/chamber** (Web site for the U.S. Chamber's international division, where you can purchase directories of AmChams abroad as well as a number of excellent publications on doing business abroad)

- **http://www.fita.org** (comprehensive resource on foreign trade provided by the Federation of International Trade Associations)

- **http://www.worldchambers.com** (access to the world's chambers of commerce)

- **http://www.iccwbo.org** (directory of international chambers of commerce)

- http://www.kompass.com (Kompass International Trade Directory)
- http://www.worldbiz.com (directories on doing business abroad)

Cruise Ships
- http://www.cruisecompete.com
- http://www.cruisemates.com

Date and Time Gateway
- http://www.bsdi.com/date

Electronic Power Support
- http://www.xantrex.com (weighing less than a pound and six inches long, the Mobile 100 gives you a single tool to sustain power for your gadgets, such as MP3 players, digital cameras, laptops, etc., and is recharged by AC or DC power)

Expatriate Living
- http://www.internationalliving.com
- http://www.livingabroad.com
- http://www.liveabroad.com
- http://www.overseasdigest.com
- http://www.talesmag.com
- http://www.expatnetwork.com
- http://www.expatworld.net

- http://www.expatriates.com
- http://www.expat-moms.com

Hotels
- http://www.unusualhotelsoftheworld.com
- http://www.hostels.com
- http://www.hotels.com

Luggage and Accessories
- http://www.letravelstore.com
- http://www.aceluggage.com
- http://www.magellans.com/store

Maps and Geography
- http://www.geography.about.com (tons of geographical resources)
- http://www.mapquest.com (the popular Web site also works internationally)
- http://www.worldtimeserver.com (provides world time for most countries along with maps; superb when you're multitasking in two time zones)
- http://www.maporama.com (maps to help in organizing trips)

News Sources
- http://www.findnewspapers.com (locate the world's newspapers)

- http://www.ft.com (*Financial Times*)
- http://www.cnn.com
- http://www.onlinenewspapers.com
- http://www.iht.com (*International Herald Tribune*)
- http://www.internationalwallstreetjournal.com (published by the *International Wall Street Journal*)
- http://www.channelnewsasia.com (news on Asia)
- http://www.lanic.utexas.edu/la/region/news (Latin-American links)
- http://www.foreignwire.com (international news)
- http://www.budgettravelonline.com (*Budget Travel* magazine)

Online Air Ticketing
- http://www.sidestep.com
- http://www.farecompare.com
- http://www.orbitz.com
- http://www.kayak.com

Satellite Phone Rentals
- http://www.rentaphone.com
- http://www.4satellitephones.com

Shatter-Resistant Film (for residential, commercial, and vehicular use)
- http://www.3m.com
- http://www.shattergard.com

Tipping

- http://www.tipping.org

Travel Products

- **http://www.travelproducts.com** (resource for ordering products of use to international travelers, such as batteries, travel clocks, health products, laptop accessories, packing aids, security products, first aid, etc.)

- **http://www.travelon.com** (source for Secure-a-Bag cable ties, which make it easy to secure luggage compartments and zippered sections without locks yet permit airport security screeners to randomly screen bags and place their own seals on your bag to safeguard contents; a package of 60 plastic ties comes with a small set of nail clippers that can be left in a small unsecured outer compartment)

- **http://www.traveloasis.com**

- **http://www.travelsentry.com** (luggage locks approved by the U.S. Transportation Security Administration [TSA]; lock design permits TSA to use a special key bypass to open the lock if random screening is necessary and then relock it)

- **http://www.members.tripod.com/~Travel_us/ index.html** (Web site for Travel Aides International, which provides travelers with disabilities equipment to facilitate their travel)

Glossary

al-Qaeda: An Islamic fundamentalist terrorist organization founded by Saudi exile Osama bin Laden, who masterminded the attacks on the U.S. embassies in Tanzania and Kenya in 1998, on the USS *Cole* in 2000, and on New York and Washington, D.C., on September 11, 2001. In recent years, many terrorist threats and attacks have been conducted by homegrown extremists who have embraced bin Laden's violent agenda against the West, even though they are not directed by bin Laden's organization.

Bureau of Diplomatic Security: Known as DS, the law enforcement and security arm of the U.S. State Department. DS oversees the Regional Security Officers (RSO), who are assigned to protect U.S. diplomatic and consular posts throughout the world.

CDMA: Cellular technology (Code Division Multiple Access) that is used in 26 countries.

Chokepoint: A predictable location where a criminal's or terrorist's target can always be expected because of a location having only one way in and one way out; a location at which a target can be expected to be at a particular time.

CIA: Central Intelligence Agency.

DEA: Drug Enforcement Administration.

Developed nation: The 31 industrialized, high-income, and advanced economies, as defined by the International Monetary Fund (IMF).

Developing nation: A nation that is not industrialized or technologically advanced and that has a high percentage of poverty; substandard social welfare systems; ineffective public safety, prosecutorial, and judicial systems; deteriorating infrastructure; and a per capita income below $11,000.

Dirty bomb: One type of a "radiological dispersal device" that combines explosive materials with radioactive material. Normally, a dirty bomb does not contain enough radioactive substance to kill large numbers of people, but it is designed to create fear and panic, contaminate property, and necessitate a costly cleanup. A dirty bomb is not a weapon of mass destruction (WMD) but rather a weapon of mass *disruption*.

EEA: Economic Espionage Act (of 1996).

Express kidnapping: A short-term abduction of an individual for the purpose of robbery, forced withdrawal from an ATM, extortion, or other crime.

FARC: Revolutionary Armed Forces of Colombia, the largest and most active armed rebel group in Colombia. It is known for using ransom kidnapping and narcotics trafficking to fund its political agenda of disrupting the operations of the government, energy pipelines, and commerce. A product of Fidel Castro's liberation philosophy of the 1960s, the FARC boasts nearly 6,000 armed fighters.

FAV: Fully armored vehicle.

FBI: Federal Bureau of Investigation.

FCPA: Foreign Corrupt Practices Acts (of 1977).

FMLN: A major leftist terrorist group in El Salvador during the 1970s–1990s. A sub-group of the FMLN, the Central American Revolutionary Workers' Party (PRTC), was responsible for the 1983 assassination of LtCdr Albert Shaufelberger, USN, who was assigned to the U.S. Embassy in San Salvador.

GA: General aviation.

GSM: Cellular technology (Global System Mobile) that is used in 185 countries.

Hard Target: a governmental or vital installation that possesses maximum levels of physical, procedural and technical security designed to prevent criminal or terrorist attacks.

Hezbollah: An Iranian-supported terrorist group. Also known as the Party of God.

Improvised explosive device (IED): A bomb that is nonmilitary in design and constructed of high explosives, commercially made or improvised, and uses differing types of energy sources and detonation initiators.

Improvised incendiary device (IID): In a post-9/11 world, all bombs are incorrectly defined as IEDs, when, in fact, they not. There are also IIDs, which have been grossly underestimated. Like IEDs, these devices, which are essentially defined as "thrown or remotely detonated incendiary bombs," are designed to cause mass casualties. IIDs are constructed of differing types of igniting fuels and gases, including propane. Included in IIDs are Molotov cocktails.

IPMS: In-place monitoring system. A system installed in a specific space to permit countermeasures specialists to monitor the system during meetings to identify any electronic penetrations.

LARF: Lebanese Armed Revolutionary Front, a terrorist group that attacked countless U.S. and Israeli targets during the 1980s and 1990s.

LAV: Light-armored vehicle.

MRTA: The Tupac Amaru Revolutionary Movement, a leftist Peruvian terrorist group that was very active in the 1980s and 1990s but is now dormant.

NGO: Nongovernmental organization. Examples of an NGO in an international setting would be Save the Children, CARE, Doctors without Borders, and companies and associations involved in aid projects.

NPA: New People's Army, a leftist terrorist organization indigenous to the Philippines.

November 17 Group: A leftist terrorist group indigenous to Greece and one of the most successful groups in the world (without being neutralized) that terrorized Greek, British, and U.S. targets for more than 30 years. The group was broken up, and most of its members were convicted and incarcerated.

PRTC: Central American Revolutionary Workers' Party, a subgroup of the Farabundo Marti National Liberation Front.

RAF: The Red Army Faction, the long-defunct German terrorist group, popular during the 1970s and 1980s, that targeted German and U.S. interests. It previously was known as the Bader-Meinholf Gang.

Regional Security Officer (RSO): A special agent employed by the Department of State's Bureau of

Diplomatic Security whose duties are to protect U.S. diplomatic and consular missions abroad, serve as a security advisor to ambassadors, conduct investigations, respond to crises and incidents against the United States and its interests, and work closely with foreign police agencies.

RPG: Rocket-propelled grenade.

SIM card: A small card that is purchased in each country and that provides a local telephone number that can be placed in GSM cellular phones.

Soft Target: An installation or structure that requires frequent access to the public and which is not designed to have formidable levels of security due to the need for access. Soft targets include hotels, shopping malls, schools and universities, tourist destinations, etc.

TSCM: Technical security countermeasures survey, a means of determining whether electronic eavesdropping is occurring in a specific space. A TSCM also includes an analysis of phone and computer systems.

U.S. Foreign Service: That component of DOS that recruits, hires, trains, and assigns diplomats and others abroad for most of their careers.

U.S. State Department (DOS): That cabinet department in the U.S. Government that is responsible for foreign affairs.

USSS: U.S. Secret Service.

U.S. Transportation Security Administration (TSA): An agency that falls under the U.S. Department of Homeland Security that is responsible for aviation and transit security. This agency is best recognized by its uniformed employees who screen passengers before they board scheduled airliners.

Vetting: The process of determining the bona fides, credibility, and reliability of an individual, company, or organization.

Weapon of Mass Destruction (WMDs): An atomic, biological, or chemical weapon; improvised explosive or incendiary device; or directed conveyance (aircraft, vessel, train, truck, or automobile) designed to inflict mass casualties on a civilian population.

About the Author

Ed Lee retired from the U.S. State Department in 1986 after serving as a special agent; a regional security officer at a number of embassies in the Middle East, Asia, and Latin America; director of training; associate director of security for Latin America; and director of security of the U.S. Agency for International Development, where he was promoted into the Senior Executive Service. Prior to joining the State Department, Ed served six years in the U.S. Marines, including service in South Vietnam.

From 1988 to 2001, Ed served as a "Personal Security Abroad" trainer at the U.S. Foreign Service Institute, where he taught more than 8,000 diplomats and their families how to avoid being victims of crime and terrorism abroad and conducted briefings for the Overseas Security Advisory Council. He also served as the security advisor to the Inter-American Development Bank for more than 10 years. From 1996 to 1998, he was chief investigator of the Cyprus Missing Persons Program in Nicosia, where his efforts led to the location and exhumation of the remains of a U.S. citizen who disappeared during the Turkish invasion of the island in 1974.

Following the events of September 11, 2001, Ed was asked to return to the State Department to serve as a senior manager in the Diplomatic Security Office of Anti-terrorism Assistance (DS/ATA), where he doubled the number of strategic, operational, and tactical anti-terrorism courses delivered to more than 70 foreign governments. Two of his major accomplishments while at State were the development of a six-week course entitled "Preventing, Interdicting, and Investigating Acts of Terrorism" and a two-week course entitled "Preventing Attacks on Soft Targets."

After his retirement from the Bureau of Diplomatic Security in April 2006, Ed established a security consulting firm, Sleeping Bear Risk Solutions LLC (**http://www. sbrisksolutions.com**), which specializes in training development and delivery, policy development, crisis management planning, business continuity, investigations, and response services for the expatriate community and multinational companies operating abroad. He is also a frequent speaker before corporate and government audiences.

Ed lives in Traverse City, Michigan, which he considers one of the most beautiful places on Earth. He has two daughters, Vicki and Jen, both of whom live in Bend, Oregon. He spends his time writing, hiking, kayaking, fishing, traveling, and pursuing his lifelong passion, photography.

How to Order This Book

To order *Staying Safe Abroad: Traveling, Working & Living in a Post-9/11 World*, please:

☐ Contact **http://www.amazon.com** or **http://www.bn.com**

☐ Contact your nearest bookseller

☐ Order directly from our website: **http://www.sbrisksolutions.com**

We offer substantial discounts for quantity orders when ordered from our website and also offer additional discounts to non-profit organizations, government organizations, educational institutions and libraries.

New Books from Sleeping Bear Risk Solutions

Economic Espionage: Protecting Laptops, Trade Secrets, and Proprietary Information, to be released in February 2009

Managing an Overseas Security Program, to be released in September 2009